Light from the West

Light from the West

THE IRISH MISSION AND THE EMERGENCE OF MODERN EUROPE

William H. Marnell

A Crossroad Book

THE SEABURY PRESS · NEW YORK

1978
The Seabury Press
815 Second Avenue
New York, N.Y. 10017

Printed in the United States of America
Library of Congress Cataloging in Publication Data

Marnell, William H   Light from the West.
"A Crossroad book."
1. Christian saints—Ireland—Biography. 2. Missions, Irish. 3.
Missions—Europe. 4. Ireland—Church history—To 1172. 5. Great
Briton—Church history—Anglo-Saxon period, 449-1066. I. Title.
BX4659.I7M28   282'.094   77-18708   ISBN 0-8164-0389-9

In front, the sun climbs slow, how slowly,
But westward, look, the land is bright.
—ARTHUR HUGH CLOUGH

To the memory of a student of Irish culture
and a lover of Irish life
Rev. Martin P. Harney, s.j.
(1896–1976)

The author acknowledges with gratitude
the generous grant-in-aid
which he received from
THE AMERICAN IRISH FOUNDATION
to facilitate this contribution
to Irish studies.

Contents

IRELAND

† site of monastery

† Derry

BELFAST †
Bangor

† Armagh

Cul-drebene
● SLIGO

† Kells

† Tara

† Killfursa

† Clonard

† Inisquin

† Durrow
● GALWAY
Clonmacnois

DUBLIN ●

Inishmor

† Kildare

Teampall an †
Cheathair Alain

Glendalough †

Ardmore †

Cork ●

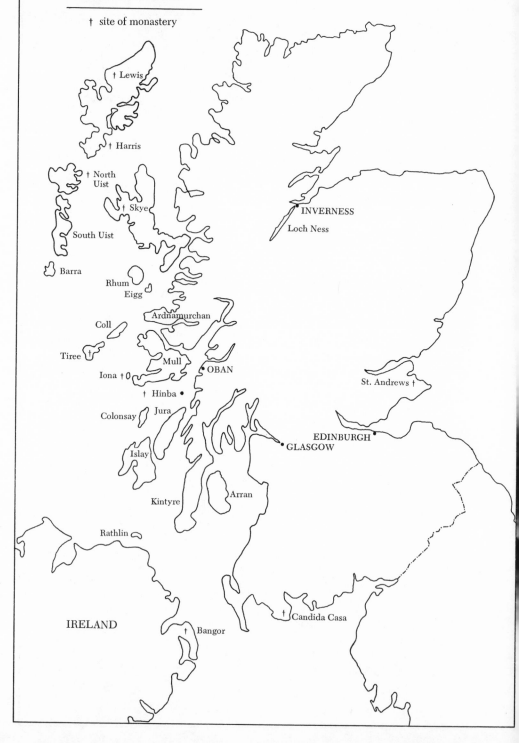

SCOTLAND

† site of monastery

† Lewis

† Harris

† North Uist

† Skye

South Uist

Barra

Rhum

Eigg

Ardnamurchan

Coll

Tiree †

Mull

Iona † O

OBAN

† Hinba

Jura

Colonsay

Islay

Kintyre

Arran

Rathlin

IRELAND

† Bangor

• INVERNESS

Loch Ness

St. Andrews †

EDINBURGH

• GLASGOW

† Candida Casa

ENGLAND

† site of monastery

EDINBURGH •

Coldingham †

Melrose †

Bamburgh

† Lindisfarne

Farne Islands

NEWCASTLE •
Gateshead †

† Candida Casa

Hartlepool †

Lastingham †

† Whitby

Ripon †

† YORK

• CHESTER

Burgh Castle †

Tilbury †

† Malmesbury
• BRISTOL

LONDON •
Rochester †

† Canterbury †

† Glastonbury

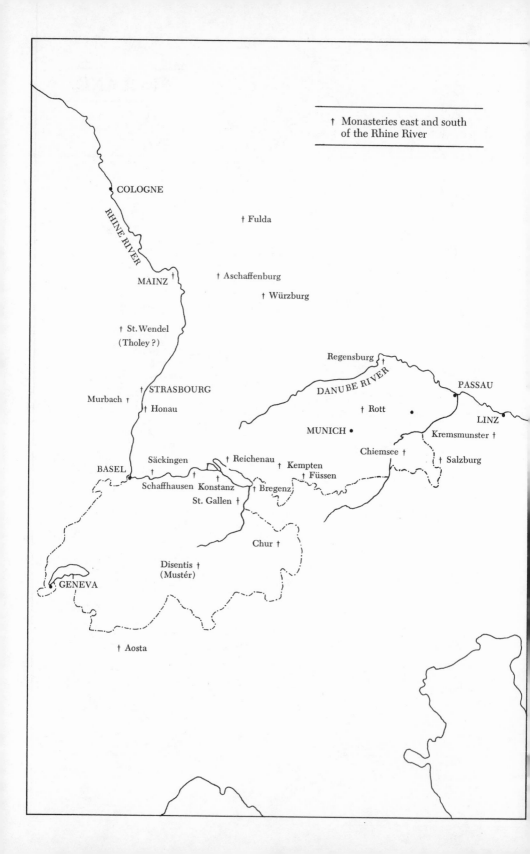

† Monasteries east and south of the Rhine River

COLOGNE

RHINE RIVER

† Fulda

MAINZ †

† Aschaffenburg

† Würzburg

† St. Wendel
(Tholey ?)

Regensburg †

DANUBE RIVER

PASSAU

† STRASBOURG

Murbach †

† Honau

† Rott

MUNICH •

LINZ

Kremsmunster †

Chiemsee †

† Salzburg

BASEL

Säckingen
†

Schaffhausen
†

† Reichenau

Konstanz
†

St. Gallen †

† Kempten

† Füssen

† Bregenz

Chur †

Disentis †
(Mustér)

GENEVA

† Aosta

† Monasteries observing
  Rule of Columbanus
Ⴔ Monastic foundations
  linked to Péronne

Ⴔ Mechelen
● BRUSSELS
† Sithiu   Ⴔ Nivelles
              Ⴔ Fosse
† Leucone

AMIENS ● Ⴔ Péronne
        † Fontenelle   † Corbie † Laon
Le Havre ● ROUEN Noyon †   † Hautvilliers
Jumièges † † Pentale † Jouarre
            Ⴔ Lagny   † Rebais
                    † Meaux
PARIS ●   † Faremoutiers
        † Chelles † Reuil   † Montierender

                        † Remirmont
              Annegray † † Luxeuil
         Fontaines †   † Lure
              † Beze   ● BASEL

DIJON   Besançon † Grandval
                      † Joussamoutier
              St. Paul †   † St. Ursanne
         Romain-Moutier † ● LAUSANNE
                          ● GENEVA

† Noirmoutier

● LIMOGES
  † Solignac

                              Bobbio †
                          GENOA ●

Light from the West

1

The Age of the Saints

A<small>N</small> ancient tradition has it that the Church in Ireland passed
through three ages, and the first and most glorious was the Age
of the Saints. The Age of the Saints is our concern, but our concern
is with its magnificent and still bewildering development which took
place all over western Europe. Christianity, which had been bruised
and beaten by the surging hordes of barbarians that poured out of the
unknown to flood what had been the proud empire of the Romans,
was given once more the breath of life by monks from Ireland. It was
greatly strengthened as Irish monks slowly taught the barbarians
Christian values and their converts came more slowly still to accept
Christian ideals.

History has often recorded the sweep of military might across the
face of Europe. In the Age of the Saints wave after wave swept across
it, Suevians and Bavarians, Franks and Alamanni, Angles and Saxons.
In the modern age Napoleon did it, and in the yesterday of history
the Nazis under Hitler. Only once in history has there been a quiet,
all but imperceptible flooding of Europe by the Word of God,
preached by ascetics at once rude and inspired. They all stemmed
directly or indirectly from the last outpost of the western world, the
tiny land of Ireland.

In a sense St. Patrick comes before the Age of the Saints, but in a
deeper sense he is its foundation. The Word had to come to Ireland
before Ireland could bring the Word back to a Europe desperately
in need of its message. The work in Ireland of St. Patrick, prototype
of all the wandering exiles living in strange lands among barbaric
peoples in the name of Christ, was the necessary prelude to the work

that his successors would do for centuries over the entire face of western Europe. The work began within a century of the presumptive date of Patrick's death, starting, as was logical, in Scotland where the Irish already had a foothold and where language was at most a minor problem, extending throughout Scotland and the northern part of England, probing down into the south, crossing the Channel, and then spreading east and south.

As geography makes logical, it was most widespread in France, with Irish monks established in at least twelve French centers including Paris, Besançon, Rouen, and Strasbourg. It moved eastward into what is now Belgium. It followed the valley of the Main to Mainz and Würzburg, and moved south to Munich and the Inn River beyond. Bern and Rheinau in Switzerland had their Irish monastic establishments north of the mountains, as did St. Gallen nestled in the Grissons. The saints pierced the mountain barrier and brought the light to Salzburg in Austria; to Piacenza, Bobbio, and Fiesole in northern Italy; to Rome itself, and beyond Rome to Taranto and Palermo. The Irish monks ranged from the Faroes and Iceland in the north to Sicily in the south. Never in human history has another nation as small as Ireland done so much missionary work in so many lands over so many decades as did the Irish in what, save for them, would indeed have been the unrelieved Dark Ages. By that measure should the importance be understood of the work started by that alien in the name of Christ who lived and died in the strange and foreign land forever inseparable from his own name, St. Patrick.

It is a story certainly worth telling for its own sake, but it also has messages worth pondering in an age so different from the Age of the Saints that to forge the mental link between that age and our own is supremely difficult. One starts with the word *saint.* In most cases, these saints were not such by virtue of formal canonization in the Catholic Church. They were holy men of God, honored for their holiness and wondered at for the self-discipline and self-denial of their lives. At St. Gallen in Switzerland is one of the greatest repositories in the world of ancient manuscripts and early printed books, its greatest treasures displayed in a room that is itself a work of priceless art. In one form or another the traveler constantly meets St. Gall in the city that bears his name, a stylized St. Gall arrayed in priestly vestments. There are two oddities to the St. Gall of stained glass windows, colored plates, and picture postcards. He has in his hands a loaf of bread, and by him stands a bear holding in its paws a log of wood. The saint of the stained glass window, with the sunlight streaming through him, is one of Yeats's "sages standing in God's holy fire," and the diminutive bear beside him is appealing.

But the St. Gall of cold and sober history did live in a cave and, by legend at least, shared the cave and life's necessities with a bear. The self-discipline and self-denial of his life did attract a company of wondering and devout followers; a simple, loosely organized protomonastery did come into being about him; and out of it grew the great cathedral and the abbey library of St. Gallen, with all that they have meant to art, literature, and learning from the Middle Ages to the present day. The sage standing in God's holy fire is statuesque and the bear is engaging, but the reality behind the stylized picture should be calculated to make the world wonder. What gleam of holy fire did this man follow, so many miles from home, across such waters, through such forests, deep into such mountains to bring the faith to a barbaric people called the Alamanni?

It is a problem to know what these saints did, since the sixth, seventh, and eighth centuries are far more distant from us, in terms not merely of literary records but of recognizable patterns of life and thought, than many centuries before them. It is a far greater problem to understand why they did it. It is little cause for surprise that when later generations wrote their lives they produced tissues of endless wonder, lives in which miracle is commonplace and the world of present reality is absorbed into an all-encompassing, all-pervading supernatural. To the medieval hagiographers their subjects must have been men of a different mold, saints loaned by eternity to guide this present life, and they must have had at their command the flashing swords of archangels. To call naïve the faith that inspired the saints in their self-discipline and self-denial, as the modern age is prone to do, is itself naïve. There is nothing naïve about the faith that moves mountains, and little wonder that the saints move mountains literally in hagiography when they moved mountains metaphorically in what they endured and accomplished. The biographer of the twelfth century deems them wonder-workers; the pragmatist of the twentieth century calls their faith childlike. Each pays tribute to an inspiration beyond his understanding. The hagiographer pays it the tribute of wonder, the pragmatist the tribute of denigration. The one exalts the saint to the skies, the other degrades him to the pavement. Neither understands him.

It is not our purpose to explain their act of faith but to record the acts to which it inspired them. In its externals, their story is inspiration enough, but it is important that the story never obscure what lies behind the story. Their faith led them into paths no other motive has ever led men to follow, and there is no other achievement in human history, after the achievement of the twelve apostles and the immediate disciples, that was motivated in the same manner and with results comparably beneficial and enduring. The Vandal and the Hun have gone their way, and so have Napoleon and Hitler, and the ruin in their wake has largely been restored. The monks of the Age of Saints went their way more than a thousand years ago, and infidelity, cynicism, and evil have not entirely eroded the good that they achieved. There may well be a pertinent message in this for our own century, in which the institutional Churches are steadily dwindling in membership as Church leaders turn away from the traditional goal of personal sanctification and substitute for it the objectives of secular humanism. Saints have never moved mountains in the name of economics or sociology.

There remains by way of preface one word of explanation. Convenience dictates the use of such terms as Celtic Church, Roman Church, Irish Church, Church in Scotland, Church of Northumbria, English Church, and the like. Such terms are geographic and national, not theological. We may say of them all what St. Bede of the Northumbrian Church said of St. Aidan of the Celtic Church: he "kept in his heart, revered and preached nothing other than we do, that is the redemption of mankind through the passion, resurrection and ascension of the mediator between God and man, the man Christ Jesus." The geographic Churches were all united in a single faith, however much they differed in such matters as monastic organization, diocesan patterns, Easter observance, tonsure, and the other distinguishing marks, important and often hotly contested, but never fundamental tenets of faith. There is much to wonder at in their faith —the inspiration it afforded, the austerities and hardships it elicited, and the triumphs it achieved—but there is no reason to wonder about its unity. The Irish Culdee in Iceland and his brother monk on Monreale in Sicily were both and equally sons of Rome.

2

The Dawn in Britain

CHRISTIANITY entered Britain as it entered the other remote reaches of the Roman Empire, slowly, imperceptibly, much as spring enters a northern land. Possibly some trader from Gaul brought the new creed along with his traditional wares, and somewhere on the shores of that great and ancient highway into Britain, the Bristol Channel, it took root. And conceivably, some trader from Britain found human love in Gaul, and with it the new divine love, and brought home Christian bride and creed to what is now the coast of south Wales. It is known, but for some reason never explained, that Christianity spread more rapidly in the Roman army than among the general population. Perhaps some Roman officer, with a hundred restless barbarians at his command and an uncounted horde of other barbarians waiting in the distant hills, scratched the Chi Rho on the red stone of the rugged outpost that now is Chester, and found comfort and strength in the symbol. The Christian trader and the soldier may well have reached Britain before the priest, and the faith before the Church.

The Dawn in Literature

We first meet Christianity in Britain in the phrases of rhetoric and the imaginative stories of romance. Chrysostom says of the twelve apostles: ". . . not satisfied with the world known to us they went out as far as the Ocean itself and enclosed in their own nets the countries of the barbarians and the British Isles." As sober history this is most certainly false, but in terms of the special sort of truth that rhetoric

5

can express it may just possibly be true. The Roman officer who scratched the Chi Rho in the red stone outcropping at Chester may once have served at Ephesus or Antioch, and have received the faith at not too many removes from an apostle. Nennius says that in 167 the British king, Leucius, and all the sub-kings of Britain were baptized by papal envoys from Rome. Once more, as sober history this is nonsense, but the kernel of truth may be at the heart of the rhetorical exaggeration. Tertullian, who was born about 150, and Origen, who was born a generation later, speak in vague and general terms of Christianity in Britain. No Briton was more apt to become Romanized than the petty king who owed survival to the conqueror's tolerance, and with his acceptance of the fasces as a symbol might go acceptance of another symbol, the cross. The Church has no British history in the second and third centuries, but that is not to say that Britain did not have the Church. The most promising place to look for its beginnings is Glastonbury.

Glastonbury

There is something about Glastonbury suggestive of a Christian antiquity so remote as not yet to have been probed. There are the ruins of St. Mary's abbey. These are the customary Benedictine ruins that commemorate in their melancholy fashion the dissolution of the monasteries. There is also the conical tor with the ruined chapel on its summit suggestive of something older and more mysterious. Something more tangible than the aura of antiquity shrouds the chapel. There has been revealed by excavation the existence of another chapel, thirteen feet wide, seventeen feet long, with a dirt floor embedded with bits of pottery, some as old as the first century. The tiny chapel is Celtic and dates from the fifth century. If those shards could speak, they might have a tale vastly older and stranger than any archaeology can tell. Giraldus Cambrensis, a Welsh clergyman of the twelfth century and a man of stormy life but active pen, says that the tomb of Arthur and Guinevere was discovered at Glastonbury in the time of Henry II. He adds that Glastonbury is Avalon, the place of mystery to which Arthur was carried after death. Closer to our purpose is the tale that after the crucifixion Joseph of Arimathea brought to England the Holy Grail—the cup from which Christ drank at the Last Supper and the cup in which Joseph caught the blood of Christ as he hung on the cross—and that Joseph of Arimathea founded Glastonbury Abbey. Thus legend brings Glastonbury into immediate relationship to the central act of Christian faith as well as into the most important body of quasi-religious legend evolved in Britain. This is the stuff of legend, not of truth, but the kernel of truth can be at the heart of legend quite as truly as at the heart of rhetoric. Glastonbury is on the River Brue, a bare ten miles or so from Burnham on Bridgewater Bay. It is of easy access from the Bristol Channel and inland the distance requisite for forewarning of attack by sea. Behind the cluster of old legend which brings together into the suggestion of a synthesis the Last Supper, the cup of Christ, Arthur and his passing, and the central quest of Arthur's court may be the dim, confused, barely recalled memory of a very early Christian settlement in Britain. If any British city is suggestive of ancient, imperceptible Christian beginnings, it is Glastonbury.

The Evidence of Archaeology

As we move toward the fourth century, archaeology begins to offer evidence more concrete and substantial than may be shrouded in rhetoric and romance. On the plaster of a Roman house in Cirencester is a vertical and horizontal inscription reading PATER NOSTER. The words are flanked by A on the left and O on the right, alpha and omega, the first and final letters of the Greek alphabet and the ancient symbol of Christ in whom everything begins and ends. There are Christian villas at Frampton and Hinton St. Mary, and a fountain marked with crosses at Chedworth. There are fragmentary remains of what were Christian churches at Silchester and Caerwent, and a room survives at Lullingstone with wall paintings that make it clear the room was a Christian chapel. None of these remains are later than the fourth century, and except for the churches they are in what were private dwellings of the well-to-do. Once more we have the suggestion that the wealthy Briton became Romanized first, and that by the fourth century to be Romanized was to be Christianized. The words were becoming interchangable, a process completed in St. Patrick who was both Roman and Christian, and who always thought himself a foreigner in the land from which his name is inseparable.

The Earliest British Church

There was not a Roman literature in Britain worthy of even the most modest of names and not infrequently the testimony of the continent must be sought to piece out what little British letters tell us. We learn of three shadowy British holders of the martyr's crown, Alban, Aaron, and Julius, in the *Life of Germanus* by Constantius, which dates to the end of the fifth century, and we further learn from Gildas, who testifies in the mid-sixth century, that Alban won his crown at Verulamium and Aaron and Julius in Caerleon. More substantial is the report that five Britons attended the Council of Arles in 314, and Athanasius records with satisfaction that the British Church was at the Council of Nicaea in 325 and supported him in 343 when a council was again convened. In 358 Hilary of Poitiers considered the bishops of Britain sufficiently important to enlist on the side of orthodoxy in the Arian struggle. The Council of Ariminum was held a year later and a number of British bishops attended, including three too poor to pay their traveling expenses. It is not impossible that these three were monks living under the vow of poverty, since the fact of their poverty elicited the praise of Sulpicius Severus.

There is a certain cumulative evidence here that mounts toward certainty. A Christian cryptogram at Cirencester attests to a Christian residence. A Christian chapel at Lullingstone attests to Christian worship. Traces of Christian churches at Silchester and Caerwent attest to Christian congregations. The presence of British bishops at fourth-century councils, however, attests to the existence of a British Church.

Furthermore the British clerics who attended the Council of Arles in 314 included the bishops of York, London, and a place called Colonia Londinensium, which has been variously identified with Caerleon-on-Usk, Colchester, and Lincoln. There is evidence here of a British Church organized on something at least analogous to diocesan lines. The conclusion that by the fourth century there were enough Christians in Britain to comprise an organized Church functioning after the pattern of the Church on the continent is justified. It probably was a Church of the town and not the country, and quite possibly of the upper classes and not the lower. It was certainly a Church related in the fact of its existence to the other fact of Roman occupation. Already the grounds were present for the identification of Roman and Christian. It seems likely that it was stronger in the west than in the east, although this may be an illusion created by the fact that the Anglo-Saxon obliteration of the Celtic past was more nearly complete in the east than in the west.

Monasticism in Britain

We have referred above to the three British bishops too poor to pay their expenses to the Council of Ariminum, and the suggestion that their poverty might have been the holy poverty of the monk. When monasticism reached Britain is a question utterly incapable of an answer, beyond the answer that it was certainly there before the time of St. Patrick. Organized monasticism was brought to Gaul from its Egyptian and Syrian seedbeds by the late fourth century. The presence of a strong monastic movement in Gaul early in the fifth century makes likely its introduction to Britain before the century was over and perhaps much earlier. As usual the evidence that first appears is oblique and tantalizingly fragmentary. In 407 three emperors of Rome were elevated in Britain; and Orosius, who is our authority on this unique occurrence, makes it clear that one of them, Constans, abandoned the cowl for the imperial purple.

There is evidence, far too fragmentary to assess let alone to believe, that the late fourth-century heretic Pelagius, who was certainly a Briton, was also a monk whose name prior to its Latinization was Morgan. It is at least conceivable that the vigor with which Germanus of Auxerre combated the Pelagian doctrine of unlimited free will and denial of original sin was fueled in part by the knowledge that the heretic had fallen not only from the usual Christian grace but from the special graces appropriate to a monk. The suggestion that British monasticism may have received its initial impulse from the potent influence of St. Martin of Tours, who is known to have been especially venerated in the Irish Church, has a certain appeal. Then there is the evidence of the ancient wattled chapel at Glastonbury, which was certainly Celtic and certainly of the fifth century. The evidence finally ceases to be oblique and at least some fragments fall into place when we reach St. Ninian, Whithorn, and the Candida Casa.

St. Ninian and Candida Casa

Deep in the south of Scotland and far to the west, north of the Isle of Man and across the narrow North Channel from Bangor and Belfast in Northern Iréland, is the small and thinly settled shire of Wigtown. It comprises two peninsulas. Toward the base of the more easterly of the peninsulas are clusters of crudely rounded hills, narrow glens, and the flat, low lying fields called the Machars. In the heart of the Machars is Whithorn. Whithorn has always been associated with the name of St. Ninian, and modern archaeology has verified the association, and incidentally justified the traditional name of his church, Candida Casa, "the white house." Mid-twentieth-century excavations have revealed the foundations of a rectangular building fifteen feet in width, with walls more than three feet thick. The *Official Guide* states that the foundations are of "roughly split, undressed blocks of local stone set in clay. Outside the masonry has been daubed with a cream-coloured plaster, portions of which were still found adhering to the base of the wall face." The creamcolored plaster justifies the name, White House, applied to this stone church, the foundation of which is today the most modest of appendages at the eastern end of what was the site of the later priory.

That the church at Whithorn was white in fact as it always was in name has an important significance. The association of white with purity is very ancient and there is evidence that among the earliest Celtic Christians white plaster on a church had a symbolic meaning. Daphne Pochin Mould quotes from a tract preserved in the ancient Irish compilation, the *Leabhar Breac,* dealing with the colors of the vestments used in Mass and their significance where the wearer is concerned: "the priest's mind should be pure like the foam on the wave, or a swan in the sunshine, or the chalk on the gable of an oratory." Just enough of Candida Casa remains to justify its name and vindicate tradition, but it was a place of substantial importance in the history of British and Irish Christianity. Archaeology dates it to the fifth century, probably to the earlier part. There is a gravestone at Whithorn and two Celtic crosses in the nearby cemetery at Kirkmadrine, all dating to the fifth century, and the gravestone inscription making highly probable a date early in the century.

For the founder, St. Ninian, we must turn to literature. All but invariably, for this remote and ill-illumined period, the first and only entirely reliable resource is the Venerable Bede, who gives in the fourth chapter of Book III some basic facts about Ninian, whom he knows as St. Nynia. Bede says that Ninian was a bishop, a native of Britain and by race a Briton, "who had been regularly instructed at Rome." Since every word is precious in matters such as these, it should be pointed out that Bede, whose ancestry was Anglo-Saxon, always distinguishes between the Britons, who spoke the Cymric dialect of Celtic and may be equated for identification purposes with the modern Welsh, and the Scots who had emigrated in great numbers from Ireland to what is now northern Wales and Scotland, spoke the Goidelic dialect of Celtic, and may be equated with the modern Irish. When Bede says that Ninian was by race a Briton, he is saying that he spoke the Cymric dialect and was not a Scot.

Bede tells us that Ninian did his missionary work among the southern Picts who lived amidst high and difficult mountains. There is in this a certain plausibility if the mountains are identified as the Grampians, since it is known that by the sixth century the Picts controlled Scotland north of the Forth-Clyde line except for Dalriada which corresponded roughly to Argyll and was held by Scots from Ireland. At this point anything that smacks of certainty ceases. The Picts are the darkest of the peoples of Dark Age Britain. They left no literature, and what archaeology can tell of them is complimentary but scanty. There is fine silver work of Pictish origin, the finest being the silver hoard unearthed in 1955–1959 in a pre-Norse church of the Pictish period located in a place of alluring name, St. Ninian's Isle in the Shetlands. However there were many churches that bore the name of St. Ninian, who seems to have enjoyed an early medieval vogue, and the presence of his name upon a church indicates no personal link. One has said all that can be said with safety when he says that in the early fifth century a native British bishop named Ninian built at Whithorn, deep in the eastern peninsula of Wigtown and across the North Channel from Ireland, a monastic church called Candida Casa. From it he brought the Word to his presumptive kinsmen or close relations, the Picts who lived north of the Forth and the Clyde. There is no proof that he established a Church among the Picts, nor indeed that he built churches, and the churches that bear his name present an illusion of his presence since they belong in the main to the twelfth century. Nevertheless he is a figure of importance. His is the first entirely reliable name that we meet in the history of missionary activity in the British Church, and the monastery he established at Whithorn had an important formative influence on Irish monasticism. That is an established fact; all else is conjecture. St. Ninian would not be the first man in history whose basic importance came after his death through the influence of the institution he created.

When we reach St. Ninian we reach the period of St. Patrick. By the mid-fifth century the Church in Britain was well established, there were British bishops and bishoprics, there were British monasteries, and missionary work in the farther reaches of Britain had begun. It is from the established background of the Church in Britain that the Church in Ireland develops. It was destined for a Dark Age development far more glorious than its compeer in Britain, and for a role in the history of Christianity quite distinct from the role of the Church in any other nation. The Christian dawn was already bright in Britain, however, when the Christian dawn was breaking across the hills of Ireland.

Bibliographical Note

A short but excellent summation of the little that is known of primitive Christianity in Britain may be found in R. P. C. Hanson, *St. Patrick, His Origins and Career* (Oxford University Press, 1968); chap. II, "The British Church in the Fifth Century." References in the above chapter to Chrysostom, *Homiliae viii;* Nennius, *Historia Britonum*, pp. 22, 164; Tertullian, Origen, and the presence of British bishops at Church councils are from this source. The archaeological evidence is presented in Jocelyn Toynbee, "Christianity in Roman Britain," *Journal of the British Archaeological Association*, 3rd series XVI (1953), pp. 1–24, and in W. H. C. Frend, "Religion in Roman Britain in the Fourth Century A.D.," *ibid.*, 3rd series XVIII (1955), pp. 1–18.

There are four sources of information, varying enormously in worth, about St. Ninian: Venerable Bede, an early *Miracles of Bishop Nynia,* a poem about him apparently written at Whithorn, and a Life of Ninnian by St. Aelred, a twelfth century abbot of Rievaulx in Yorkshire. The best edition and translation of Venerable Bede, *Ecclesiastical History of the English People*, is that of Bertram Colgrave and R. A. B. Mynors (Oxford, 1969). The *Miracula Nynie Epi-*

scopi, which contains an occasional kernel of fact nestling in the husks of wonder, is in *Monumenta Germaniae Historica: Poetae Latini Aevi Carolini* IV (Hannover, 1902), pp. 943–62. (This collection is referred to hereafter as *MGH*.) The poem on St. Ninian is available in both Latin and English translation in the *Dumfriesshire and Galloway Transactions*, 3rd series XXXVII (1961), pp. 21–51. The Life by St. Aelred, described by its modern editor as "almost worthless as a historical tract," is in Alexander P. Forbes, *Lives of St. Ninian and St. Kentigern Compiled in the Twelfth Century* (Edinburgh, 1874); Latin, pp. 137–57 with English translation, pp. 6–26. The archaeological findings at Whithorn are detailed in C. Ralegh Radford and G. Donaldson, *Whithorn and Kirkmadrine: Official Guide* (Edinburgh, 1953). For the physical description of the Whithorn findings quoted in this chapter, see p. 34.

Scholarly writing about St. Ninian concentrates on the nature and extent of his missionary activities. The most extreme example of what is almost certainly exaggeration is G. A. Frank Knight, *Archaeological Light on the Early Christianizing of Scotland*, 2 vols. (London, 1933). Knight attributes to Ninian very extensive travels and church foundations, and pictures Christianity in Scotland as extensive before the time of St. Columba. A more scholarly but seemingly exaggerated picture of the travels and evangelical activities of the saint is to be found in the works of W. Douglas Simpson: *The Historical St. Columba* (Aberdeen, 1927), *The Celtic Church in Scotland* (Aberdeen, 1935), and *St. Ninian and the Origins of the Christian Church in Scotland* (Edinburgh, 1940). The work of Simpson is criticized and a more moderate view of the work of St. Ninian is presented in a series of articles in *Analecta Bollandiana* by Paul Grosjean, S.J., a French scholar of Celtic antiquities, and by A. C. Thomas in M. W. Bailey and R. P. C. Hanson, eds., *Christianity in Britain 300–700* (Leicester University Press, 1968). John MacQueen, *St. Nynia: A Study Based on Literary and Linguistic Evidence* (Edinburgh, 1961), limits to a similar extent the work of St. Ninian, holding that it began after 400 and extended far enough east to include the present city of Carlisle.

3

The Dawn in Ireland

D URING the centuries when the western world was split into two
stark divisions, Rome and Not Rome, Not Rome masked some
of its mysteries behind such vague names for ill-defined land masses
as Germania, Scythia, and Sarmatia. Other parts of Not Rome, such
as Persia and India, were somewhat more definitely conceived. Not
Rome lay to the east, vast regions with great human hordes to be kept
from Rome by the distant ramparts of empire along the Rhine, the
Danube, and the Black Sea. All the time there was also one tiny
segment of Not Rome in the distant west, the last and most remote
land before the world ends in a watery waste, the tiny segment called
Ireland. Ultimately, Ireland was conquered by Rome, but it was a
conquest willingly accepted as time progressed and the conquest was
by the Rome of Peter, not the Rome of Caesar.

That Ireland was never part of imperial Rome has ramifications,
some perhaps unexpected. If Roman arms, laws, and government
never reached Ireland, neither did Roman masonry. Consequently
archaeology can offer little help to those who try to trace the dawn
of Christianity in Ireland. Ireland has its share of antiquities, but
Roman ruins are not among them. The result is that those who
investigate what Christian beginnings there may have been in Ireland before the coming of St. Patrick must fall back upon the record
of literature, and it is both late and extremely uncertain. Archaeology
does offer one slight bit of evidence to bolster recorded legend. The
wine merchants of Burilaga, now Bordeaux, had an emporium in
Ireland called Bordgal. According to legend, the Corcu Loidge were
the first in Ireland to accept Christianity. Archaeology has revealed

that the wine trade was conducted among them at Garranes in county Cork, possibly in return for the bronze, glass, and pottery products made there. The inference that the new faith may have followed the wine trade into Ireland is at least as enticing as the similar inference where Britain is concerned.

The Pre-Patrician Saints

Legend with virtually no substance to support it proffers the names of various Irish saints who either lived before the time of Patrick or had their faith and their sanctity independent of him. The oldest is St. Ciaran of Saigher. Of him it is recorded that he was an Irish John the Baptist, living in the wilderness and attended by wild animals; that he was a native of Ossory and famed as patron of the area; that he founded a convent for virgins near Saigher and placed it, possibly with a prudence greater than logic, under the care of his mother; and that the hawthorne bush which stands on a little island in the road at Clareen near Birr and is hung with rags and ribbons is so hung in his memory, for the tree is sacred to his name. Behind the practice is the cult of bushes and the magic powers they possess of absorbing the ills of humans who hang such votive offerings, and one recalls that at Glastonbury there is a thorn sacred to Joseph of Arimathea.

The saint of the presumptive pre-Patrician group who best retains a clear identity is Saint Declan. He was of the royal house of the Desi and the medieval life of him has it that when he was born Ireland was a pagan land. Christianity was beginning to creep in, however, and a priest named Colman came to the palace when Declan was born and induced his parents to allow the baptism of the infant. Declan grew up a Christian, went to Rome, was consecrated a bishop by the pope, returned to Ireland, presented himself at Cashel, and preached before King Aongus. The king was convinced of the truth of the new creed, but insisted on waiting for Patrick to come south and baptize him. He and Declan were of different clans, and the king was not of a mind to accept incorporation into the Church at the hands of a rival clansman. The king was duly baptized by the neutral foreigner, Patrick, and Declan returned to preach among his own people, the Desi. The ruins of the church at Ardmore in County Waterford, and the great round tower that stands beside it, are his memorial, although neither dates to his period.

While one is on the flood tide of legend, one should add that there is at Ardmore a rock sacred to St. Declan. It is the rock on which by accident he left his bell when leaving Wales for Ireland. Happily the rock with the bell on it floated along behind his boat and then took over the lead as the two neared land, indicating by the place at which it selected to land the site of the monastery he was to build. The choice was a wise one since Ardmore is a fine headland with a splendid beach. The rock is still there, and to crawl beneath it is beneficial for those with rheumatism, but it is a feat impossible for any in a state of mortal sin. Pilgrims still visit Ardmore on St. Declan's day, and amidst the multitude of Patricks who dot school rolls in Ireland, now and then appears an iconoclastic Declan. The veneration of St. Declan is one of the oldest threads in Irish Christianity, unbroken from its very first days.

Palladius

We come a little closer to solid ground when we meet Palladius in the pages of Prosper of Aquitaine. Little is known of Palladius or, for that matter, of Prosper who lived and wrote in the first half of the fifth century. Prosper states that in 431 Pope Celestine consecrated one Deacon Palladius a bishop and sent him to be the first bishop of the Christians in Ireland. The inferences are important: if Prosper is to be trusted, there were enough Christians in Ireland before St. Patrick arrived to require a bishop, and the organization of the Church in Ireland started in Rome as Columbanus later states. Prosper adds, possibly with more rhetorical balance than historical accuracy, that while others were striving to keep the Roman (British) island Catholic, Palladius made the pagan (Irish) island Christian. Others, who wrote from a bias that was Irish rather than Roman, make it clear that Palladius did very little to make the pagan island Christian. Muirchu, one of St. Patrick's earliest biographers, has Palladius deterred by Irish hostility, fall victim to homesickness, and die in Britain shortly after his return. With minor variations, his is the story accepted by the early Irish historians.

Another early biographer of St. Patrick, Tírechán, really set the wild goose flying with his statement that Palladius was also called Patrick. Out of this statement arose the concept of the two Patricks, with Palladius the Old Patrick, Sen-Patric of the *Chronicum Scot-*

torum. Those who chase the wild goose in the twentieth century hold to the thesis that Palladius was sent to Ireland by Pope Celestine, worked there for about twenty years, and was the Sen-Patric. After him came the other Patrick, the St. Patrick who wrote the *Confession* and the *Epistle* and who worked in Ireland in the last third of the fifth century. While the truth in these matters is seldom a matter of certainty, it would seem likely that there was a fifth-century papal mission to Ireland headed by Palladius, that it met with scant success, that Palladius soon moved over to Britain and shortly thereafter died, that as time passed his shadowy memory fused with the bright, enduring memory of St. Patrick and they emerged two men with one name and one solid nugget of truth at the heart of the legend: there may have been enough Christians in Ireland before the coming of St. Patrick to warrant Pope Celestine sending them a bishop.

The St. Patrick of History

When we reach Saint Patrick it is dawn in Ireland, and glorious sunrise as well. Ireland is the only land on earth with a saint as the central figure in its history. There are always three St. Patricks to be considered, the St. Patrick of history, the St. Patrick of tradition, and the St. Patrick of legend. The story of the first St. Patrick is true, but its details are lamentably scanty. The story of the second St. Patrick may be true, but it takes the most delicate of hands to separate the true from the false. The story of the third St. Patrick marches resolutely into the land of fable. We have no concern with the St. Patrick of legend, except when legend is made to serve a very pragmatic purpose. Our concern must be with the St. Patrick of history and tradition, and we must wrest as much of the former from the latter as is possible.

We know the St. Patrick of history from his two unquestioned writings, his *Confession* and his *Letter to the Soldiers of Coroticus*. The former tells, in sixty-two short chapters, the story of his spiritual conversion, his struggles with inadequate education, his vocation to bring the Christian light to the pagan land where once he was a slave, his problems and his perils as he gave the rest of his days to the call he answered. Permeating all is the spirit of thanksgiving to the Lord who was ever by his side. It is a confession, a report to persons unidentified, and an act of thanksgiving. It is not an autobiography, and yet it tells us almost everything we know about the Patrick of history. The *Letter* excoriates a Welsh raider, whom Patrick calls Coroticus, who had raided a settlement of Patrick's newly baptized and confirmed Irish Christians, massacred many, and sold the rest into slavery. Patrick excommunicates Coroticus and calls his men to repentance and atonement.

The Patrick of history, as we learn from the *Confession*, was born at a place called Bonnavem Taburniae, "where three roads meet." His father, whose name was Calpornius, was a minor local magistrate, a decurion, and had become a deacon. Patrick's grandfather was a priest named Potitus. No odium was attached to the marriage of priests in the fourth century. Patrick confesses to a wayward youth in which he "knew not the true God," but standards of waywardness vary, and it is an old man with a life of self-sacrifice behind him who makes the charge. He must have lived in a region vulnerable to piratical raids across the Irish Sea, since he was kidnapped when about sixteen and brought to Ireland. He tended flocks for six years, and in the solitude of fields and moors he learned to pray. The day came when a voice heard in a dream told him that the hour of release was near, but the ship to carry him to safety was some two hundred miles away. He left his master, found the ship, and was let on board by a reluctant ship master. The ship made land and all aboard wandered in a wilderness for twenty-eight days and were saved from famine only when God answered Patrick's prayer by sending them a herd of swine. He was received back in Britain by a loving family which pleaded with him never again to leave. He had a dream, however, in which a man named Victoricus brought him letters from Ireland and, as he read one headed "The Voice of the Irish," he heard the voices of those who dwelt in Ireland by the wood of Folcut near the Western Sea plead with him to return.

Before his return was possible he had to overcome the opposition of certain of his elders who held that he was unworthy of the Irish mission and even raked up a sin of his youth that he had once disclosed to a faithless friend. Once more he sensed that God was with him and he persevered until the Irish mission was his. It was a mission of problems and perils, with the dark shadow of slavery always over him and the darker shadow of death. Yet he persevered, baptizing and confirming converts and ordaining clerics to share his task. He rejoiced that so many highborn sons and daughters of the Irish became monks and nuns. He rejoiced as well that some of his bravest converts were slaves who could be monks and nuns of the Lord only in desire. He had a human longing to return to Britain, once more to see his parents, and to go to Gaul to see his brethren, but his divinely appointed task was in Ireland. His final words are perfectly consistent with the spirit that pervades his *Confession:* "I pray those who believe and fear God, whosoever shall have deigned to look upon or receive this writing which Patrick, a sinner and unlearned as everybody knows, composed in Ireland, that no one ever say it was my ignorance that did whatever small matter I did, or proved in accordance with God's good pleasure. But judge ye, and let it be most truly believed, that it was the gift of God. And this is my confession before I die."

But Patrick did not die. He lives immortal in history, and the Patrick who lives in the imagination of the simple countryman of Ireland's remote west is the Patrick of history in every sense that is essential. We know very little of the Patrick of history, but we know the very little that matters.

The St. Patrick of Tradition

We know the Patrick of tradition partly from writings attributed to him and partly from early lives. The writings attributed to him with varying degrees of probability are three isolated sayings known as the *Dicta Patricii;* certain canonical writings that bear his name; and the *Lorica,* "The Breastplate of St. Patrick," which is known in Irish as *Faeth Fiada,* "Deer's Cry," a hymn invoking God's protection against a number of dangers. The probability that the *Dicta* are authentic is lessened by the fact that the third urges upon all churches the Greek invocation, *Kyrie eleison,* which was introduced to the West by Pope Gelasius (492–496). The canonical writings are suspect because they seem designed to quiet controversies in the Irish Church that flared up in the seventh century. The *Lorica* is dubiously attributed to Patrick because, although it is in Irish of great antiquity, linguists competent in that recondite field hold that it is not of the period of Patrick.

The earliest Lives of St. Patrick are contained in the ninth-century manuscript called the *Book of Armagh.* One is by Tírechán, a native of Tirawley and a man who wrote with a purpose. His Life, which probably dates to the last third of the seventh century, is largely devoted to activities ascribed to St. Patrick but uniformly designed to buttress the ecclesiastical and territorial claims made by the monastery of Armagh. In the first part Patrick tours northern Ireland, accepting grants of land from local kings and land owners in Meath, Connacht, the land of the northern Uí Néill, and the coast to the northwest. He builds churches as he goes and ordains clergy for them. In the second part Patrick makes a similar tour of the south, ending at Cashel. It is entirely possible that Tírechán presents a fairly accurate transcript of church lands granted and the names of the grantors. The use of St. Patrick as the omnipresent "onlie begetter" of all the churches claimed by Armagh, which meant in effect churches unattached to monasteries, is the part that is suspect. The one who would travel Ireland with Tírechán as guide is more likely to be hot upon the traces of some later bishop of Armagh.

The other Life of Patrick in the *Book of Armagh* is by Muirchu moccu Machtheni, a cleric of the church of Sletty who led the life of a hermit and died in 700. Bishop Aed of Sletty assigned him the task of writing the Life. Muirchu uses Patrick's *Confession* for the early part of the work. After Patrick's escape from Ireland, Muirchu has him set out for Rome but, attracted by the fame of Germanus of Auxerre, he becomes his student and studies under him for some thirty or forty years. He is then urged in a vision to return to Ireland, tells the vision to Germanus, and Germanus sends him to Ireland with a priest named Segitius. In the meantime the mission of Palladius is taking place. When Patrick hears of the death of Palladius, he betakes himself to a Bishop Amathorex who consecrates him a bishop and he then proceeds to Ireland. There follows a series of incidents culminating in a meeting with King Loeghaire who gives Patrick permission to preach in Ireland. These incidents are designed to buttress the claims of Tara and Armagh. Muirchu's Life, like Tírechán's, is enlivened by miracles and concludes with an account of Patrick's death and burial. In addition to these early Lives there are a number of later Lives, starting with the early ninth-century Life by Nennius in his *History of the Britons* and a homiletic Life mainly in Irish with Latin sections called the *Vita Tripartita* which Irish scholars variously date from the eighth to the eleventh century.

We are not done with the tradition when we enumerate its ancient sources. In 1904 J. B. Bury, the historian of Rome, published a brilliant *Life of Patrick*. So influential has this work been that it is hardly an exaggeration to say that all writing about St. Patrick since 1904 has been in one way or another a commentary on Bury. Bury accepted much of the tradition. He believed that Patrick visited Rome and lived in Gaul; he accepted as historical the meeting with King Loeghaire; he viewed as authentic the *Dicta* and much of the canonical writing. Most important of all, he believed that a valid life of Patrick could be based on Tírechán and Muirchu. On the whole, a majority of Patrician scholars belong to the school of Bury and tradition, although they make such exceptions to what they consider the excessive credulity of the master as they deem necessary. The most competent of them all, the Austrian born expert on Ireland, Ludwig Bieler, puts succinctly the philosophy behind the school of tradition in his *The Life and Legend of St. Patrick:* "accept as probable all traditions which existed at the end of the seventh century unless they are demonstrably false; . . . unless a later piece of evidence is in itself suspect, or runs counter to fifth century evidence that is unequivocal, it ought to be accepted."

The scholars who reject the tradition as either false or at least unprovable take their major stand on two issues: Patrick's place and date of birth and, what looms considerably larger in the scholarly debate, the question of his residence in Gaul. Where Patrick's place of birth is concerned, neither the traditionalists nor the antitraditionalists have much to go on. He named it Bonnavem Taburniae and the only other indisputable fact about it is that it must have been close enough to the western sea to be raided by Irish slavers. The *Vita Tripartita* adds that Patrick was born among the Britons of Ail-Cluaide, which is to be identified with Dumbarton on the north bank of the Strathclyde fourteen miles northeast of Glasgow. Those who accept this Scottish birthplace find support for the thesis in the identification of Coroticus with Ceretic Wledig of Strathclyde in the Welsh genealogies. Others counter with the contention that Patrick's father owned a substantial villa of the Roman sort and as a decurion was a member of a local municipal council, and that such villas and such offices did not exist in Strathclyde. They favor a birthplace in the south of Wales or the southwest of England.

There is less dispute where the date of his birth is concerned, except when the issue is clouded by the matter of the two Patricks.

If Palladius went to Ireland in 431, Patrick could not have gone before 432 and this date finds support in the *Annals*. A life span for St. Patrick somewhere in the order of 390–460 would seem likely, with the last three decades spent on the Irish mission. The matter of his spending some thirty or forty years in study under Germanus can be lightly dismissed as part of the Patrick legend which, with the finest kind of chauvinism, would have Patrick equal the 120-year life span of Moses.

The prime crux of all is the matter of his residence in Gaul. Nothing Patrick ever wrote has aroused more controversy than the first of the *Dicta:* "I had the fear of God to guide my way through the parts of Gaul and Italy, as well as in the islands of the Tyrrhenian Sea." Some traditionalists have Patrick land in Gaul after his escape from slavery in Ireland and wander for his twenty-eight days in a man-made wilderness caused by the ravages of German invaders. Those who incline to question the tradition have him wander through the hills of Wales or by the Strathclyde. It could be significant that the early Lives on which the tradition is founded leave implicit a return to Britain from slavery in Ireland and have his period in Gaul come later. The traditional view has Patrick spend some years under St. Honoratus at the monastery of Lerins off the southeast coast of Gaul and then proceed for a longer period to Auxerre where he studied and prayed under Germanus. He was then consecrated a bishop either by Germanus or his successor and after overcoming the obstacles referred to above undertook the Irish mission to which he devoted the rest of his life.

Those who reject the tradition deny that Patrick had his training in Gaul, rejecting the tradition with the verdict of "Not Proven" despite the wish he expresses in the *Confession* to go to Gaul to see his brethren. Their contention is that his background was exclusively British. It rests in no small measure on the unquestionable fact that Patrick is often guilty of bad Latin, or perhaps more accurately, of the sort of vulgar Latin that may have been spoken in Britain in his day. His relative incompetence in Latin is unchallenged. Patrick acknowledges it himself, calling himself in the *Confession* "a rustic, an exile, unlearned surely as one who knows not how to provide for the future" (ch. 12). But he asks the "lordly rhetoricians" who despised him and tried to block his assignment to the Irish mission at a time when, as he says in chapter 32, he was not in Britain, to ponder this: "Who was it that exalted me, fool though I be, from the midst of those who seem to be wise and skilled in the law, and powerful in word and in everything else?" (ch. 13). The thesis of those who hold that no one with an academic background in Gallic Latinity could be guilty of the frequently bad Latin of the *Confession* and the *Letter* stands or falls with belief in the unerring success of the Latin instruction in the monasteries of Gaul and the verbal purity of conversation within their walls. St. Patrick was most certainly a man of action, and a temperament such as his does not always easily abide attention to verbal niceties. Against his verbal infelicities may be counterbalanced his intimate knowledge of Scripture shown by the constant scriptural echoes in his writing. What is at least as significant as verbal felicity in taking the intellectual measure of the man, is his repeated demonstration of a particular interest in St. Paul's Epistle to the Romans and a thorough understanding of its often difficult doctrine.

The question of Patrick's academic background cannot be separated from the question of the origin of his mission. The *Confession* is essentially an *apologia* in the Greek sense, but there is also a sense in which it is a report. He says in chapter 51, "I spent money for you that they might receive me. And both amongst you and wherever I journeyed for your sake, through many perils, even in remote parts where no man dwelt, and where never had anyone come to baptize, or to ordain clergy, or to confirm the people, I have, by the bounty of the Lord, done everything, carefully and most gladly, for your salvation." In chapter 53 he says, "You know also how much I spent on those who ruled in all the districts to which I used to come more frequently," and in the next chapter, "Nor would I write to you that there may be an occasion of flattering words or gain, nor that I hope for honor from any of you." No certain answer can be given to the identity of the persons to whom these chapters are addressed. It is possible that they were addressed to his Irish converts, but it would seem more likely that they were addressed to those who sent him on his mission and to some extent at least financed it. The Church was strong enough in Britain by Patrick's day to organize and finance a mission of conversion to Ireland. However the tradition that he was sent to Ireland from Gaul is equally consistent with the interpretation that his *Confession* is in part a report to Gallic patrons who rejected the advice of those who held him incapable of the mission and backed him with their confidence and their money.

If the ancient tradition is of very little value where a knowledge of Patrick's activities in Ireland is concerned, there is a genial modern tradition derived from it which is equally misleading. By this tradition Patrick was a wonder-worker eagerly welcomed by a people receptive on instinct of the new faith and impatiently waiting its coming. He does his magic work without let or hindrance, and lo, Ireland has been converted. It is a tradition reaching an annual climax on March 17, when it finds eloquent expression at dinners held to celebrate the saint and the day. It is an oral tradition, to be sure, but oral tradition can be as enduring in the twentieth century as in the seventh.

The St. Patrick of Actuality

The St. Patrick of actuality whom we meet in the *Confession* and to a lesser degree in the *Letter* is a very different and far more convincing person than the wonder-worker of ancient or modern tradition, and one vastly better calculated to command our belief and our respect. He is not a wonder-worker. There is not a single miracle recorded in the *Confession.* There are repeated instances of the special providence of God working on Patrick's behalf or directing him on his uncertain way, but special providence is a concept very different from miracle. Patrick did not come to an eagerly receptive people; "Most assuredly I believe that I have received from God what I am. And so I dwell in the midst of barbarous heathens, a stranger and an exile for the love of God" are opening sentences from the *Letter.* On one occasion in his ministry he was held captive for fourteen days, as he records in chapter 52: "Sometimes I used to give presents to the kings, besides the hire that I gave to their sons, who accompany me. Nevertheless they seized me with my companions. And on that day they most eagerly desired to kill me; but my time had not yet come. And everything they found with us they plundered and myself they bound in iron chains. And on the fourteenth day the Lord freed me from their power; and whatever was ours was restored to us for God's sake, and for the sake of the good friends whom we had provided beforehand." On another occasion he was held captive for sixty days but as he says in chapter 35: "Now, it would be a tedious task to narrate the whole of my toil in all its details, or even partially. I shall briefly say in what manner the most gracious God often rescued me from slavery and from the twelve dangers in which my life was imperiled, besides many plots, which I am not able to express in words, lest I should weary my readers." He had to face the mockery of all who are fools for the sake of Christ: ". . . they kept saying, 'Why does this fellow thrust himself into danger amongst enemies who have no knowledge of God?' " (chapter 46). His constant answer is simple and direct: "I have part with those whom He called and predestined to preach the Gospel amidst no small persecutions even unto the very ends of the earth. . . ." (*Letter,* chapter 6). And again, in chapter 10: "In short, I am a slave in Christ to a foreign nation on account of the unspeakable glory of the eternal life which is in Christ Jesus our Lord."

This is the St. Patrick of actuality, and immortality, and no studied tribute to him can reflect more luster on his name than do the simple, usually labored, and often incoherent sentences of the *Confession* and *Letter.* It was the St. Patrick of actuality, the slave of Christ and his follower in exile but not the wonder-worker of tradition old or new, who established the tradition in which the Irish monks who brought Christianity back to Europe in the sixth, seventh, and eighth centuries lived, worked, and suffered. A frequent part of the pattern was the martyr's violent death.

Bibliographical Note

For the pre-Patrician saints, see Daphne Pochin Mould, *Ireland of the Saints* (London, 1952), with John J. Ryan, *Irish Monasticism: Its Origins and Early Development* (London and Dublin, 1931; Cornell University Press, 1972), as an occasional corrective.

The mission of Palladius is first mentioned in Prosper of Aquitaine whose *Chronicon* is available in Theodor Mommsen, ed., *MGH: Chronica Minora Saeculorum IV, V, VI, VII,* vol. I (Berlin, 1892), pp. 341–499. The confusion of Palladius and Patrick is very old. Tírechán of Tirawley (see below), c. 664–700, refers to "Palladius who is called by the other name Patrick"; the *Hymn of Fiacc,* c. 700, says "the other Patrick joined his greater namesake in Heaven"; the *Martyrology of Oengus,* c. 800, calls Palladius *Sen-Patraic* ("the old Patrick") and the *Annals of Ulster* date to the year 457 "the repose of the Old Patrick."

T. F. O'Rahilly, *The Two Patricks* (Dublin, 1942), identifies the "Old

Patrick" with Palladius and brings St. Patrick to Ireland in 462, more than thirty years after the mission of Palladius. The problem is rehearsed also in James Carney, *The Problem of St. Patrick* (Dublin, 1942; reprinted, 1961). The case for two Patricks is reviewed and rejected by Ludwig Bieler in "The Mission of Palladius," *Traditio* 6 (1948), pp. 1–32. Bieler believes that Palladius was not the "Old Patrick" but that he was in the Wicklow region for some years, and that he founded three churches and suffered martyrdom there.

Martin P. Harney, S. J., ed. and trans., *The Legacy of Saint Patrick* (Boston, 1972), contains the *Confession, Letter to the Soldiers of Coroticus, Hymn of St. Secundinus,* and the *Lorica.* All quotations from the writings of St. Patrick are from this edition. The authentic writings are also available in Newport J. D. White, *The Writings of St. Patrick* (London, 1932), and Ludwig Bieler, *The Works of St. Patrick* (London, 1952).

The early Lives by Muirchu and Tírechán are in Whitley Stokes, trans., *Book of Armagh,* Rolls Series, 2 vols. (London, 1887), and in Kathleen Mulchrone, trans., *Book of Armagh,* 2 vols. (Dublin, 1939). The *Vita Tripartita* is also in the *Book of Armagh.* The *Vita Patricii* of Nennius is in his *Historia Brittonum cum addiatamentis Nennii,* chaps. 50–55, ed. T. Mommsen, *MGH: Auctores Antiquissimi* XIII (Berlin, 1898). In addition several eighth- and ninth-century Lives were printed by John Colgan in his *Acta Sanctorum Hiberniae* (1645).

Among the modern comprehensive studies of St. Patrick may be singled out J. B. Bury, *The Life of St. Patrick and His Place in History* (London, 1904); Newport J. D. White, *St. Patrick, His Life, Times and Writings* (London, 1920); Ludwig Bieler, *The Life and Legend of St. Patrick* (Dublin, 1949); and R. P. C. Hanson, *St. Patrick a British Missionary Bishop* (Leicester University Press, 1965), and *St. Patrick, His Origins and Career* (Oxford University Press, 1968). Hanson is the most competent of the scholars who break with the Patrick tradition. Important critiques of St. Patrick's biographers are found in Paul Grosjean, S. J., "Notes sur les documents anciens concernant S. Patrice," *Analecta Bollandiana* LXII (1944), pp. 42–73, and D. C. Binchy, "Patrick and His Biographers: Ancient and Modern," *Studia Hibernica* II (1962), pp. 7–173.

On St. Patrick's Latin style see M. Esposito, "Notes on the Latin Writings of St. Patrick," *Journal of Theological Studies* XIX (July 1918), pp. 342–46, and Christine Mohrmann, *The Latin of St. Patrick* (Dublin, 1961).

4

The Dawn in Scotland

DURING the century that separated the presumptive date of Patrick's coming and the entry of St. Columba into the religious life the Church became established in Ireland and then started to consolidate itself. These hundred years began with Patrick's preaching, baptizing, confirming, and ordaining. The modest story that he tells in his *Confession* has the flavor of the Acts of the Apostles, and in all probability the reality was apostolic. There is a slight suggestion of the monastic in the religious establishments he brought into being; Patrick speaks of the newly converted monks and virgins who gathered in the name of Christ. If we knew what pattern of church organization he had in mind, we could speak with greater confidence, but probably it was the pattern familiar to him at home, the episcopal pattern of Roman Britain in which bishops exercised administrative authority and monasteries and their abbots were subject to them.

The Irish Monastic Church

This was not the pattern that Ireland was to know, and no one has ever offered a complete explanation of that fact. The likely explanation of this failure is that there was no single reason but rather a complex of reasons. One reason is fairly obvious. In a missionary country the monastery and not the parish is the obvious pattern of organization. The monastery is the focal point from which missionaries can go out to a partially converted people as from a base of supplies that are both spiritual and physical, and the focal point to which they can return when the need arises, and the need may quite

27

as well be physical as spiritual. When conversion is complete, and with conversion the danger of hostility has vanished, the parish becomes the obvious pattern of organization. Furthermore, the monastery is a logical center of secular learning as well as religious instruction, and pagan Ireland had a tradition of centralized learning at the bardic colleges where druids and brehons were trained in their often esoteric crafts. The druid vanished with paganism but the bard and the brehon did not, and not infrequently the bard and the brehon taught the monk his literature and law as the bard Gemman taught St. Columba.

The divergence from the usual pattern, which found Irish bishops as well as priests under the administrative authority of abbots, was not without a logic of its own in a land where the process of conversion was continuing. There are certain church functions that only the bishop can perform: confirmation, ordination, and consecration of church property. These are precisely the functions most commonly in demand in a missionary country as the Church becomes established, and so bishops are in a demand at least as great as the demand for priests. But in such a country the ordinary daily functions of the two orders are identical, and both bishop and priest can do their work more effectively if freed from administrative responsibility of the religious headquarters, the monastery out of which they work. There is no particular paradox in a bishop being under the administrative authority of an abbot in a missionary country in which the Church is organized on a monastic basis. Bishop and priest do the work of Mary; the abbot can do the tasks of Martha.

Major Irish Monasteries

There is a passage in Tírechán descriptive of St. Patrick's foundation of Trim near Tara. It is no doubt true that Tírechán reflects back to the fifth century what prevailed in the seventh century in which he lived, but the pattern is probably valid for the post-Patrician century with which we are concerned. The lord of Trim gave the land for the monastery and its church, with the proviso that the monastery was to educate the children of the district. To perpetuate the monastery, one child in seven so educated was to enter the monastic life. A member of the founder's family was to be abbot if a member was available; the hereditary nature of the position was one of its marked Irish peculiarities. As with other monasteries, Trim was linked in a monastic series called a *paruchia,* a series under one ultimate authority and roughly analogous to the *province* which is the organizational principle of some contemporary religious orders. Monks moved from one establishment to another within the *paruchia* almost at their free will.

Certain monasteries can be singled out for their preeminence. There was Clonard in Meath, some thirty-five miles west of Dublin, which was founded about 520 by St. Finnian. This was the seedbed of monasticism, with the most celebrated of the older generation of missionaries, the group known as "the Twelve Apostles of Ireland," among Finnian's disciples. From Clonard came St. Ciaran, St. Brendan of Birr, St. Brendan the Voyager, and preeminent among the Twelve, St. Columba. There was Clonmacnois in Offaly, a few miles south of Athlone, the foundation of St. Ciaran who lived to the mid-sixth century. This was the great collegiate monastery, a massive institution with thousands living and studying there. The great nursery of missionaries stood far to the north upon the coast east of Belfast, the monastery of Bangor which was founded by St. Comgall who is believed to have been an Irish Pict. There was a close link between Bangor and Candida Casa and later between Bangor and Iona, as Bangor became a stepping-stone for Christianity when it passed from Ireland to Scotland.

Farther south was the monastery at Glendalough in the Valley of the Lakes in County Wicklow, southeast of Dublin, a site which is still a prime tourist objective. This was the foundation of St. Kevin, a member of the royal family of Leinster whose instincts were for the hermitage and not the castle. He selected a site ideal for a hermitage between the upper and the lower lakes, but its isolation was destroyed by the enthusiasm of the admirers who sought him out and brought into being a protomonastery by the waters. Kevin himself was forced to seek a less accessible place for contemplation, selecting the grotto by the upper lake which the more energetic tourists know as St. Kevin's Bed. Glendalough was a very early foundation, the date of St. Kevin's death being about 615. There is nothing at Glendalough today which dates to his foundation. The stone church called Kevin's Kitchen and the ruins by it were of later construction.

The most splendid of the monastic churches of the nascent period of Irish Christianity was at Kildare, in the valley of the Liffey. This stood by the foundation which St. Brigid brought into being at a date so early that accounts of her personal acquaintance with St. Patrick, although fictional, are plausible. From the cluster of legends which surround her name, recounted in pleasant fashion by her seventh-century biographer, Cogitosus, a few kernels of fact at least can be extracted with a measure of confidence. They concern her birth and childhood. She was the daughter of Dubhthach, to anticipate a title, poet laureate to King Loeghaire, and his concubine Brotsech, and is reputed to have been brought up in the household of a druid. She managed to escape an arranged marriage and to become a nun, founding her nunnery at Kildare on the site of an ancient pagan temple. Her identity came to be fused with that of the pagan goddess Brigit, patroness of poetry and the useful arts. The perpetual fire which burned in her honor at Kildare and was seen by Giraldus Cambrensis as late as 1186 may have been a dim memory of the pagan cult of the goddess Brigit, perpetuated in a flame that honored Mary of the Gael. St. Brigid induced the head of a group of hermits of the area to accept consecration as a bishop and to join her in the establishment of the monastery at Kildare, the one authenticated double monastery, or monastery for both sexes, in Ireland. She met abbots and bishops on equal terms and, with an administrative competence at least as great as theirs, proceeded to construct one of Ireland's most important *paruchiae*. She is remembered and venerated to this day, as St. Brigid in Ireland, St. Bride of the Kine in the Hebrides, St. Bride elsewhere in Scotland, and St. Ffraid in Wales.

Irish Monastic Life

In general the Irish monastic regimen was stricter than the Benedictine. One might note that St. Benedict of Nursia (c. 480–543) lived in the century under discussion and that Irish monasticism developed at a date too early to show his influence in its formation. A number of formulations of the Irish penitential code exist, a code far more severe for the clergy than for the laity. A psychological principle underlies them: sin is a disease of the soul and a penance is not a penalty but a cure. The cure was the opposite of the disease, penance being imposed on the thesis that an evil is cured by the virtue antithetical to it.

Irish monasticism succeeded in effecting the implausible combination of the anchorite's life with the life of service to the people. The hermits lived apart from the monastery but under the jurisdiction of the abbot, but they were neither isolated from the needs of the people nor indifferent to the principle of service. They were a leaven for the crude mixture of barbaric practices, primitive passions, and yet simple rudimentary virtues that marked a people new to Christianity. They aided peoples capable of civilization, and starting the painful process of attaining it, to sense the difference between Rome and Not Rome and the superiority of the former.

A typical Irish monastery was built within an enclosure, frequently a fort of pagan days, and comprised one or more small churches, a graveyard, some huts of the beehive sort in which individual monks or small groups lived, a larger hut for the abbot which might approach the dignity of a house, as well as work buildings and quite possibly some standing crosses. As the numbers in a monastery grew until the monastic church would no longer accommodate all, instead of the church being enlarged, another small church was built, and quite possibly still another until one reached the multiple churches of Glendalough. Sometimes, as at Armagh, one church was for the clergy and another for the laity. Sometimes, as at Kildare, one side of the church was for men and the other side for women. The greater the celebrity of the monastery, the greater the sanctity of its graveyard, until one reaches in the Life of St. Finnian the logical, ultimate assurance that was given by an angel. No one buried in the graveyard of St. Finnian's monastery would go to hell. The same comforting assurance lay behind the burial of kings at Armagh, Clonmacnois, and Glendalough, nor should the visitor to Iona be surprised by the discovery that forty-eight Scottish kings rest in guaranteed peace on the sacred island, along with four Irish kings and eight Norwegian.

Such was the monastic pattern which St. Columba contributed to in Ireland and then transported to Iona in the Hebrides, and perhaps from there to the Scottish mainland. With modifications and variations, it was the pattern Irish missionaries brought to western Europe when the Dark Ages were darkest, and Rome had desperate need for the light from the tiny segment of Not Rome by the western sea. The long and intricate story of how that light was brought from land to land begins with St. Columba and the monastery at Iona, that tiny Hebridean outpost off the Ross of Mull which became the Holy Island revered throughout Scotland and Britain.

Adomnan's Life of St. Columba

What we know of St. Columba with reasonable certainty comes from his Life as written by Adomnan, a seventh-century successor as abbot of Iona. Adomnan was a man of very substantial ability, a church diplomat with relationships that extended far from his insular outpost to the Church in Northumbria and England to the south. He wrote the *Vita Sancti Columbae* before 704. It exists in a manuscript written by 713 and preserved at Schaffhausen in Switzerland, as well as in several ninth-century transcripts. One must understand that the *Vita* is the life of a saint as the seventh century understood the term. A saint's life so understood is lived in constant contact with the supernatural. It is a life compounded of miracle and wonder, lived by one whose sanctity elevates him above the normal powers of man and gives him something of the vision granted to the saints and angels in heaven. A biography of this sort rests upon the premise that our life on earth is lived within a cloud which is constantly pierced with radiance from heaven for those whose austerities, penances, and prayers win them the vision. Thus Book I of the Life of St. Columba concerns chiefly his powers of prophecy and his intuitive knowledge of events taking place elsewhere. Book II concerns his miracles, his changing water to wine and bitter fruit to sweet, hastening the ripening of grain, and the like. Book III concerns his angelic visions, mainly of angels conducting the souls of the blessed to paradise. As is always true in early hagiography, what the modern age considers biographical and historical details are incidental to the theme.

And yet, relatively trivial as such matters were to Adomnan, he had an instinct for accuracy in them. He makes it clear that he used both written sources and the traditions handed down at Iona. It is thought that the written sources might have been the work of Cuimine, abbot of Iona some sixty years after Columba's death. Bede, who makes no reference to the work of Adomnan, does say (III, 4) that some of Columba's disciples are believed to have written about him.

Adomnan's Second Preface states, "The holy Columba was born of noble parents, having as his father Fedelmith, Fergus's son, and his mother Ethne by name, whose father may be called in Latin 'son of a ship' and in the Irish tongue Mac-naue. In the second year after the battle of Cul-drebene, the forty-second year of his age, Columba sailed away from Ireland to Britain, wishing to be a pilgrim for Christ." This information dovetails with information in the Irish annals. The original name of St. Columba was Cremthann, meaning *fox*. It was Latinized and moderated for church use into Columba, meaning *dove*, and amplified into Columcille, *dove of the Church*, presumably in recognition of his hours of devotion. His grandfather Fergus was the son of Conall Gulban, founder of the branch of the northern Uí-Néill to which Columba belonged. Fergus was grandson of the great central figure in this long dominant Irish dynasty, Neill of the Nine Hostages. Thus Columba was of royal stock and indeed his relationship to Ainmere, the king reigning at Tara in his youth, made it not impossible that he might succeed to the throne of Tara.

In accordance with an ancient and long enduring Celtic and Germanic custom where the young of nobility were concerned, Columba spent his early years with a foster father, Cruithnechan, the priest who baptized him. While quite young he rejected the crown for the cross, and became a monastery novice under Finnian of Moville, whose own training had been at Candida Casa. His secular training was entrusted to the bard Gemman, a Christian in faith but the inheritor of a literary tradition far older than Christianity. When in the mid-thirties Columba joined the monastery of Clonard, St. Finnian wanted him to be consecrated a bishop, but by some inadvertence he was ordained a priest. Columba accepted this as the will of God and never sought the higher rank. At Clonard he was one of "the Twelve Apostles of Ireland," and when one of the Twelve, St. Mobhi, founded the monastery of Glasnevin, Columba joined him there. In 543 the plague forced the closing of the monastery and Columba returned to the north and founded the monastery of Derry on Lough Foyle.

The sort of legend that made St. Patrick the founder of a most extraordinary number of churches, dedicated at least as much to the glory of Armagh as to the glory of God, made St. Columba founder of a comparable monastic chain. The record of his foundation at Derry seems clear. The monastery was located on Lough Foyle at a fort which belonged to Aid, son of King Ainmere and therefore Columba's first cousin once removed, who deeded him the land for his foundation in 545. There is a comparably reliable if factually less detailed ascription to him of the monastery of Durrow in Offaly. Adomnan says (I, 3): "At one time, when for some months the blessed man remained in the midland district of Ireland, while by God's will founding the monastery that is called in Irish *Dairmag* [Durrow], it pleased him to visit the brothers who lived in the monastery of Clóin of Saint Ceran [Clonmacnoise]." A much more dubious link joins his name to that of the monastery of Kells, in Meath. All the rest is legend rooted perhaps in piety but not in truth.

"To Every Cow Belongs Its Calf"

The central historic event linked to Columba by Adomnan as a dating device is the battle of Cul-drebene. This battle between the southern Uí-Néill and the northern was fought at a site between Drumcliff and Sligo in northern Connacht. When legend linked the name of Columba to this battle it had a moment of high inspiration and concocted a tale vastly preferable on artistic grounds to what one must fear is sober truth. Legend has it that Columba borrowed from Finnian a manuscript of St. Jerome's text of the Psalter and Gospels which he had brought from Rome. Columba then proceeded to copy the manuscript without Finnian's knowledge or permission. When Finnian learned of this, he demanded both manuscript and copy. Columba would grant him the former but not the latter, and the matter came before Diarmit, head of the southern Uí-Néill and then king at Tara. King Diarmit pondered this strange and unprecedented case involving what a later age would call copyright, and made his ruling by the clause in Brehon law which he considered best applicable by analogy to the problem. "To every cow belongs its calf" was the clause, and by that principle the king ruled that the copy belonged with the manuscript and thus both were the property of Finnian.

An outraged Columba then gathered the forces of the northern Uí-Néill, attacked the southern forces under Diarmit at Cul-drebene, and defeated them. There followed reflection, remorse, and confession. Columba's confessor, St. Molaise, imposed upon him as his penance exile from Ireland with the injunction never again to see his native land, and the further injunction to convert to Christ a number as large as had fallen at Cul-drebene. And so legend has a penitent and mournful Columba leave Ireland for the Hebrides, with the task of converting the northern Picts, and the high destiny of starting the Irish missionary movement of the Dark Ages that has made his name immortal. The legend is a splendid one, and lacks no merit except verifiable truth. If Adomnan knew of the legend, he does not refer to it, and he does record that Columba returned several times to Ireland. And yet there is in Adomnan something difficult to explain. In 562, the year after the battle, Columba was excommunicated. It was for a trivial and easily pardonable offense, Adomnan assures his reader, an assurance which leads one to suspect that the motivation may have been political rather than theological. In any event the supernatural came to the rescue. St. Brendan had a vision of a pillar of fire preceding Columba, and on the head of this vision his excommunication was rescinded and honor paid to him. It may perhaps be graceless to add that if Columba had been tempted to disobey his father confessor and see Ireland again, he could have done so on a clear day by climbing the hill on Iona and looking south.

The Synod of Druimm-cete

On one occasion Columba certainly returned to Ireland. According to the Forespeech of the *Amra Choluim Chilli*, which is partly a poem of welcome written to greet Columba on his return to Ireland and partly a poetic lamentation on his death, Columba returned to Ireland to attend the Synod of Druimm-cete. He came for three reasons: to redeem a young prince held hostage by the high king; to protect the *filid*, scholars of the realm who were threatened with banishment; and most important of all, to make peace between the Irish and their kinsmen the Scots of Dalriada. But as the *Amra* has it, Columba never saw Ireland again. J. O'Beirne Crowe translates the pertinent passage as follows:

... they say that Colum Cille by no means saw Eriu that time, for there used to be a bandage over his eyes; and it is it that caused that, because he promised before that at going past it, that he would not view Eriu from that forth, saying:

> There is a gray eye
> That will view Eriu backwards;
> By no means will it see afterwards
> The men of Eriu or its women.

An affiliated legend may be added. *Dallan* means blind. The blind man, whose name was Eochaid, was the son of a woman named Forchella. It is part of the legend that the *Amra* was written by a blind man known as Dallan Forgaill, "Forchella's blind son," to honor the returning Columba. As the synod was ending with Columba triumphant on all three counts, he read the poem to the returning hero who showed a complacency that little befitted his sanctity. Fortunately his companion, St. Baithene, observed a troop of scoffing demons triumphantly circling the head of Columba and warned the holy man of the insecurity of his holiness. Columba forbade further reading, but the blind man asked permission to finish the poem after the saint died. On hearing from an angel of Columba's death, the blind man finished his work, whereupon he regained his sight. One might add for the benefit of any baffled by the grammar of the passage quoted that a good translation into standard English to replace the century-old and painfully verbatim translation by Crowe is one of the desiderata of Irish studies. What is more, the reliability of legend about the return of Columba to Ireland, embroidered though it is by the Celtic imagination, fades before Adomnan's assurance that he returned a number of times, and no mention is made by Adomnan of the bandage.

Scottish Dalriada

We return to our starting point. Whether inspired by the spirit of penitence, adventure, or missionary zeal, and quite possibly by a combination of the three, in the spring of 563 Columba sailed out of Derry. His coracle of wicker and hides was capacious enough for twelve companions and supplies for the voyage. He was accompanied by an uncle, two cousins, Mochonna whose father was a king, and eight other men. They coasted around the northern shore of what now is County Antrim, crossed the North Channel to the Mull of Kintyre, and then followed the coast of that long and narrow Scottish peninsula up to Dunadd at the head of the Sound of Jura. Here was the castle of his cousin Conall, ruler of the Scottish Dalriada.

The Scottish Dalriada was a settlement from Irish Dalriada in Ulster. The settlement seems to have started in the fifth century and, as the Scots poured in from Ireland the indigenous Picts were driven to the east and north. By the time of Columba's coming, the power of the invading Scots had reached and passed its high-water mark. In 563 it was approximately coterminous with modern Argyllshire. The Picts had already rallied under King Brude mac Maelchon, stopped further Scot expansion, won back some of the territory they had lost, and reduced Columba's cousin Conall to vassalage. The power of the Scots in the Inner Hebrides was substantial, however, and the monastery that Columba was to found on Iona was probably within the Scottish and Christian realm of his cousin Conall. From Conall's castle Columba had a relatively short passage between the islands of Jura and Scarba across to the long and westward pointing peninsula, the Ross of Mull, and so to Iona off its western extremity. Landing was made here on May 12, 563, at the bay variously called Port à Churaich (Port of the Coracle), and St. Columba's Bay.

Iona

The modern pilgrim to Iona, and on a pleasant summer weekend his name can be legion, ordinarily takes the auto ferry from Oban on the mainland to Craignure on the island of Mull. He then proceeds by bus across the fascinating, and on occasion dramatic, island of Mull, beneath Ben More and through the long, desolate, strangely beautiful Highland defile called Glen More, with now a sea loch on one side and a herd of deer high on the hill opposite. He passes through bonny Bunessen where Mull finds light and laughter, out the long Ross of Mull always toward the west until he comes to microscopic Fionnphort, the motor launch, and the rolling, tossing, tidal current ride over to Iona. This was the route Columba would parallel by sea as he was to make his way to the Isles of the Sea and Dalriada beyond. His arrival, at least as legend has it, was at the tiny bay that bears his name, at the extreme south of the island. Certainly now, and just as certainly then, the southern half of the island with its rolling moors, knobby knolls, and weathered cliffs had no habitations. From the start the village was where it is today, two-thirds of the way up the east coast across the Sound of Iona from the Ross of Mull.

Bede and the Irish annals agree that Iona was granted to Columba by the Pictish king, Brude, and the Scottish king, Conall. There is a plausibility to this, since Brude was quite possibly a Christian and his current vassal, Conall, was Columba's cousin. There were people living on Iona when Columba came and, in the absence of actual evidence, one must rely on logic and call them Christian Scots. Columba may not have been Iona's first saint. St. Oran is thought by some to have preceded him and before he died in 549 to have brought into being the Reilig Oran, burial ground for the kings of Dalriada and later for the kings of Scotland, which still exists and perpetuates his name. Columba decided that his monastery should stand beside the Reilig Oran. One should record, however, an alternate tradition which makes Oran a follower of Columba, the first monk to die at Iona, and the first occupant of the Reilig Oran.

Columba's monastery on Iona was constructed after the fashion familiar to him in his native Ireland. The church was, of course, central to the whole. Each monk had his own hut, and the huts of the monks surrounded Columba's hut which stood on the top of a small mound still called Tor Abb, "the abbot's hill." There were a refectory and kitchen, a scriptorium and library, such working buildings as a mill, smithy, and kiln, and there was a guest house. The entire monastery was surrounded by a thick earthen wall.

Neither time nor the beautifully restored Benedictine monastery of a later date has entirely obliterated Columba's primitive establishment. The Tor Abb faces the west door of the abbey. On its top there have been excavated the stone foundations on which his cell rested as well as the granite supports of a table or seat. Beside the cell is a socket for a wooden cross. Around the abbot's cell were ranged the beehive cells of the monks, traces of which have been discovered, as have minimal remains of two larger buildings somewhat to the west of Tor Abb. The outline of the boundary wall is still visible and makes it clear that Columba's monastic area extended a substantial distance to the west of the present abbey block and was much larger than it. The purpose of the wall in all probability was to keep in animals, not to keep out enemies. It is unusual in being rectangular in shape rather than circular, measuring about 1100 feet by 500. Excavation has also unearthed charcoal and other burnt material within the enclosure, probably evidence to the Norse burnings of the eighth century and later. Iona was attacked by the Vikings in 795, 802, 805, and later years until the monks who survived the repeated raids were forced to take refuge at Kells in Ireland. It is thought that the monastery was rebuilt of stone late in the ninth century and that such antiquities as the three High Crosses by the abbey and St. Oran's Chapel to the east of the abbey date to the ninth or tenth century. The Benedictine abbey which the modern visitor sees in splendidly restored form was founded by Reginald, son of the Lord of Argyll, at some date between 1164 and 1203.

The pattern of activity in the Iona monastery was that of the Irish monasteries. The monks were not hermits. Each monk had his tiny cell in which to keep his possessions and to sleep, but the monks worked, ate, and worshiped together. They were divided into three grades: the seniors, the juniors, and the workers. The workers farmed, fished, and, for reasons not entirely clear, engaged in the hunting of seals at the neighboring island of Erraid, which is joined to the coast of Mull at low tide and gave Robert Louis Stevenson a secluded retreat in which to write *Kidnapped*. The true monastic work was performed by the seniors and juniors. The seniors were the literate and educated; they conducted the religious services and worked as copyists in the scriptorium. The juniors were aspirants to their rank, following their own studies and working under the direction of the seniors. Life was of the most austere simplicity, meals rivalling in scantiness their simplicity. Clothes were of the coarsest cloth, and beds were of the hardest rock. Columba himself slept on a bare rock, and the stone that is reputed to have been his pillow is now on display at Iona. Discipline was as austere as life, and those who broke discipline were given ample time for reflection and contrition at the island of Tiree, then a flat and windswept piece of desolation far out in the Atlantic.

Hinba

In addition to the monastery on Iona the name of St. Columba is associated with a monastery at an enigmatic place which Adomnan calls Hinba. It was governed by a prior under supervision from Iona, and provided Columba with a place of spiritual retreat. The most commonly accepted but not unchallenged surmise about the locale of Hinba is to identify it with a mile-long island off the Argyll coast between Mull and Jura called Eileach an Naoimh (Elachnave), one of the group called alternately the Garvellachs and the Isles of the Sea. The little island has a beautifully sheltered landing place and in a nearby hollow are the ruins of a chapel and monastic buildings, an ancient burial place, and a crude standing cross. Excavations in 1937 by the Ministry of Works unearthed two beehive cells, one of which has been reconstructed. The isolation of Elachnave and the absence of habitation have preserved structures of the sort that were largely obliterated by later building at Iona. Those who challenge the identification of Hinba with Elachnave do so on the grounds that reference in Adomnan to a "great sea-bay" on Hinba is geographically inconsistent with the Elachnave terrain and that other considerations make more probable the identification of Hinba with the island of Jura, which lies off the Argyll coast conveniently close to the site of King Conall's fortress. Wherever Hinba may have been, it is the one monastic foundation in Scotland that we may be reasonably certain was the work of St. Columba.

Columba as a Missionary

No question about the activities of St. Columba is quite so thorny as the question of the nature and extent of his missionary activities. We have three potential sources of information: Adomnan, Bede, and Cuimine Ailbe, the seventh abbot of Iona to whom the Irish Life of Columba is attributed. Adomnan's Life makes it clear that once he had settled at Iona, Columba looked to the islands and the Scottish mainland. Adomnan refers to a visit to Ardnamurchan, the long, westward extending peninsula that juts from the mainland north of Mull and in Columba's time marked the northern limit of Scottish Dalriada. Another reference is to a visit to the island of Rathlin in the North Channel directly north of County Antrim; there are two references to visits to Skye in the Inner Hebrides; two references to visits to Loch Ness; three references to visits to the province of the Picts and three references to visits to "the spine of Britain." The spine of Britain is the chain of mountains running from Cape Wrath in Sutherland directly south. It is probably a fair assumption that Columba's visits brought him to the eastern limits of Dalriada and so to the boundary between the Scots and the Picts, approximately where Argyll meets Perth.

If one accepts the visits to Ardnamurchan and the spine of Britain as reaching at least as far as the borders of Pictland, and if one assumes that Skye, which lies far to the north of the known limits of Dalriada, was in Pictish hands, there are in Adomnan eleven references to visits made by Columba to the territory of the Picts. There is no way of determining to how many separate visits these references pertain, but it is upon them that belief in a successful mission by Columba to the northern Picts must rest if the statement of Bede is to obtain external confirmation. The closest Adomnan comes to claiming that Columba made such a mission is his statement that the success of the Picts and Scots in escaping a plague that ravaged Europe was the influence in heaven of ". . . St. Columba, whose monasteries, placed within the boundaries of both peoples, are down to the present time held in great honour by them both." The difficulty with accepting this as confirmatory evidence of what Bede says is that St. Columba, when he interceded for his people, might quite as well have been in heaven as on earth.

There is no question that a widespread *paruchia* linked to the name of Columba was established throughout Scotland after the saint's death. William Reeves, who edited Adomnan in 1857, lists forty Irish churches and fifty-six Scottish as comprising the *paruchia* of St. Columba or associated with his veneration. It is, of course, an unquestioned fact that the Irish monks of Iona undertook a mission to Northumbria a generation after the saint's death and that for a full century Iona held religious primacy over northern Ireland, Scotland, and even Northumbria. As already indicated, Bede gives testimony to this fact, and the record of that religious sovereignty will be in large measure the subject of our next chapter. But that is to ascribe neither the missionary activities nor the foundations to St. Columba himself. The three foundations one can ascribe with certainty to St. Columba are Derry, Durrow, and Iona. Everything else is specula-tion. The soundest grounds for skepticism about the reputed missionary activities of Columba—which in the Irish Life bear a disquieting resemblance to the myriad church foundations ascribed to St. Patrick by writers with the primacy of Armagh dear to their hearts—arises from the silence of Adomnan. His Life is the record of the supernatural experiences and achievements of an abbot living a monastic life on Iona, withdrawing on occasion to the spiritual solitude of Hinba, and making visits to the Picts—Christian, one should recall, as well as pagan—who lived beyond the borders of the Irish territory called Dalriada. The Columba we meet in Adomnan is a monk and not a missionary. As to whether he was the latter and the former as well, Adomnan is silent.

Columba and the Loch Ness Monster

Even when Columba was on his travels in Pictland, it is Columba the prophet, Columba of the intuitive knowledge, Columba the worker of miracles, Columba of the mystical vision of whom we read in Adomnan. One instance, with a certain contemporary interest, may suffice for illustration. Columba had been some days in the province of the Picts and had reached Loch Ness where a group was burying the body of a man killed by a water monster. Columba imposed upon a follower named Lugne mocu-Min a test of loyalty surpassing the draconic in severity: he was to plunge into the same waters, swim across, and sail back a boat that rested on the opposite bank. Without hesitation Lugne plunged in, whereupon the monster surfaced and made for him with lightning speed. "While all that were there, barbarians and even the brothers, were struck down with extreme terror, the blessed man, who was watching, raised his holy hand and drew the saving sign of the cross in the empty air; and then, invoking the name of God, he commanded the savage beast, and said: 'You will go no further. Do not touch the man; turn backward speedily.' Then, hearing this command of the saint, the beast, as if pulled back with ropes, fled terrified in swift retreat; although it had before approached so close to Lugne as he swam that there was no more than the length of one short pole between man and beast.

"Then, seeing that the beast had withdrawn and that their fellow-soldier Lugne had returned to them unharmed and safe, in the boat, the brothers with great amazement glorified God in the blessed man. And also the pagan barbarians who were there at the time, impelled by the magnitude of this miracle that they themselves had seen, magnified the God of the Christians" (II, 27).

It is pleasant to record simultaneously this clear record of a conversion and to establish the reality of the Loch Ness monster, but it is well to let the matter rest at that. One may say with certainty that St. Columba, by founding the monastery at Iona, started the process which led to the conversion of that part of Scotland still pagan. Iona was the seedbed from which grew a monastic chain that stretched across Scotland and northern England to Lindisfarne on the eastern coast. But beyond that, by carrying the cross over the North Channel to the Hebrides, St. Columba initiated the all but incredible centuries of missionary activity that were to see Irish monks bring the light to the Dark Ages, a light that was to shine on Europe from the Orkneys to Sicily. That much one can claim for St. Columba with certainty, and it is not necessary to claim more.

Bibliographical Note

The best general study of Irish monasticism is John J. Ryan, *Irish Monasticism: Its Origins and Early Development* (London and Dublin, 1931; Cornell University Press, 1972). See also John T. McNeill, *The Celtic Churches: A History A.D. 200 to 1200* (University of Chicago Press, 1974), and Kathleen Hughes, *Early Christian Ireland* (Cornell University Press, 1972).

The three sources of information about St. Columba are Adomnan's Life, Bede's *Ecclesiastical History of the English People,* and an Irish Life attributed to Abbot Cuimine. The standard edition and translation of Adomnan, *Vita Sancti Columbae,* is by A. O. and M. O. Anderson (*Adomnan's Life of Columba,* New York, 1961). All quotations in the text are from this translation. There are earlier editions by William Reeves, *The Life of St. Columba, Founder of Hy, written by Adamnan* (Dublin, 1857), and J. T. Fowler, *Adamni Vita S. Columbae* (Oxford, 1920). The Irish Life attributed to Abbot Cuimine is available in W. M. Metcalfe, *Pinkerton's Lives of the Scottish Saints* (Paisley, 1889), pp. xviii–xx, 51–69, and in Gertrud Brüning, *Zeitschrift für celtische Philologie* XI, ii (1917), pp. 260–72, 291–304. An Irish Life by Manus O'Donnell (d. 1567), *Betha Colaim Chilli, The Life of Columcille,* has been edited and translated by A. O. Kelleher and G. Schoepperle (University of Illinois Press, 1918).

Behind Adomnan's Life is a chronicle kept at Iona and embedded in the early Irish annals; see Dr. John Banneyman, "Notes on the Scottish Entries in the Early Irish Annals," *Scottish Gaelic Studies* XI (1968), pp. 149–70. The Iona entries in the Irish annals contain many references to the politics of Dalriada and the Picts from 563, the year of Columba's arrival, with exactly dated entries from 686 to 740. This Iona chronicle was available to Adomnan who became abbot of Iona in 679 and lived until about 704. The references in Adomnan to visits by Columba to the islands and the Scottish mainland are as follows: Ardnamurchan, I, 12; Skye, I, 33; II, 26; Loch Ness, II, 33; III, 14; the province of the Picts, II, 11; II, 27; II, 31; the spine of Britain, I, 34; II, 31; II, 42.

Bede has relatively little to say about Columba, other than to state that he came to Iona in 565 (sic) after founding Durrow and that he converted the northern Picts. Bede's Book III deals chiefly with the post-Columban spread of the Celtic church in Northumbria. Abbot

Cuimine was the great-grandson of a first cousin of Columba and his seventh successor as abbot of Iona (657–669). His misnamed Life comprises, with expansions and additions, Book III of Adomnan. It is debated whether this is an original work by Cuimine later incorporated into his Life by Adomnan and therefore the oldest extant example of Irish hagiography or a later abridgment of Adomnan's work identified with a lost Life by Cuimine.

The three Latin hymns attributed to St. Columba are available in Guido M. Dreves and Clemens Blume, *Analecta Hymnica Medii Aevi* (Leipzig, 1908), vol. 51. Dallan Forgaill, *Amra Choluim Chilli* is available in an execrable translation by J. O'Beirne Crowe (Dublin, 1871).

There are twentieth-century lives of St. Columba available: Aodh Sandrach De Blacam, *The Saints of Ireland: The Life-Stories of SS. Brigid and Columcille* (Milwaukee, c. 1942), and Lucy Menzies, *St. Columba of Iona: A Study of His Life, His Times, and His Influence* (New York, 1920). The latter is vitiated by an untenable theory of the separation of the Church in Scotland from the main stream of sixth-century Christianity.

The following are important critical studies of St. Columba, his biographers, and the Iona monastery: Ludwig Bieler, "The Celtic Hagiographer," *Studia Patristica V* (1962), pp. 243–65 (on Adomnan); Gertrud Brüning, "Adamnans Vita Columbae und ihre Ableitungen," *Zeitschrift für celtische Philologie* XI (1917), pp. 213–304 (for the models and sources of passages in the *Vita*); James B. E. Bulloch, "Columba, Adamnan, and the Achievement of Iona," *Scottish Historical Review* 43 (1969), pp. 111–50 and 44 (1970), pp. 17–33; and Whitley Stokes, "The Bodleian Amra Choluimb Chille," five articles in *Revue Celtique* 20 (1899) and 21 (1900).

A description of the Iona site prior to the restoration of the abbey may be found in Alexander Ewing, *The Cathedral, or Abbey Church, of Iona: A Series of Drawings and Descriptive Letterpress of the Ruins* (London, 1866), and in E. C. Trenholme, *The Story of Iona* (Edinburgh, 1909). A brief sketch of Iona history and a description of the restored abbey is available in the Iona Community brochure by Tom Graham and Grant Hicks, *Iona Abbey: a Short Tour* (Glasgow, n.d.). For the island of Iona and the Hebrides in general, see W. H. Murray, *The Hebrides* (New York, 1966).

For the identification of Elachnave as Hinba, see Murray, chap. 8,

"The Isles of the Sea," pp. 77–80. Murray offers etymological evidence that *Hinba* means "Isles of the Sea." For the identification of Hinba with the island of Jura, see M. O. Anderson, "Columba and Other Irish Saints in Scotland," *Irish Conference of Historians: Historical Studies* V (1965), pp. 30–31, and William J. Watson, *The History of Celtic Place Names in Scotland* (Edinburgh, 1926; Shannon, 1973), p. 81.

5

Lindisfarne

THE racial composition of Scotland was complete when Columba came to Iona. North of the Firth of Forth-Firth of Clyde line were the Picts, and south of the line were the Britons. This generalization is subject to one important limitation. North of the line in what is approximately modern Argyll were the immigrant Scots from Ireland and the kingdom they had established there, Dalriada, to which probably belonged the southern Inner Hebrides including Iona. South of Dalriada were the Britons of the Strathclyde and east of the Britons the Angles of Northumbria. The Britons were already Christian as were the southern Picts when Columba's coracle beached on the south shore of Iona. The northern Picts were pagan and so, at least by way of generalization, were the Angles. Here were the first two mission fields of the Irish monks. Language aided them among the Picts, who were their kinsmen, and Rome aided them among the Angles.

The Picts Arrive

Legend has a way of reducing to pleasant, human proportions the waves of humanity that swept across Europe in the ages of migration. Thus legend has the Picts emerge from Scythia, that convenient catchall term for the unknown that was Not Rome, and reach the shores of Ireland. They asked, with courtesy, permission to settle, and the Irish, with equal courtesy, offered them the portion of the larger island to the east now called Scotland. They further asked for wives, since they had left their own in Scythia, and once more the Irish obliged. The Irish set one stipulation, however, which the Picts accepted: whenever the matter would be in doubt, succession to the Pictish throne should follow the female line. This gave the Irish a toehold in the Pictish royal house.

Less is known of the Picts than of the other divisions of the Celts since they left no literature beyond the names of their kings. The few inscriptions surviving in their tongue appear to indicate that it belonged to p-Celtic, the division of the Celtic language best exemplified by modern Welsh, but even this has been contested. Their artistic creativity was substantial, as archaeological digs have revealed and a visit to the Royal Scottish Museum in Edinburgh will attest. Beyond this they are a people without a history, and it is the destiny of such that the importance of what is done among them dwindles by comparison with achievement among peoples with annals. The Irish, Welsh, and English are rich in annals.

Conversion of the Picts

Conversion of the Picts who lived south of the Grampian Hills was the work of St. Ninian, as tradition has it. Making appropriate allowance for the way that tradition in these matters tends to personalize the work of a missionary group in the name of its dominant member, one may say that the conversion of the southern Picts was the work of Ninian and the monastic establishment he brought into being at Candida Casa and the activity emanating from it. Bede says flatly that St. Columba converted the northern Picts. Adomnan says nothing on the subject one way or the other. Since the northern Picts were indeed converted, the most likely explanation is that, in the case of Columba as in the case of Ninian, the work of a monastic establishment and its members has been personalized in the name of its dominant member. As we have already seen, it is Columba the monk, the anchorite, and the saint we meet in Adomnan, not the missionary.

Specific details about the missionary work of St. Columba approach the nonexistent. He did some missionary work among the northern Picts on the island of Skye, if a record of individual baptisms may be expanded to justify the term, and there was all but certainly a monastery established there out of Iona, but there is no evidence that it was founded by St. Columba. There was a monastery on Hinba under the jurisdiction of Iona in Columba's time to which he would retire for solitude and contemplation. There was certainly a monastery established on remote Tiree, if only a rudimentary retreat house to which those who fell short of the austere demands of monastic life on Iona might be sent for proper contemplation of their failings, a purpose to which Tiree was ideally suited. The monastery on Tiree is attributed to St. Brendan, although Columba's pupil and successor, Baithene, presided over it. All in all, the few fragments of evidence available would suggest that what missionary activity Columba did in person was largely limited to the Inner Hebrides, with the possibility that he did more on the mainland not ruled out but necessarily given the Scottish verdict, Not Proven.

We are, if anything, worse off where information about the missionary activity of other Iona monks is concerned. The one colorful figure in an otherwise undifferentiated group is Cormac. On the occasion of Columba's visit to the court of King Brude he was informed through his supernatural ability to know distant events that Cormac and other Iona monks were in grave danger, and he managed, through his ability to project thought, to transmit to Cormac the information necessary to save their lives. They were sailing at the time in far northern waters, possibly about the Orkneys. Adomnan records two such voyages by Cormac, one of which brought him into waters too thick for rowing. One may interpret this as a reference to floating ice and, according to the quality of daring present in one's power of surmise, identify the locale with the Orkneys, Shetlands, Faroes, or with a giant leap of the imagination, Iceland. There is nothing in Adomnan to indicate that they were on a mission more sanctified than exploration. What could be deemed a rational barrier to such surmise, the question of the sort of boat that would carry voyagers to such distant parts, is actually no barrier at all. St. Columba's ship is often referred to as a coracle, and one with any knowledge of such matters might picture the river coracle or basket boat not entirely unknown today in Ireland, with its framework of hazel laths and its ovoid shape. There is a delightful stained glass window in the cathedral of Dol in Brittany showing St. Samson with two companions sailing to Dol in what looks like a tub, all three with edifying expressions, the saint slightly larger than his companions as befits a saint. They are in a river coracle. One should think rather of the curragh, the traditional fishing craft of the Celts, the long boat with trim lines, light and maneuverable, with tarred canvas sides pulled taut over a frame of wooden laths. This is the modern descendant of the skin boat of Columba's time, and the curragh can go great distances in heavy weather. The aura of the supernatural shrouds the episode of Cormac's voyage, but it has nothing to do with his boat or his seamanship.

Beyond this record, which at best is only peripheral to our concern, there are a few references to other missionaries of the early Iona days: to St. Chattan who did missionary work in Dalriada, to St. Moluag who preached in Pictland, and to St. Maelrubha who worked in the Hebrides. We are forced back to the lists of Columban foundations with some assurance that we are on the right track since they are on the whole more numerous where in logic they should be more numerous. Most of them are in the Inner Hebrides including Skye; some are in the Outer Hebrides, including Lewis, Harris, and the Uists; there are more of them west of the spine of Britain than east, and the ones east of the ridge, like the ones in Strathclyde, are more suspect than those closer to Iona. Even when foundations are far later than the lifetime of the saint they commemorate, they give evidence since they are often revivals of the memory of a great man once associated with their locales. The evidence of foundations would indicate that the missionary activity from Iona followed the predictable course where the Picts were concerned. It gradually suffused the land of the northern Picts, insular and mainland alike, and the prestige of Iona made it dominant within its sphere of influence for a full century after Columba's death. There is no reason to doubt the literal accuracy of Bede's summation: "The island called Hii [Iona], whose monastery was for a long time the chief of almost all those of the northern Irish, and all those of the Picts, and had the direction of their people" (III, 3).

St. Augustine's Mission

To this point we have been striving to push through the misty mid-regions of protohistory. In 597, however, the year that St. Columba died, we suddenly move out of the mists into the light of true history. In 597 St. Augustine came to Kent.

Ethelbert, the pagan king of Kent, was married to Bertha, the Christian daughter of Charibert II, king of the Franks. She came to

Kent fortified by the presence of her bishop Liudhard. Since there seems never to be an actual beginning in these matters, there was already at Canterbury a decayed and ancient church of Celtic origin. Bede identifies it as St. Martin's and the modern visitor to Canterbury may observe its crumbled relics in that fascinating field behind the cathedral where archaeology has bared a church history in Canterbury 800 years older than the cathedral itself. This became Liudhard's church, and once more there was Christianity in Kent.

It attracted the attention of Pope Gregory. In 596 he sent a mission of forty Benedictine monks headed by Augustine, a Frenchman who had headed the Benedictine monastery of St. Andrew in Rome, on a task of awesome proportions, to convert Anglo-Saxon Britain. The mission landed on the island of Thanet, the forty-square-mile northeast tip of Kent, and notified King Aethelbert of its presence. He welcomed the monks to Canterbury in the name of his wife, authorized them to preach, and assured them that he himself would not listen. They held services in St. Martin's, made some converts, and eventually the king did listen and was converted. Such is the account Bede gives in chapters 25–26 of his first book, and its authenticity is beyond question. Albinus, who became abbot at Canterbury early in the eighth century, and would seem to have been the same age as Bede, sent to Bede a priest named Notheld with written documents and oral information. Notheld subsequently went to Rome and brought back to Bede letters of Pope Gregory and other pontiffs for the *History*. Even more to the point, it was largely at the urging of Albinus that Bede undertook the *History* in the first place, and Albinus was always Bede's chief source of information about Kent and other parts of southern England.

In all, Bede devotes eleven chapters to the mission of Augustine, about two-thirds of which is devoted to the letters of Pope Gregory. The Pope had systematic plans for a converted England. Augustine was authorized to consecrate twelve bishops of his own selection, the appropriate apostolic number. He was to send a bishop to York and if the conversion of Northumbria proceeded well, to authorize the bishop of York to consecrate twelve bishops for the northern dioceses. It is clear that Gregory considered London and York the first and second cities of England, that the bishop of each was independent of the other, that the one first consecrated should have precedence over the other but that during his lifetime Augustine should have precedence over all the bishops of England. He thought of Augustine only in terms of London. Not gifted with St. Columba's foreknowledge, he had no inkling of what Canterbury would become.

Augustine's achievements must be counterbalanced against Pope Gregory's plans, since all too often the two have been silently equated. In 602 Augustine held a fateful meeting with seven British bishops and a number of monks from Bangor-is-Coed (Bancornaburg) in Wales. Augustine was seated when they entered. They watched to see if he would arise. He remained seated. He offered them a share in the task of converting the Anglo-Saxons provided they would accept the Roman system for dating Easter and the Roman form of baptism, and made it clear that his terms were not negotiable. The British bishops said that since he would not rise to greet them, agreement would not mean that they joined him in the mission but that they submitted to him, and they would be treated thereafter with more studied contempt. Bede says that Augustine threatened them with disaster if they did not accept his authority, and that the price the British paid was the death of 12,000 monks of Bangor-is-Coed at the hands of Ethelfrith, whose invasion of Wales was "the working of divine judgment" as Bede saw it. Bede saw things with urbanity where the Irish were concerned, a people remote from Northumbria, but his urbanity slipped and slid where the neighboring British were concerned. The Pope had given Augustine the authority, but wisdom in its exercise was not vouchsafed and his treatment of the British bishops delayed literally for centuries the completion of Pope Gregory's plans for an organized and unified Church in Britain.

The tangible achievements of Augustine's mission were either negligible or substantial, according to the viewpoint from which one judges. It achieved nothing that even by impossible exaggeration could be called the conversion of the Anglo-Saxons. Except for a brief extension to London, the mission never left Kent and the conversion even of Kent was markedly incomplete. Yet under Augustine the first, simple foundations, now all but totally obliterated, of three of the supreme cathedrals of England were laid at Canterbury, London, and Rochester. St. Martin's at Canterbury was enlarged and three other churches built there. It is quite possible that if we knew as much of the personal achievements of Saints Ninian and Columba as we do of St. Augustine and his immediate successors, we would see that the scale of accomplishment was comparable, and if the very establishment of Candida Casa and Iona had an importance in the future far transcending the importance that was immediate, surely the same can be said of Canterbury. What forty Roman monks did in a far-off and enigmatic land where they were tossed about on the swirling tides of palace politics, where even their coreligionists were not the fellow soldiers in the cause they had anticipated—and perhaps had a right to anticipate—and where death struck so often and so quickly, was not negligible. Neither was it so great as often has been claimed.

Mission to Northumbria

As a matter of fact, more was done in Northumbria by the Romans than in Kent. A geographic excursus is here necessary, supplemented by a bit of politics. Seventh-century Northumbria was the eastern part of England and Scotland, from the River Humber to the Firth of Forth. It was divided into two parts, Deira and Bernicia. Deira extended northward from the River Humber at least to Tees Bay and sometimes to the Tyne. It included modern Yorkshire but not Lancashire, which was British. Bernicia extended at least from the Tyne and sometimes from Tees Bay to the Firth of Forth. It comprised modern Northumberland and the eastern half of Scotland north to the Forth. Modern Durham was a no man's land of varying allegiance between the two. Lancashire and the western half of Scotland to the Clyde comprised Strathclyde which was British and Christian.

We pass to politics. King Edwin of Northumbria married Aethelburh, daughter of the now Christian king of Kent, after satisfying her father that he consented to her being a Christian and, if satisfied with the truth of her religion, would consider adopting it himself. Time passed, and a juxtaposition occurred that seemed to the pagan king evidence that a power beyond human ken was operating in his behalf. An amazing escape from assassination and the birth of an infant daughter on the same Easter night led him to consider seriously the matter of a change of faith. Word of this must have been relayed quickly to Kent and with equal speed to Rome, and clerical machinery began at once to move.

There was in Kent a priest named Paulinus. He had come in 601, subsequent to the coming of Augustine but, like him, coming from Rome. In 625 he was consecrated a bishop and went with Aethelburh to Northumbria in the same year. One year later he baptized the infant Eanflaed whose birth had set her father pondering the theological. The time was ripe for Rome to undertake the conversion of Northumbria and the establishment of an independent see at York for the supervision of Christianity in the north, as Pope Gregory had envisaged. In 625 Boniface V was pope. He had been one of Pope Gregory's clerical staff and was entirely cognizant of Gregory's far-sighted plans for the ecclesiastical organization of Britain. Pope Boniface proceeded to write a long letter to King Edwin, urging Christianity on him and demonstrating his affection by the gift of an embroidered tunic and cloak for the pagan king and a silver mirror and inlaid ivory comb for his Christian queen. The Pope then died and presumably carried on the struggle for Edwin from a celestial vantage point. Edwin killed in battle the king of the West Saxons who had sent the assassin to murder him, and then added to the realm of Northumberland the distant West Saxon throne. Paulinus made it clear to Edwin that the time had come to show his gratitude to God.

Edwin expressed a desire first to discuss the issue with his council. He was surprised and Paulinus heartened when the chief pagan priest, Coifi, expressed his personal disillusionment with the pagan religion. Then another chief arose and spoke, and there follows in Bede one of the set pieces of Old English literature:

This is how the present life of man on earth, King, appears to me in comparison with that time which is unknown to us. You are sitting feasting with your ealdormen and thegns in winter time; the fire is burning on the hearth in the middle of the hall and all inside is warm, while outside the wintry storms of rain and snow are raging; and a sparrow flies swiftly through the hall. It enters in at one door and quickly flies out through the other. For a few moments it is inside, the storm and wintry tempest cannot touch it, but after the briefest moment of calm, it flits from your sight, out of the wintry storm and into it again. So this life of man appears but for a moment; what follows or indeed what went before, we know not at all. If this new doctrine brings us more certain information, it seems right that we should accept it.

The chief priest then called on Paulinus to speak and after he presented the Christian explanation of life and the Christian promise, Coifi announced his readiness to become a Christian. The king and court joined him, and on Easter Sunday, April 12, 627, king, court, and enormous numbers of the people were baptized. The king then established an episcopal see for Paulinus at York, where the baptism had taken place. Six years later Edwin fell in battle at Heath-field against the forces of a rugged old pagan, Penda, king of Mercia, and of Caedwalla, king of the western Britons, who was fighting for the freedom of his people.

One faces the customary difficulty in trying to determine the precise amount of missionary success achieved by Paulinus and the Roman mission which he headed. The conversion of king, court, and people in great numbers obviously eclipses anything done by Augustine and his fellow Romans in the south. Bede makes it clear that Paulinus preached mainly in Deira, as was logical since his see was at York, but in Bernicia as well. He built a church at Campodunum, site of a Roman camp near Dewsbury in Yorkshire and of a royal palace as well. He went south of the Humber to preach in the king-dom of Lindsey, building a church at Lincoln. No churches of the monastic sort are associated with the name of Paulinus, nor is there evidence that he was a monk. He preached at the royal palace at Yeavering in Northumbria, where excavations have unearthed a long wooden hall with a fire pit midway, doors at either end, and windows in the middle through which sparrows might fly in and out. "He was tall, with a slight stoop, black hair, a thin face, a slender aquiline nose, and at the same time he was both venerable and awe-inspiring in appearance," an old man whom Paulinus had baptized told Bede (II, 16).

In contrasting the achievements of Paulinus with those of the far better publicized Augustine, one must bear in mind the difference between the problems the two missionaries faced. The pagan Jutes and Saxons had been entrenched in the south for a century and a half before Augustine came, and nothing Christian remained in the southeast of England but a few possible withered, all but dead roots. On the other hand, the Angles were just becoming entrenched when Paulinus arrived, and west of Deira lay the Christian Strathclyde and beyond it and to the south the Welsh Church. Similarly, west of Bernicia was the land of the Christian southern Picts, Christian Dal-riada, and beyond them Iona and Ireland, the seedbed of northern Christianity. Christianity was at least known in the north, as was that mystic entity which was neither a city nor a nation but a pattern of culture called Rome. There were men of sound and open mind, like the pagan high priest Coifi ready to listen to the message of Rome and to accept it when it seemed valid. The north was ready for conversion but the south was not. Paulinus did much, and had dynastic strife not undone much that he achieved his name would be larger in the history of religion. As the pattern of life worked out, however, the enduring conversion of Northumbria was not to be Roman but Irish, and to be personalized not in the name of the Roman Paulinus but in the name of the Irish Aidan. There is no evidence that the well-informed and scholarly Adomnan had ever heard of Augustine and Paulinus.

King Oswald of Northumbria

Once more the groundwork of history must be laid. King Edwin was the son of Aella, king of Deira. When Aella died, King Aethelfrith of Bernicia usurped the throne of Deira and united the two kingdoms under the name of Northumbria. Edwin was forced into exile, was received by King Raedwald of East Anglia, plotted revenge with him, and in 616 after Raedwald defeated and killed Aethelfrith, Edwin became king of Northumbria, with the results recounted above. The three sons of Aethelfrith, whose names were Eanfrid, Oswald, and Oswiu, were forced into exile. Eanfrid took refuge with the Picts, Oswald and Oswiu with the Irish, probably in Dalriada and quite possibly at Iona. Oswald and Oswiu were converted, Oswald becoming a sincere and dedicated Christian and Oswiu a nominal one. Eanfrid remained a pagan.

In 635 Oswald, who had returned from exile, reunited the crowns of Deira and Bernicia by force of arms and reigned as king of Northumbria. After seven years on the throne, seven of the most fruitful years in the history of British Christianity, Oswald fell in battle at the hands of the all but permanent nemesis of the Christians, Penda of Mercia.

There are few things more fascinating about the Dark Ages, in which Rome was almost prostrate beneath the repeated and devastating onslaughts of Not Rome, than the occasional appearance in the barbarian ranks of a fine mind attuned to what was best in Rome and well aware of its superiority to what his own people had. Charlemagne had such a mind, and Alfred the Great; and operating in a much more limited field of action and period of time, so did Oswald, king of Northumbria for seven short years during which Northumbria became Christian and Oswald earned canonization as a saint. The greatest blessing of his life was its greatest trial, his exile from Northumbria to the land of the Irish. There was in Ireland a native culture, centuries old, developed in total isolation from Rome and the entire tradition of Greco-Roman culture, a culture that centered about religious belief, legal tradition, and literary achievement. Then St. Patrick came, and with him and after him a basic change in religious belief but in no sense an abandonment of legal tradition and literary achievement. Rather they were incorporated into the framework of Christianity, and continued to flourish. Great monastic schools came into being, with numbers in attendance not completely dwarfed by the numbers that attend our contemporary colleges. Aerial photography of their nearly obliterated dimensions bears out their amazing size.

Whether the exiled Oswald came to know this culture at first hand in Ireland itself, at the ascetic outpost of Iona or in attenuated form in Dalriada, he came to appreciate its worth, to accept its religious convictions, and, when he came to the throne, to dedicate his short but amazingly constructive reign to planting its values among the Angles in Northumbria. Logically he turned first to Iona for assistance, asking for a bishop for the English people. He was sent one Bishop Corman, who soon returned discouraged. There followed a long and anxious consultation on Iona, where one is certainly justified in picturing a bitter disappointment that this most promising sequel to the conversion of the Picts should peter out in so humiliating a fashion. Then Bishop Aidan spoke, suggesting that Corman may have expected more of the still barbaric Angles than was reasonable, and urging that St. Paul's sensible and pragmatic injunction about milk for babes be followed. Not unnaturally, the assignment was his.

St. Aidan

Some miles south of Berwick upon Tweed is the little seaside resort of Bamburgh. On a massive headland towering above it is a gaunt and menacing reminder of centuries when Northumbria was as powerful a kingdom as Britain knew. It is Bamburgh Castle, ancient enough for Sir Thomas Malory to think it the Joyous Gard of Lancelot of the Lake, but in actuality the historic seat of Northumbrian kings, and today a valued setting for film companies making pictures of medieval derring-do. Some prototype of Bamburgh Castle stood upon that eminence when Aidan came to Northumbria and in it King Oswald held his court. Not far away was the two-square-mile island called Lindisfarne. At low tide one could reach it on foot. Unlike Iona, which still has relics of Columba's period, the modern pilgrim to Lindisfarne will find nothing that dates to the age of Aidan. The Danes, in the days when they were the scourge of Europe, saw to that. He will find in the parish church of St. Mary relics of a Norman church of the twelfth century, a southwest front that dates in part to the Norman period, Norman arches ornamented on the north arcade with alternating red and white stones, and the red sandstone ruins of a twelfth-century priory. The castle, now a National Trust property, is a modern reconstruction of a sixteenth-century structure, a fortress in miniature crowning a cone-shaped rock. For the rest the pilgrim must trust to history and his sympathetic imagination.

Aidan came to Bamburgh and Oswald gave him Lindisfarne as the seat for his diocese, following the ancient Irish principle that islands are ideal for that purpose. A monastery was built on Lindisfarne and a group of Irish monks established there. Then the two men started the crusade to convert Northumbria, Aidan the monk and Oswald the king. The king had become proficient in Irish during his years of exile, a proficiency which the monk could in no way match in English. And so Aidan preached and Oswald interpreted, and the presence of their king beside the preacher certainly did not impede the process of conversion. What we know of Aidan we learn in all but its entirety from Bede, who lived in Northumbria in a day when Aidan and Oswald were still in living memory. Bede is generous in his praise of those he admires, but he is discriminating in his judgments. He devotes the fifth chapter of his third book to the praises of Aidan as a man and as a priest, and present as well is an awareness that his king and collaborator, Oswald, was a man of fine ability and true religious fervor. From 635 until Oswald's death in 642 they preached the word in Northumbria and, aided by the work done before them by Paulinus but fundamentally by their own energetic and soundly inspired efforts, they turned the tide against paganism and made Northumbria a Christian land.

Bede makes it clear that at Lindisfarne, contrary to what was so often true in Ireland, the bishop was not subject in terms of jurisdiction to the abbot. Aidan lived in the monastery that he founded with the monks whom he recruited, and he directed all its operations. He founded a church at Bamburgh not far from the royal palace and found it a convenient center from which to make his missionary journeys with his royal associate and interpreter. Bede refers to the founding of churches by Aidan and to the endowment of monasteries by Oswald, but it would appear that the monasteries were centers of education, the establishment of which was Oswald's secondary but important motive in furthering the work of Lindisfarne and bringing to his people the cultural resources of Ireland as well as its religious faith. These monasteries would appear to have been attached to churches and not to comprise a *paruchia* after the Iona and the general Irish model. Just as St. Columba had his place of retirement at Hinba, where he found spiritual as well as physical rest and the opportunity for meditation, from which grew a clearer concept of his mission and the way to its fulfillment, so St. Aidan had his hermitage at Farne Island, the largest of a group of islands off the Northumbrian coast, close to Bamburgh and about seven miles from Lindisfarne. What fame Farne has today comes from the memory not of St. Aidan but of his English successor at Lindisfarne, St. Cuthbert, who lived there when he could and died in his isolated cell upon the island.

Mention of St. Cuthbert suggests a point fundamental to missionary work that is often overlooked. An entirely successful mission is entirely self-liquidating. The object of a mission is primarily to convert the pagan, but also to bring into being among the converted pagans a native clergy. Aidan's purpose, like the purpose of Patrick, Columba, and all who followed them in Ireland, Scotland, and England, was not merely to convert but to make conversion self-perpetuating. By way of example, Bede tells us (III, 26) of twelve English boys, again the apostolic number, whose education Aidan undertook at the start of his episcopate. One of them, Eata, later became first abbot of Melrose and then bishop of Lindisfarne. As time passed, the Irish influence in English Christianity dwindled and finally disappeared. To attribute this to the setback administered the Irish conservatives at the Synod of Whitby over the issues of the dating of Easter and the form of tonsure is simplistic. The setback played its part, but the basic cause of the "failure" of the Irish mission was its success. Within a generation there was a native English clergy ready to continue the work the Irish had started among their people. St. Aidan died in 651, his great English successor as bishop of Lindisfarne, St. Cuthbert, died in 687. It is true that between the two dates occurred the Synod of Whitby and the withdrawal from Lindisfarne of the Irish monks, but equally essential to a full understanding of what happened is the fact that there was brought into being in a single generation a native English clergy ready to do the work of Lindisfarne. The Irish missionary effort had not ended. It had done its basic work in Northumbria and moved to other lands.

After Oswald's death Aidan continued his missionary work, aided by Oswin who became king of Deira, and ignored by his cousin Oswiu who ruled in Bernicia. Nine years passed and Oswiu slowly came to recognize that what Aidan and Oswald had initiated was continuing, increasing, and now was dominant. Northumbria was Christian and would remain so. Furthermore, it was spreading south into the once pagan domain of the soon to be eliminated Penda. Oswiu was ready to accept the permanency of Christianity if not its precepts. He had his cousin Oswin assassinated in 651 and three years later killed Penda on the field of battle, but he dedicated his daughter Elfled to virginity from the cradle in a fine show of surrogate piety. As it turned out, the child grew into the reality of piety, her pragmatic father came to sense a value higher than the pragmatic, and he endowed her with land for a community of nuns and eventually she became abbess of Whitby.

All this was after the death of Aidan. The Irish monk, worn by years of labor in the rugged realm east of the Pennines, desolated but not broken by the death of his royal associate Oswald, heartened by the help of Oswin and then brokenhearted by his murder, succumbed to years and to sorrow on August 31, 651, twelve days after Oswin was assassinated. He died on Farne Island, attended at the end by Lindisfarne associates. "They erected a tent for him during his illness," Bede says (III, 17), "at the west end of the church, the tent itself being attached to the church wall. So it happened that he breathed his last, leaning against the buttress which supported the church on the outside. He died on 31 August, in the seventeenth year of his episcopate. His body was shortly afterwards translated to the island of Lindisfarne and buried in the cemetery of the brothers. Some time afterwards, when a larger church had been built there and dedicated in honour of the most blessed chief of the apostles, his bones were translated to it and buried on the right side of the altar, with the honour due to so great a bishop." A fair appraisal of what St. Aidan accomplished when brought together with the work emanating from Lindisfarne, which he established, justifies the judgment that Aidan, far more than Augustine, was the apostle of England.

Conversion of the Midlands

After the death of Aidan an Irishman named Finan was conse- crated his successor as bishop of Lindisfarne. During his ten-year tenure the conversion of the midlands started. One recalls that in 654 Oswiu had eliminated, in the customary fashion, the doughty cham- pion of paganism, Penda, on the battlefield. Penda's son Peada was a Christian and Oswiu's own Christianity had warmed considerably now that he saw in it the wave of the future. Oswiu proceeded to induce Sigebert the Little, king of the East Saxons, to accept a Chris- tian mission. The choice of missionary is significant: it was an English Northumbrian named Cedd, who had been trained at Lindisfarne by Aidan and had tested his wings in Mercia, a land ripe for Christianity now that Christian Peada was king. Cedd moved into Essex where the missionary activity of Bishop Mellitus, a colleague of St. Augus- tine, had long since been obliterated. On Bede's authority we know that Cedd established churches in Essex and ordained priests, but specific names and places are scanty in the record. Cedd's most noteworthy foundation was at Lastingham in the North Riding of Yorkshire, but this alumnus of Lindisfarne worked as far south as the Thames estuary, founding a church at Tilbury, a few miles down- stream from London. Cedd was English but in the Irish tradition, as were so many English trained in Ireland and Irish institutions. At the Synod of Whitby he defended the Irish dating of Easter, although he accepted in better grace than the Irish monks the finding in favor of the Roman dating. Cedd died at Lastingham directly after the Synod.

The ripening of Mercia for conversion was speeded mightily by the death of Penda, but even while his father lived, his Christian son Peada had made efforts to plant the Christian seed. Mercia was the great central heart of England, south of Northumbria, east of Wales, and north of Wessex. In 653 Finan had baptized Peada and when the land of Mercia was fully opened to Christian missionaries Finan con- secrated an Irishman, Diuma, its first bishop. To anticipate matters, we may add that his successor Ceollach was also Irish, but the third bishop, Trumere, was English although educated by the Irish, as was the fourth bishop, Jaruman. Vitally important as was the conversion of Mercia, little or nothing is known of its details beyond the names of the bishops who guided the process. It is clear that they looked to Lindisfarne for guidance and inspiration, that they had no apparent contact with Canterbury, and that whether racially Irish or English they were ideologically Irish on the twin areas of incipient dispute: the Easter dating and the tonsure styling.

The Lindisfarne Foundations

Some of the monasteries founded out of Lindisfarne can be named. There was the monastery of Gateshead, across the Tyne from Newcastle, where Utta was abbot. There was a monastery at an unidentified place called Paegnalaech, where Tuda, the fourth bishop of Lindisfarne, was buried. Bishop Tuda's appointment was a masterly piece of face-saving politics. He was an Irishman who considered correct the Roman dating of Easter, and as successor to Bishop Colman, who chose return to Iona rather than submission to King Oswiu's decision about Easter, he perpetuated the Irish tradition at Lindisfarne and yet accepted the Roman dating of Easter which the southern Irish accepted anyway. Of far more familiar ring are the next two, the monasteries at Melrose and Ripon. Melrose was the personal foundation of St. Aidan, on the Tweed some forty miles west of Lindisfarne but north of the Cheviots and so in Scotland. Beneath the picturesque ruins of the Cistercian abbey that survive at Melrose are stones of more ancient date, unseen memorials to St. Aidan, Lindisfarne, and the seventh century. The same is true of the lovely old cathedral of St. Wilfrid at Ripon, which was in its earliest form a foundation out of Melrose. Willibrord, an Englishman and, as apostle to the Frisians, one who shared the continental mission field with the Irish, was a son of Ripon who went first to Ireland for training and then to north Holland as a *peregrinus* in the Irish fashion. St. Aidan brought into being foundations for women as well, Coldingham in Berwickshire where Aebba, the half sister of Oswiu, was abbess, and Hartlepool in Northumbria where Heiu was abbess. The latter establishment started a sequence of events of major significance in church history. Hilda, grandniece of King Edwin and one baptized by Paulinus and so a link between two traditions, succeeded Heiu at Hartlepool and then built at Whitby at the mouth of the Esk on the Yorkshire coast the most celebrated of the double monasteries and one that was to be the site of the most celebrated synod in English history. The site was magnificent, high on the cliff above the picturesque ravine of the Esk, and today its ruins etched against an evening sky and crowning the tierlike red-brick town below are among the finest sights on the coast of Yorkshire and Northumberland.

Thus Northumbria was converted from Lindisfarne, as so much of Scotland had been converted from the primal seedbed of the Irish Church in the northland, Iona. From Lindisfarne the Christian message was carried down into Mercia and Essex, and missions stemming from Lindisfarne carried the Word through the midlands down to the Thames and the outskirts of London. It had been carried as well from both Lindisfarne and Iona to the Firth of Forth and beyond. From the Firth of Forth to the River Thames, the east of Scotland and England was now Christian, and the capital of Christian England was Lindisfarne just as the capital of Christian Scotland was Iona. The work of the Irish *peregrini* was finished in the main, where the east of Scotland and England was concerned. Already names like Cedd and Trumhere, Willibrord and Hilda, the names of English men and English women were becoming key names in the continuing process of conversion. The second part of the task, the creation of a native clergy, was well underway when the Synod of Whitby was convened and the self-liquidation of the Irish mission, always one of its main objectives, was proceeding as it should. There remained the area west of Kent, where German paganism was inured and the mutual hatred of Celt and German certainly inhibited, if not indeed prohibited, missionary activity in areas where Christian Celt and pagan Saxon were immediate neighbors. In this area missionaries from Ireland in the geographic sense, or from that newly created Ireland of the spirit with its twin capitals Iona and Lindisfarne, played a major but not a dominant role in the process of conversion.

Briton and Saxon

As we move to the south and west of England there comes into play the influence of another Christian Church, closely allied to the Irish but distinct from it and quite possibly one of its major formative influences, the Church of Wales. Welsh monasticism was very similar to Irish in organization and purpose, and the missionary spirit was strong. Llantwit Major on the coast of Glamorganshire on the north coast of the Bristol Channel was a center of learning after the Celtic fashion that prevailed in Ireland, and the penitentials to which monks who resided there were subject were similar in severity to the Irish penitentials. St. Samson of Dol, an important early figure in the Welsh Church, had a career very similar to that of an Irish missionary and indeed linked in his own person the Church of Wales, of Ireland, of Cornwall, and of Brittany. His first recorded post was abbot of the monastery of Caldey Island. He was called from there to Ireland to head a monastery the abbot of which had gone insane. When the latter recovered his sanity he returned to his post, and Samson returned to Wales where he became abbot of Llantwit. From there he was called to Cornwall where he founded four monasteries, and ultimately to Brittany where his monastic labors centered at Dol. There is evidence to indicate that St. Samson was an outstanding figure in a steady migration of Welsh clerics from Wales down through Devon and Cornwall across to Brittany. The conversion of the southwest of England and the solidifying of Christianity in Brittany were basically the work of the Welsh Church, affected by the Irish only to the extent that the relationship between ecclesiastical Wales and Ireland was extremely close throughout the age of the saints.

On the other hand, there is an irrefutable abundance of evidence that the Welsh Church never involved itself in the conversion of the Anglo-Saxons. Racial antagonism ran far too high for the Christian Welsh to consider the problem or for the pagan Saxons to accept the solution. As Christianity gradually seeped down into the pagan south of England from the now Christian north, and out from Christian Kent, and as a native Anglo-Saxon clergy came into being, the old antagonism, far from disappearing, simply took on a new but equally bitter form. Even Bede, always benign where the Irish were concerned, loses his suavity when he thinks of the Britons and expresses his total acceptance of the thesis advanced by the Welsh historian Gildas, that the Anglo-Saxon conquest was the proper administration of God's vengeance against an evil, luxury-loving people. He further held it against the Christian Britons that they did not preach the Gospel to the pagan Saxons. The melancholy truth is that Christian

Celt hated Christian Saxon quite as much as pagan Saxon, and Celtic priest hated Saxon priest. In 705 Aldhelm, Saxon bishop of Sherborne, wrote that the British priests of south Wales ". . . will neither pray with us in church, nor eat with us at table. Worse, they throw out the food left over from our meals to dogs waiting open mouthed and to foul pigs; they give orders that the dishes and bowls which we have used must be scraped and scoured with sand or with cinders before they are fit to be placed upon their tables."

This antagonism must be borne in mind when one considers the Celtic intransigence over the dating of Easter and the form of the tonsure. There were factors involved quite different from convictions about the church calendar and the cutting of hair. The closer the Celts were to the Anglo-Saxons, the more tenacious their convictions. Nowhere were they more tenacious than in Wales. Like so many other aspects of life through the centuries in the British Isles, these convictions were in no small measure corollaries to the ancient and never-ending rift between Celt and German, which can simmer down to rivalry or heat up into conflict. It is well to remember that Saxon forays into Welsh territory were unending during these troubled centuries, that Welsh churches were prime targets for pillage, and that the Saxon marauder with a touch of piety in his makeup, who balanced accounts with the Lord by donating to a Saxon priest the chalice and vestments he had stolen from a Welsh priest, was not necessarily less moral than the Saxon priest who happily received them without giving disturbing thought to the fact that there was only one possible way in which such sacred objects could have come into marauding hands. The tenacity of the Welsh to their Easter and tonsure convictions and their repugnance at the thought of preaching the Gospel to the Saxon was not necessarily due exclusively to perversity. Neither is it entirely surprising that the tenacity of the Irish of Lindisfarne and Iona to such convictions was substantially stronger than the tenacity of the Irish at spots of idyllic remoteness from the Angles like Kells and Clonard. Religious convictions are frequently a curious mixture of disparate elements.

Mission to East Anglia

The result was that there was no missionary activity from Wales in areas not yet considered but closer to Wales than to Ireland. We may start with East Anglia, which corresponded approximately to modern Norfolk and Suffolk and so was least susceptible to Welsh influence. As in the case of Oswald of Northumbria, the exile of a king facilitated the conversion of East Anglia. King Sigebert was driven into exile in Gaul and remained there from about 616 to 630, becoming a Christian, as Oswald had, and a lover of learning. He was the first English king to show a genuine susceptibility to scholarship, and Bede appropriately calls him *doctissimus.* He had all the piety of Oswald, but with a quietism that led him ultimately to relinquish his throne, become a monk in a monastery he had founded, refuse to fight the inescapable Penda, and to die on the battlefield to which his bewildered and outraged compatriots had dragged him. While on the throne he brought from Burgundy one Felix and gave him an episcopal see, probably at Dunwich. Felix came to East Anglia by way of Kent, bringing to aid him in his task what Bede calls "masters and teachers as in the Kentish school" (III, 18). The name Felix masks the racial identity of its bearer quite as effectively as the name Paulinus. One may toy with the thought that Burgundy was the center of Irish missionary activity in Gaul, as will presently be demonstrated, and therefore link Sigebert's conversion and Felix's ordination with the Irish center at Luxeuil, but there is not a vestige of evidence to raise the thought above the level of a bare hypothesis.

On the other hand, there is no question about the other chief missionary to East Anglia. He was St. Fursa, an Irishman who came to England after 640, a *peregrinus* for the love of God. Bede tells us that King Sigebert gave him as the site for his monastery a Roman camp later called Cnobheresburg. Abandoned Roman camps made excellent sites for monasteries since their walls made fine cashels or outer ramparts. St. Fursa's monastery was at Burgh Castle near Yarmouth. It would appear that he came to East Anglia accompanied by his two brothers and two other priests, and that the five men dedicated themselves for some years to the conversion of East Anglia. Then St. Fursa, satisfied that monastery and mission were prospering, decided to leave the active field and become a hermit. He did so for a year, and then followed St. Columbanus into the missionary field of Gaul. The rest of St. Fursa's life belongs elsewhere in our story, and we shall meet him again at the appropriate time.

West Saxons and South Saxons

There remain the West Saxons and the South Saxons, the mysteries of Glastonbury, and the later and clearer history of Malmesbury. Much ink has flowed on the subject of the Irish at Glastonbury, and it has flowed to little purpose. In the tenth century, St. Dunstan speaks of the Irish colony there who "cherished that place of Glastonbury . . . with great affection, especially in honour of the blessed Patrick the Younger [*Patricii Junioris*] who is said to rest there happily in the Lord." All one can say with safety is that there is indeed evidence of a very ancient Christian settlement at Glastonbury, that there was a cult of St. Patrick there, but whether it was St. Patrick the apostle of Ireland, Palladius-Patrick, or some other Patrick whose annals otherwise are silent is beyond human ken.

The situation at Malmesbury, which is in Wiltshire a hundred miles or so west of London, is both later and clearer. There were, successively, a Roman settlement at Malmesbury, then a British town, later a castle, and finally a monastery founded by an Irishman named Maildubh. His one recorded achievement was the training of the Englishman Aldhelm who became bishop of Sherborne, a newly created see in Wessex associated with Canterbury. Aldhelm was a stouthearted warrior in the Roman cause with a passion for learning, "a man of universal erudition" according to Bede, and the first Englishman to write Latin prose and verse in what Bede considered an elegant style and modern scholars a barbaric one. Actually the first figure in the conversion of the West Saxons was neither Irish nor English, but a Bishop Birinus sent from Rome by Pope Honorius. Aided by Oswald, who was wooing the daughter of the West Saxon king, Birinus converted king and court and then was given an episcopal seat at Dorchester-on-Thames from which he conducted his missions and built his churches. What Birinus started was continued after a short reversion toward paganism by a Gaul, Bishop Agilbert, who had an Irish education. Falling out of royal favor, he was replaced briefly by an Englishman named Wine who received Winchester as his see and under whom the Old Minster at Winchester probably was built. The Irish contribution to the conversion of Wessex was minimal. On the whole Wessex was essentially an English mission conducted by the English.

The South Saxons were the last pagans to yield. The key figure in their conversion was Wilfrid, archbishop of York whose endless trials and tribulations, of which expulsion and exile from first one place and then another would make a tragedy of many cantos. In the view of his biographer, his own resourcefulness, reinforced by timely miracles, pulled him through and let him settle for a time at Selsey which became an episcopal see and a center for conversion. As an indication of the disappearance of an abiding influence from the mission of St. Augustine outside of Kent, one might point out that Wilfrid came to pagan Sussex, which adjoined Kent, seventy years after the arrival of St. Augustine.

We have now passed by two decades the date of the Synod of Whitby. There was still nothing one could truly call an English Church. Northumbria was converted as was Scotland, and Christianity was strongly entrenched in much of East Anglia and in parts of Mercia. This was almost entirely the work of the Irish monks and stemmed from Iona and Lindisfarne. Kent was also Christian, and this is attributable to the abiding influence of the Augustine mission. When the synod was convened Essex was, if anything, slipping back toward paganism, and Sussex was not yet even a missionary field. If a broad generalization may be chanced, in 665 Christianity was a fairly well established fact in the north and a reasonably grounded hope for the stout of heart in the south.

The Dating of Easter

All through the Age of the Saints the controversy over the dating of Easter and the form of the tonsure simmered. In one sense it was a difference between the Celtic Church and the Roman Church; in a second sense it was a quarrel between Celt and Saxon; in still another sense it was a cleavage between progressive and traditionalist. Like so many long-lasting, pervasive, and emotional divisions in human thought, it was a melange of mingled motives, and in it, as so frequently is true, the fundamental points at issue were first obscured and then obliterated by factors that had nothing to do with them. The Celtic tonsure was cut from ear to ear, the Roman tonsure was on the top of the head. The Celtic Easter depended on one Easter cycle, the Roman Easter on another. There was no matter of faith involved, no question of morals was at stake. Yet charges of heresy and sin were hurled about, when words became weapons as they invariably do in such struggles, and differences in viewpoint became emotional chasms capable of splitting monasteries, and very capable indeed of bewildering a missionary country quite uncertain of its grasp on Christian principles but at least aware that the hatred of man for man was not one of them.

It is quite possible that if the issue of Easter were not at stake, the issue of the tonsure might have been resolved on the live-and-let-live principle. Presumably the Church was sufficiently catholic to allow two forms of ecclesiastical haircutting. The dating of Easter, however, was a different matter; every major date in the Church year except the date of Christmas depends on the date of Easter. It made no sense for one monastery to be singing Easter's joyful alleluias while the monastery across the ridge was deep in the penances of Lent. The issue arose in the first place from the attempt to solve a problem which in the literal sense does not admit of a solution. The date of Easter is keyed to the date of the Passover, which in turn is based on lunar reckoning. The lunar month of twenty-nine and a half days cannot be adjusted exactly to the month which is based on solar reckoning. Consequently no Easter cycle is exactly correct.

An Easter cycle was constructed in the third century for the years 213–312. It was amended in 312, accepted at Rome under the title *Supputatio Romana,* and brought back to Britain by the British delegates to the Council of Arles in 314. It was accepted as the Easter cycle in Britain, Wales, and Ireland by the earliest Christians of the regions. It was still accepted in much of the Celtic Church in the mid-seventh century. In 457 a scholar named Victorius worked out a cycle of 532 years. The *Cursus Paschalis* of Victorius was amended in 525 and gained acceptance on the continent under the name, *Table of Dionysius Exiguus.* When St. Augustine came to Kent in 597 he brought with him the revision of the Victorine cycle, but he brought it to a country that had used the *Supputatio Romana* for 283 years. As Hanson puts it (p. 69): "By the time knowledge of Victorius's *Cursus Paschalis* reached the British Church the observance of the older calculation had become so much a matter of ancient tradition and corporate pride that even the sense of allegiance to the Roman see felt by that Church (a sentiment whose existence we need not doubt) was not strong enough to break the old bonds."

The actual differences between the older and the newer cycles were not great, since each was competently constructed. Under the older cycle which the Celtic churches observed, Easter might be celebrated between the fourteenth and twentieth day of the moon; under the newer cycle which the English of Roman training accepted, between the fifteenth and twenty-first days. The differences which seem minimal when put that way could produce very substantial differences in practice. An extreme example occurred in the year 631, when the Roman Easter came on March 24 and the Celtic Easter on April 21.

The Celtic Easter was certain to be the long-term loser, since nowhere but in the British Isles was it observed. There was constant travel between Celtic Britain and Gaul, where the Roman Easter was observed, and substantial travel between Celtic Britain and Rome itself. Gradually the Roman Easter came to be known in the Celtic west, and the obvious argument for a single Easter observance accepted. By the mid-seventh century, the Roman Easter was accepted throughout the south of Ireland, and one monastery and then another was coming to accept it in Germanic England. The diehards were in Wales, the Strathclyde, Dalriada, and Northumbria, the Celtic regions in which hostile conflict with the Anglo-Saxons was most common. These were the areas in which Celtic Church and Celtic people came to be equated, English Church and Anglo-Saxon people, the regions in which traditionalism in the observance of Easter was a mark of defiance directed by the Celt at the Anglo-Saxon conqueror. Two popes pleaded with the Celtic west to accept the otherwise universal dating of Easter. Pope Honorius sent a pastoral letter to the Irish early in the seventh century urging them to join the rest of Christendom in the Easter observance. The southern Irish, happily isolated from the racial struggles of Britain, complied; the northern Irish, the clerical staging area from which the mission field in Scotland and England was manned and so the area closest to that struggle, did not. Pope John, the second pope after Honorius, wrote to the Irish warning them of the Pelagian heresy and urging them to accept the Roman Easter. The Pelagian heresy had nothing to do with the Easter dating, but the juxtaposition of warning and exhortation had its overtones. Even the southern Irish tried to win over their recalcitrant brethren as Cummian, abbot of Durrow, who had sent emissaries to Rome in 631 and with their assistance had formalized at the Synod of Mag Léne the Roman Easter for southern Ireland, wrote to his colleague, Seghene, abbot of Iona, "What can be felt worse for Mother Church than to say: Rome is mistaken; Jerusalem is mistaken; Alexandria is mistaken; Antioch is mistaken; all the world is mistaken; the Scots and Britons alone have sound wisdom?"

The *coup de grâce* was readied as a result of a development at the Northumbrian court. One must turn the clock back to that memorable Easter night when King Edwin of Northumbria escaped assassination and became father of a baby girl, a coincidence of date and events that seemed to him sufficiently supernatural to make him accept the religion of his Christian queen, Aethelburh of Kent. One recalls that after Edwin's death Paulinus brought mother and child back to Kent, where the child was reared in all the orthodoxy of Christianity, the Roman dating of Easter included. The child, whose name was Eanflaed, grew to maturity and became wife of King Oswiu of Northumbria, whose calculated acceptance of Christianity we have already recorded. Included in his acceptance was the Celtic Easter. The king and queen, each having free will and ample experience in its exercise, proceeded to celebrate Easter each after his or her own fashion, he the Celtic Easter and she the Roman. "Hence it is said," remarks Bede, "that in these days it sometimes happened that Easter was celebrated twice in the same year, so that the king had finished the fast and was keeping Easter Sunday, while the queen and her people were still in Lent and observing Palm Sunday."

The Synod of Whitby (664)

This really brought matters to a head. A synod was called at Whitby, the double monastery on the Yorkshire coast north of Scarborough which Abbess Hilda headed. She entertained the synod but maintained silence at it concerning her convictions, which were Celtic. Abbot Colman of Lindisfarne headed the Celtic delegation with his interpreter Bishop Cedd, an Englishman who accepted the Celtic Easter as did many English educated under Irish auspices. Bishop Wilfrid of York headed the Roman group, supported by the queen's chaplain, an important court dignitary named Aldfrith, and other dignitaries. King Oswiu was arbiter. Colman explained the Celtic cycle, claiming for it the authority of St. John. Wilfrid explained the Roman cycle, claiming for it the authority of Saints Peter and Paul. The arguments from authority, always *de rigueur* in the Middle Ages and the ages before them, cancelled out, the more easily since none of the apostles had concerned themselves with the dating of Easter. Then Wilfrid used the one argument that really mattered, the argument from universality. Was all the world mistaken, and did only the Celtic Church, or more accurately only part of it, have the truth? Was Rome itself wrong, and Iona right? King Oswiu, predictably and also inevitably, ruled for Wilfrid and for Rome.

Thus the Roman Easter became the British Easter. St. Hilda bowed to the royal decision, as did Bishop Cedd. Abbot Colman and those who would not accept defeat returned to Lindisfarne, collected the relics of St. Aidan, returned with them to Iona, and ultimately returned to Ireland where Colman founded a monastery on the island of Innisbofin. Iona continued to observe the Celtic Easter, and still was observing it in the early eighth century when Adomnan was abbot and tried without avail to gain acceptance for the now all but universal Roman Easter. One adds the necessary footnote that the Celtic tonsure went the way of the Celtic Easter, and the shaven crown prevailed.

There has been a tendency evidenced by historians of this remote and difficult period to give to the Synod of Whitby an importance in the history both of Britain and the Church greater than is warranted. The process that the Synod all but completed had been underway for generations. There simply was no answer to the argument from virtual universality, and little by little the Celts accepted the fact that there was one generally accepted way of dating Easter and it was the Roman way. Although the influence of Lindisfarne waned and Iona shrank to a force more nearly commensurate with its physical size, and although England gradually ceased to be a missionary country and a native English clergy took on a steadily increasing portion of the task of conversion, the spiritual and intellectual influence of the Irish monasteries continued to be exercised throughout Britain long after the Synod of Whitby concluded. As Bede puts it: "At this time there were many in England, both nobles and commons, who, in the days of Bishops Finan and Colman had left their own country and retired to Ireland either for the sake of religious studies or to live a more ascetic life. In the course of time some of these devoted themselves faithfully to the monastic life, while others preferred to travel around to the cells of various teachers and apply themselves to study. The Irish welcomed them all gladly, gave them their daily food, and also provided them with books to read and with instruction, without asking for any payment."

The Fate of Lindisfarne and Iona

The fate of Lindisfarne and Iona was the fate of most insular monasteries. After Whitby, Lindisfarne had a revival of greatness under St. Cuthbert, its sixth bishop and an Englishman who had been a monk at Melrose and later its prior, but it was short lived. The sanctity of Cuthbert was recognized even during his lifetime, his relics were deemed the richest treasure of Lindisfarne, and in the Middle Ages his shrine at Durham rivaled in its number of pilgrims the shrine of St. Thomas at Canterbury. It is said that the English army fought under the banner of St. Cuthbert at Neville's Cross. It had a revival of an artistic sort under Bishop Eadfrith (698–721) when the Lindisfarne Gospels, a magnificent manuscript and one of the supreme artistic creations of what were not in the total sense the Dark Ages, was written in majuscule script and, with Saxon influence evident, decorated in the Irish style. Within a century, however, the Danes sacked Lindisfarne and destroyed the church. The survivors rebuilt it, but in 875, fearing another Danish invasion, they fled with St. Cuthbert's body and the Lindisfarne Gospels to Chester-le-Street, and later to Durham. In the eleventh century Lindisfarne was refounded out of Durham, and Holy Island became a dependent cell. What one sees at Lindisfarne today is, in its oldest parts, a relic of the second foundation. The Lindisfarne Gospels one sees at the British Museum.

The influence of Iona was necessarily circumscribed by the extension of the domain of the Angles through the Scottish lowlands. In 717 the communities established among the Picts from Iona were driven out by King Nechton, whose acceptance of the Roman Easter and whose turning to the English monastery of Wearmouth and Jarrow for spiritual guidance may well have been motivated as much by political considerations as by piety and second thoughts about the Easter cycle. The Picts had lost substantial ground to the Irish of Dalriada and may well have wanted a Northumbrian alliance. In 717 the Irish *Annals* records the "expulsion of the *familia* of Iona across the Spine of Britain by Nechton the king." One is probably justified in reading into this the expulsion of all the Irish monks who would not accept the authority of Nechton. For two centuries at least a community was maintained at Iona, with intervals when it lay prostrate under the sacking of the Danes. Indeed, for a time in the ninth century, when Kenneth mac Alpin was on the throne among the Picts, Iona recovered its old ascendency in the north of Britain. Then this passed, and there followed the dwindling and disappearing of Iona's influence as already recorded. Like Lindisfarne it had a medieval rebirth and then in our own day a fine second rebirth which Lindisfarne has not enjoyed. Furthermore, unlike Lindisfarne, there are on Iona traces of what was there in the sixth century and, meager though they are, they are precious.

They are precious for reasons more profound than the antiquarian. One pictures Columba, his relatives and comrades, pushing north and east through waters barely known, to a land where their kindred had a precarious and threatened landfall, to a people holding to their pagan concepts with that religious tenacity always typical of the Celt, yet always fortified and sustained by faith in their dedication to an exalted purpose. Iona is in size almost the last and least of the Hebrides, but from that geographic mustard seed grew the British Church. One pictures Aidan answering a call and a challenge, carrying the Word with his king and acolyte by his side to the Angles of Northumbria, and building at his insular outpost of Lindisfarne a Christian fortress from which his warriors of the Lord and those who came after them won East Anglia and Mercia to the faith, and carried it to Saxon lands beyond. Iona and Lindisfarne had their hour, and it passed, but the main reason for its passing was its very success. The day of Irish names like Chattan and Moluag, Maelrubha and Cormac, Diuma and Ceollach was destined to end if those who bore them were to succeed in their mission. The day dawned when English names like Trumhere and Cedd, Agilbert and Aldhelm, Cuthbert and Hilda replaced the Irish, and the latter had succeeded in their mission.

Faith can indeed move mountains, and one's preoccupation with dim memories and shadowy beginnings in ages when the rude North was just beginning to know Rome in all its varied meanings should not obscure the message of those distant days. In the web of miracles that hagiography wove about such names as Ninian and Patrick, Columba and Aidan, no miracle is quite so impressive as the miracle of faith and endurance by which Ireland, Scotland, and England were won to the Christian Church, and that miracle is a simple fact. Iona and Lindisfarne had their hour, but in the decades that followed their hour of greatness Ireland itself continued to be the source of wisdom and guidance for the converts made from the holy islands. Ireland "welcomed them all gladly, gave them their daily food, and also provided them with books to read and with instruction, without asking for any payment." The Irish *peregrini,* however, the exiles for God, were already opening other mission fields. Seven years before Columba died, more than half a century before the Synod of Whitby convened, the greatest of all the Irish *peregrini,* St. Columbanus, was in his retreat deep in the Vosges.

Bibliographical Note

For St. Columba, see bibliographical note to chapter 2. Efforts have been made by several to trace the missionary journeys of Columba and his Iona associates. A pioneer effort is E. C. Trenholme, *The Story of Iona* (Edinburgh, 1901), pp. 44–48. William Reeves gives a total of fifty-eight Columban foundations in his edition of Adomnan's Life (*The Life of St. Columba, Founder of Hy, written by Adamnan* [Dublin, 1857]), p. xlix. W. Douglas Simpson prunes the list to some thirty foundations, mainly in the Inner Hebrides, in his *The Historical St. Columba* (Aberdeen, 1927); for criticism of his list, see bibliographical note to chapter 3. The best, easily available treatments of the subject are M. O. Anderson, "Columba and Other Irish Saints in Scotland," Irish Conference of Historians, *Historical Studies* V (1965), pp. 26–36, and D. A. Bullough, "Columba, Adomnan, and the Achievement of Iona," *Scottish Historical Review* XLIII (1969), pp. 111–50 and XLIV, pp. 17–33.

Book III of Bede's *Ecclesiastical History* deals at length with the spread of the Celtic Church, especially in Northumbria. Bede treats in succession the achievements of Aidan; Columba; Acca, who was an English bishop trained in Ireland; Fursa; the bishops of Mercia, two of whom were Irish and the third English; Finan; Colman, who spoke for the Celtic Easter at Whitby; his English successor at Lindisfarne, Eata; and Tuda, his successor as bishop of Northumbria whose appointment was a triumph of diplomacy since he was an Irish supporter of the Roman Easter. All other sources of information about the missions stemming from Iona and Lindisfarne and those who led them are subordinate to Bede. For an excellent treatment of Bede and his *History,* see Peter Hunter Blair, *The World of Bede* (New York, 1971). There is information about the conversion of

Northumbria and Mercia in John T. McNeill, *The Celtic Churches* (University of Chicago Press, 1974), pp. 104–8, and in Nora K. Chadwick, "The Conversion of Northumbria," in *Celt and Saxon: Studies in the Early British Border* (Cambridge, 1963).

Bede devotes eleven chapters of Book I to the mission of St. Augustine in Kent and gives an account of Paulinus's work in Northumbria in Book II, chapters 9–14. In addition, see McNeill, *op. cit.*, and Peter Hunter Blair, "The Letters of Pope Boniface V and the Mission of Paulinus to Northumbria," in Peter Clemoes and Kathleen Hughes, eds., *England Before the Conquest: Studies in Primary Sources Presented to Dorothy Whitelock* (Cambridge, 1971).

For the Welsh Church, see A. W. Wade-Evans, *Welsh Christian Origins* (Oxford, 1934); for St. Samson, Thomas Taylor, trans., *The Life of Saint Samson of Dol* (London, 1925). There is information about Welsh missionary activity in the southwest of England in Gilbert H. Dole, *The Saints of Cornwall* (Chatham, 1960) and Thomas Taylor, *The Celtic Christianity of Cornwall* (London, 1961). The implacable hostility of British priest for Saxon is described by Blair, *The World of Bede.* He quotes, p. 83, the statement of Aldhelm on the subject; see R. Ehwald, ed., *Aldhelmi Opera, MGH: Auctores Antiqui* XV, p. 484.

For the Irish at Glastonbury, see James F. Kenney, *The Sources of the Early History of Ireland: Ecclesiastical* (New York, 1929 and later), pp. 606–8. The statement of St. Dunstan on the subject may be found in W. Stubbs, ed., *Memorials of St. Dunstan,* Rolls Series 63 (1874), p. 10. A revision of the *Memorials* dating to before 1050 changes Patrick the Younger to Patrick the Elder and a Glastonbury missal gives him a Mass on August 24. Patrick the Elder reappears in the Irish Martyrology of Oengus, c. 800, with a gloss which states that he is "in Glastonbury of the Gaels, that is a city in the south of England, and Irishmen used to dwell there"; see Whitley Stokes, ed., *The Martyrology of Oengus the Culdee,* Henry Bradshaw Society 29 (1905), p. 188.

For the Easter controversy consult Kenney, pp. 210–17, 220–21. Cummian's plea for the Roman Easter is in his *De Controversia Paschalis,* Migne, *Patrologia latina* 87, p. 974, and J. E. J. Oulton, "The Epistle of Cummian, 'De Controversia Paschalis,'" *Studia Patristica* I (Dublin, 1957), pt. 1, pp. 128–33. See also Paul Grosjean, S. J., "La controverse pascale chez les Celts," *Analecta Bollandiana* 64

(1946), pp. 200–243 and Nora K. Chadwick, *The Age of the Saints in the Early Celtic Church* (London, 1961), pp. 117–38.

There is a good description of the Lindisfarne Gospels in Gareth W. Dunleavy, *Colum's Other Island: The Irish at Lindisfarne* (University of Wisconsin Press, 1960). A complete facsimile edition of the Gospels was published in two volumes by T. J. Brown, R. Bruce-Mitford, and A. S. C. Ross (Olten and Lausanne, 1956–1959).

6

St. Columbanus

IN the days before nations had hardened into political reality and the continent of Europe was still turbulent from a restless mass of invading tribesmen who had overrun every corner of the far-flung Roman Empire, St. Columbanus was the first Irishman to be an emissary from civilization. He was the most important Celtic apostle of Christ to barbarians who were not yet Frenchmen, Germans, or Swiss. The mission field of Columba and his followers was Scotland, the field of Aidan and his followers was England, but the mission field of Columbanus and his followers was the heart of western Europe. By that measure is his importance to be gauged.

Columbanus was born about 550, a century after St. Patrick died and a bare generation after the birth of St. Columba. The juxtaposition of names and dates has its significance. Within a century of Patrick's death the conversion of Ireland had been completed, the conversion of Scotland all but completed, and the conversion of Anglo-Saxon Britain far advanced. Paradoxically, the Gaul that Caesar had conquered and Rome had converted was in large measure pagan and barbaric again. The work of conversion that Pothinus and Irenaeus had initiated in the second century, and that might be deemed completed by the fourth century when St. Martin of Tours was the most eminent figure in the Christian Church, had to be done once more. St. Columbanus and his followers inherited much, but much of it was fragmentary. They had a foundation on which to build, but the foundation was crumbling and desperately needed to be shored. In the late sixth century as in centuries later, our own included, the masonry was loosened and the hard rock was slipping in what had been the strong structure of Christianity, and the tireless dedication and unflagging zeal of the missionary were needed to make strong once more the human edifice constructed by the Founder on the eternal rock.

We have linked the names of Columba and Columbanus. Oddly the link is entirely between the names and not the persons. Columbanus actually called himself Columba and is known to German scholars as Columba the Younger. His Latin name is Columbanus, and today its truncated form, Columban, is commonly used. All three forms can be justified, and our choice of Columbanus rests on nothing more profound than the desire to avoid confusion between Columban the saint and Columban the adjective.

In most respects we are better off where the life of Columbanus is concerned than we are in the case of Columba. In 618 an aspirant named Jonas entered the monastery at Bobbio in northern Italy which Columbanus had founded and in which he had died three years before. Jonas served as secretary to the two abbots who succeeded Columbanus and was given the task of writing the life of Columbanus by Bertulf, who served as abbot from about 626 to 640. Thus Jonas had the advantage of living and working where Columbanus had lived and worked in his last years, and writing with the advantage which only conversation with the contemporaries and friends of the biographer's subject could give. He had the further advantage of interviews with Eustasius, who succeeded Columbanus as abbot when he was expelled from Luxeuil in 610, and with his subject's comrade in exile, St. Gall. The Life is thinnest where Columbanus's Irish period is concerned, since Jonas had no source of information at distant Bangor, and the early years at Luxeuil receive the limited treatment which betokens limited knowledge. Yet the very limitations of the work testify to its reliability. Jonas wrote of what he knew, and although Columbanus performs a number of miracles commensurate with his saintly status, the work is by no means the constant tissue of miracles so typical of early hagiography. Outside the work of Jonas there is nothing of independent value about Columbanus from his own age. The part of Jonas that deals with Columbanus's activities in Burgundy, especially his relations with the Burgundian court, may be found in an important source work for Frankish history, the continuation of Gregory of Tours's *History of the Franks* which is known as the *Chronicle of*

Fredegarius, and there is a metrical life of Columbanus by one Flodoard which is merely Jonas set to verse.

Columbanus was born in Leinster. Whatever else may be uncertain about him, there can be no doubt of his physical strength and handsome appearance. He could fell a tree with one blow of an axe and strangle a bear with his formidable fingers, the sources solemnly assure us. Due allowance must be made for exaggeration in such matters, but even that may not be necessary where the handsome appearance is concerned. Jonas is certain that Columbanus had female Ireland at his feet before he aspired to the tonsure. By a process of logic obscured in the passage of time, this seemed to an aged woman of his acquaintance a fate worse than death and she solemnly assured him that flight would be his only salvation, warning him of Irish relatives on the distaff side, likening them to Eve, Delilah, and Bathsheba. He took the hint and fled, over the prostrate body of his pleading mother by one account, to the monastery of Gleenish on Lough Erne in County Fermanagh. Here it was his fortune to be trained by Abbot Sinell, scholar and disciplinarian, and to write under his tutelage a commentary on the Psalms and some hymns, now lost. He then transferred to Bangor where Comgall was abbot, and Bangor was his home for many years.

Bangor is located on the southern side of Belfast Loch, farther out to sea than the city of Belfast and a logical stepping-stone to Scotland and the Hebrides. Comgall, abbot during the time of Columbanus, had founded the monastery in either 555 or 559, according to the Ulster *Annals.* There is nothing on which to construct a picture of the life of Columbanus at Bangor beyond what we know of the monastery itself and the assumption that the life of Columbanus accorded with the pattern of monastic life at Bangor. It is thought that as many as 400 monks resided there in the sixth century under a rule considerably stricter than that of St. Benedict, who was a contemporary of Comgall. It was a life that drew the more gifted of Ireland's youth away from the violence rampant then in Irish life, as it was in life throughout the western world, and gave them a life of the spirit and the intellect, a life of prayer, and a life of work, but a life in which, by some formula lost in the mists of time and never quite recaptured, the asceticism of the anchorite was combined with the missionary's service to the people. The life of St. Columbanus is a microcosm of the entire Irish monastic movement: he was a missionary to the pagan; a theologian who debated with bishops and even with a pope; a public figure feared and therefore courted, without success, by a regent and a king; a poet who could versify his faith but also write a rowing song; the sort of man who could fell a tree with one blow of an axe and then strangle a bear. Such men have messages for popes and barbarians alike. About 590 Columbanus left Bangor to deliver that message to a larger world.

It is likely that he went by sea from Bangor to Cornwall, crossed the peninsula to a spot near Plymouth, and then crossed the Channel to Brittany, landing at Guimoraie between Saint Malo and Mont Saint Michel, if the commemorative stone there is to be trusted. He appears to have wandered through northern France for some time, following no set plan and presumably seeking the place where he was destined to do his chosen work. It was an age of unimaginable chaos, an age of constant battles between small professional armies, with assassination a commonplace. The petty kingdoms of Austrasia, Neustria, and Burgundy were battlefields on which armies moved, checked, slew and were slain as the degenerate sons and daughters of the lamentable Merovingian line ordained in their endless maneuvering for personal supremacy. As the French historian Funck-Brentano says of the *Chronicle of Fredegarius,* which relates this sad and worthless tale: ". . . the social life presented by Fredegar is nothing but darkness and confusion. The grossest barbarism had invaded even the episcopal thrones—a thick fog which here and there was pierced with difficulty by the shy rays of some quiet candle burning on the rough wooden table of a modest monk bending, in the silence of the monastery, over a manuscript of ivory hue." Columbanus was not quite a modest monk, but he finally set up his rough wooden table in an abandoned fort at Annegray, in the foot-hills of the Vosges near the border of Burgundy and Austrasia. Permission to establish his initial monastery was granted him by Gun-trum of Burgundy (561–592) or his successor Childebert II.

The Vosges lay to the northeast, the Jura Mountains to the southeast, of his selected place. There is at least something symbolic to the modern name of the district, Franche-Comté, the "free county." It was and is a land of mountains and mountain streams, mountain lakes that mirror mountain tops, a land where winter is long, villages are small, lines of communication strung out, and men and women free. The cities are far away and always have been. The implications of

that were substantial indeed for Columbanus and the customary
twelve Irishmen who had accompanied him from distant Bangor to
this remote place which was German without being Germany, Gallic
without being France.

The First Mission

The Germanic invaders of the Roman Empire were men of the
fields and the woods, delighting in the hunt, avid for the active life,
warfare their sport, and the feast by the campfire its satisfying aftermath. The city was a place beyond their ken and foreign to their
instincts. After the universal fashion of their kind, they held in contempt what they did not understand and deemed degenerate those
who had inherited its refinements. Even the Germanic courts tended
to shun the cities and to establish themselves beyond their confines.
The Gallo-Romans, on the other hand, those whom the Franks and
Burgundians had conquered and now ruled, had an instinct for the
city which was mightily reinforced as it became a place of refuge.
The result was a long period in which the races were separated, the
Gallo-Romans in the cities with their now ancient tradition that
stemmed partly from ancient Rome and partly from Christian Rome,
and the Germans in the forest where nature perpetuated the almost
infinitely older tradition of sun and starlight, rain and snow, thunder
and tempest, Woden and Thor.

The Church was centered in the cities, serving the Christian Gallo-
Romans. It ventured into the country districts only to the Germanic
courts where temporal power was centered. The kindly interpretation is that the bishops concentrated on the kings, striving to win
them over to the Christian God and through them the people. This
missionary technique was an ancient one, used with notable success
by St. Patrick in Ireland, by Paulinus and Aidan in England. The
cynical interpretation is that they concentrated on the kings, con-
solidating their own position, enriching the Church, making themselves the ecclesiastical wing of the temporal power. Somewhere
between the two the truth presumably lies. As Jonas saw it, in the
days when Columbanus inspired those who sought him out at Annegray and Luxeuil, it lay considerably closer to the cynical view than
to the kindly.

Columbanus and his twelve associates did in the foothills of the

Vosges what their predecessors had done in the remote places of their native Ireland and in the Britain they labored to convert. The monks made the crumbling walls of the ancient fort at Annegray the walls of a monastery. They undertook the far from simple task of making the desert bloom, a desert that is more than a little recalcitrant in the foothills of the Vosges. Jonas tells us that a Gallo-Roman farmer of the area kept them alive with loads of food as heavy as his horse could carry, for which he asked as recompense prayers for his ailing wife. An abbot with the Celtic name of Caramtog also sent them food. Who was Caramtog, what brought him to the Vosges, where was his abbey, when did it come into being? Invaluable though he is in general, on these matters Jonas fails us. Caramtog existed, and helped that first desperate winter. The question elicited by the Celtic name stays unanswered: were there Irish in the Vosges before Columbanus and his twelve, or was Caramtog a Briton who had moved far to the east of the mission field of the Welsh Church?

The little group survived and became known in the district. Native Christians of the older stock began to seek out Columbanus. Word spread, and crowds grew larger. Time passed, and the crowds were great indeed. They were crowds of Christians, Gallo-Romans with a faith that was centuries old and still survived through the chaos of invasion, the disorder of a land plundered, harried, and at best uneasily ruled by an invader with the physical strength for conquest but not the political maturity for stable government. It survived despite the neglect, whether culpable or not, of a Church that was urban and bishops who were protocourtiers in the crude and violent courts of Austrasia, Neustria, and Burgundy. The crude but peaceful settlement at Annegray was different. Columbanus and his monks heard individual confessions, gave penances, and with the penance also consolation, encouragement, spiritual assistance, and what physical assistance was in their power. Columbanus himself sought from time to time the traditional refuge in solitude that brought Columba to Hinba and Aidan to Farne. His cell was a hollow in a rock where he lived on apples, wild herbs, and water. It was his after he had expelled a bear—gently, Jonas assures us. Columbanus could strangle a bear, but it was not his practice. He returned from his cell to his monastery, stronger in spirit. Always there was about him an aura of mystery proper to a giant of a man from a distant, hardly known land, who spoke Latin with an accent that was strange and another tongue that was stranger still, but who had in the secrecy of individual confession an instinctive sympathy, understanding, and a sternness unbending toward the sin but tempered by love for the sinner. Columbanus is Jonas's subject, but his hero as well, as a subject should be to a biographer.

It would be fascinating to know how many Franks, Burgundians, and Suevians, of the tiny remnant of that people left behind in the Vosges, came to Annegray and later to Luxeuil. In theory, the Franks and Burgundians were Christians, the former orthodox from the baptism of Clovis onwards, and the latter Arian when converted but later reconverted to Christian orthodoxy. Their primitive faith had been in nature and the elements of nature, and particularly in the vaguely sensed, unseen, higher powers that ruled the elements. These powers controlled what was natural, but the powers of the Christian priests transcended the natural as their miracles attested. Thus the God of the Christians was a deity more powerful than Woden and Thor and more to be placated. As Daniel-Rops puts it, "The miracle proved that the Christian God was the strongest God, and herein, as far as they were concerned, lay the essential, the *ultima ratio.*" The prophet of this mighty God was a man worthy to serve him and to perform miracles in his name, a great, powerful, hulking man, larger and more powerful than were the Franks and Burgundians whose size and physical prowess has been magnified by chauvinistic myth. But there was also in him something of the spirit beyond their ken. Hell they could understand and fear. It was the one Christian dogma they understood with ease, the one consistent with their habitual thought that deity is powerful, irascible, vindictive, and desperately hard to appease. But this imposing figure muffled in a cloak and shrouded in a cowl who listened to them and talked with them through an interpreter, the man he called Gall, held out to those who would abandon the ancient and instinctive ways of barbarism the promise of a life after death in which everything was miracle and the bloody hall of heroes was replaced by the peaceful hall of saints. How many we do not know, but Franks and Burgundians found their way to Annegray and swelled the throngs of Gallo-Romans.

The Monastery at Luxeuil

It became clear that a larger and better foundation than Annegray was needed. A site was found at Luxeuil, which the Romans had called Luxovium. There Columbanus founded the most important monastery associated with his name, the foundation that Daniel-Rops calls the French Monte Cassino. The site was shrewdly chosen. It had the crumbling Roman fort so useful, as we have seen, for conversion to a monastery. It had the hot springs which brought the Romans there in the first place, and still brings those with aching joints. It had soil more tractable than that of Annegray, eight miles away in the hills. It was some fifty miles north of Besançon, an ancient city when Caesar captured it a half century before the birth of Christ. Besançon was a center of Gallo-Roman culture to the extent that culture still existed, and furthermore it was the seat of a bishopric. In theory at least, Columbanus was subject to the bishop of Besançon, but Besançon was far away and bishops seldom ventured into the Vosges. For ten years Columbanus did his work at Luxeuil, and at a third foundation three miles to the north, Fontaines, that the success of Luxeuil made necessary. He did so free from episcopal supervision and the criticism it could invoke.

Columbanus wrote a rule for his monastery at Luxeuil which has an importance to scholars of Irish monasticism, since it clearly reflects the rule that Finnian wrote for Clonard and probably was based on the rule that Comgall penned for Bangor. The monks of Columbanus might eat half as much as the monks of Benedict, but they were to sing twice as many psalms. The basis of the cuisine was cabbage, variety being provided by other vegetables; biscuits and bread of a rudimentary sort rounded out the courses, and the dinner bell sounded well toward evening. Conduct was rigidly defined, and misconduct was corrected on the already mentioned principle of opposites: silence for the overtalkative, cultivated meekness for the bellicose, vigils for those drowsy at divine service, and beatings for sinners of every sort. All the axioms of modern psychology crumble before the facts of life at Luxeuil and Fontaines, and all the other monasteries spawned by them in the land of the Franks. Young men were not repelled by their austerities; they were drawn in great numbers by their challenge. As time passed the hardships did not blunt the challenge but more and more aspirants came forward to meet it, and monastery after monastery came into being from the seedbed of Luxeuil.

Two thoughts must be borne in mind when the phenomenon is faced. One is that all life was hard in the seventh century, life in the fields and woods, life in the camp, life in the city, but in fields and woods, camp and city there was no safety comparable to the relative safety of the monastery. The other and more elevated one is based on the sermons of St. Columbanus, of which thirteen survive. They sound the note of hell fire, but it is not the dominant note. They constantly stress the two sets of values, the earthly and the heavenly, and the meaningless quality of the former when measured by the latter. They rise to sublimity when they treat of God as Creator and Redeemer, and the note of redemption is steadily stressed. The fundamental message is that this life is a pilgrimage that has no meaning except in terms of its goal. Life does have a meaning; it is not to be found in life, however, but in the heavenly aftermath to life with its inexpressible joys for those who merit it. Young men met the challenge, but they met it because they marched to a different drum than modern psychology beats. Faith can move mountains at which rationalism quails. It has done so repeatedly in human history, and notably so in the Dark Ages which ironically were also the Age of the Saints.

The Letter to Pope Gregory

For ten years Columbanus and his monks did their work untroubled, but not unnoticed, by those who in theory had ecclesiastical supervision over the region in which Luxeuil was situated. When they did take notice, and with the notice offense, is not clear. What is clear is that their complaints about the monastery at Luxeuil were twofold: it did not recognize the authority of the bishops and it observed the Celtic Easter. We do not have their accusation but we do have an oblique reply from Columbanus in the form of a letter written about 600 to Pope Gregory the Great in which, among other things, he defends the Celtic Easter. He points out that the Celtic Easter is based on the calculations of Anatolius, a man highly praised by St. Jerome for his learning, and quoted by Eusebius in his *History of the Christian Church*. Certainly his calculation is to be preferred to that of Victorius whom the Gallic bishops follow, a calculation which the Holy Father might be quite justified in considering schismatic. It is not that the scholars of Ireland did not know the calculation of Victorius. They did know it, and rejected it with ridicule. Columbanus then proceeds to argue in elaborate detail for the superiority of the calculation of Anatolius to that of Victorius.

He then returns to the matter of bishops. What, pray, is the Holy Father to make of bishops who buy their croziers, and of clerics who keep mistresses when they are deacons and yet rise to episcopal dignity? He names no bishops, but such there are and by implication the problem they present is greater than the problem of dating Easter. He adds that he has read Pope Gregory's *Pastoral Care,* and he asks for his work on Ezekiel, which he had heard highly praised. He has read Jerome on Ezekiel, but there are parts that are not clear. He concludes by reminding the Pope that, although his emissary Candidus may be correct in expressing the Pope's view that error can be so entrenched by the passage of time that it cannot be dislodged, yet truth is older than error and ultimately prevails.

The personality of the man who wrote the letter shines in its pages. He writes with deference but not obsequiousness. He is quite aware of the other viewpoint about Easter but he considers it invalid. He says his say about the dating of Easter and then—*"Haec de Pascha sufficient."* He makes it clear to the Pope that conditions in clerical France could stand investigation, but he does not labor the point. He is acquainted with what the Pope has written, and would like to know more. It is the letter of a man of substantial dignity writing in a fundamentally friendly fashion to his superior, a man independent in his pattern of thinking, not yielding in his convictions because expediency seems to dictate compliance, and a man of learning as well, isolated from his intellectual peers by the pattern of his life but not isolated from the intellectual concerns of his time and eager to learn current trends in theological thought.

The Synod of Chalons

History now becomes silent for some three years, as it habitually does in this remote and scantily recorded era. No answer from Pope Gregory has survived, there is no record of what Columbanus and his monks did or what the bishops did in the interim. One can only assume that Luxeuil continued to be thronged, and the bishops perturbed. In 603 their perturbation developed into action. A synod of bishops was assembled at Chalons sur Saône and Columbanus was summoned before it. He did not answer the summons in person but by letter, and his letter has been preserved. He urges the bishops to conduct their meeting in a spirit of humility. By showing apostolic humility all might be reunited in harmony. It is true, he states, that he prefers to follow Anatolius rather than Victorius in the matter of the Easter dating, but he has stayed away from the synod rather than risk acrimonious debate with its members. He congratulates the assembled clerics on holding their meeting, and urges that such meetings be held as frequently as possible. The participants might discuss not merely the Easter matter which has been quite adequately aired but also the matter of the observance of those canons of the Church which have been scandalously neglected. He quotes from the first letter of St. John: One who claims to dwell in Christ must needs live and move as Christ lived and moved, and he draws the conclusion that this implies poverty in worldly goods, humility of spirit, and a willingness to suffer persecution gladly. Only those who live the Christlike life can inspire it in others.

As for himself and his monks, he says, "I ask you by Our Lord and by Him 'Who is to judge the living and the dead' that in your peace and love you let me abide in these woods and live by the bones of our seventeen dead brethren, as you have already allowed me to live among you for twelve years, and that we may pray for you as we should and hitherto have prayed" (p. 162). He asks episcopal benevolence toward his monks, "those poor old men and aged strangers in the land." He begs the bishops not to give comfort by their quarrels to the Jews, the heretics, and the pagans, and he recalls to them that all Christians are members of a single body, whether they be Gauls, Britons, Spaniards, or members of whatever race on earth. At the same time he addressed a short letter to Rome, this time to Pope Sabinian, asking that he be allowed to observe Easter according to the dating that he considers right and to do so without interference. He concludes this letter by citing the second canon of the Council of Constantinople which permitted missionaries working among barbarians to employ the church laws in vogue in the countries which sent them into the mission field.

The tone of the letter to the synod is moderate and subdued. It is clear that Columbanus wanted no trouble with the bishops, but it is equally clear that his respect for most of them is minimal. There was indeed a difference between the life of a Gallic bishop in the episcopal palace and the life of an Irish monk at Luxeuil, and the difference is implicit in the virtues Columbanus stresses: holy poverty, humility, brotherly love, tolerance, reason. Jonas is explicit about the contempt

Columbanus felt for the bishops as a group, but the reader can infer his attitude toward them from the very qualities appropriate to the priesthood which he pleads with them to manifest in their lives.

Yet the bishops also had a case. Rulers whose closest approach to religion was superstition, who knew the emotion of fear all too well but had no concept of divine love, were their allies because the God of the bishops was stronger than the gods of the Teutoberg Forest. There were nominal Christians close to the court, more Christians of the same sort outside the court, and unconverted pagans in abundance among the people. Should conscientious bishops, like Bishop Donatus of Besançon whom Columbanus reared and trained at Luxeuil, do what they could within the framework life had imposed upon them, with all the time-serving and compromise with principles that necessarily involved, or should they have the independence of Columbanus and lose what influence for good they might exert in court and city? Not all the bishops of the Dark Ages were hypocritical sinners. As the editor of Gregory of Tours puts it: "The blood of the martyrs was the seed of the Church, but the patronage of a Lothar withered like an ill wind. Intending good, the Church had allied herself with wanton power, and she was now caught in a dilemma. It is not easy for us to judge the bishops who found themselves in these straits. They trusted that by turning the hearts of the kings they could save the people; but they found the Merovingian nature infinitely hard to change."

Columbanus Expelled from Luxeuil

Silence once more closes in, this time for seven years, and when trouble next came to Columbanus so far as history records, it came from Brunhilda, regent of Austrasia for her grandson Theudebert II and regent of Burgundy for her grandson Theuderic II. Once more an excursus into history is necessary. When Clovis died in 511, his Franks had conquered Gaul and made it France. By the middle of the century the three Frankish kingdoms, Austrasia, Neustria, and by conquest Burgundy, had begun to take shape. Austrasia, the eastern kingdom, lay between the Meuse and the Rhine; Neustria, the new kingdom, lay between the Meuse and the Loire; Burgundy, land of the Burgundians but now Frankish by conquest, along the upper waters of these rivers and the Saône as well. Luxeuil was in Burgundy, near its northern border with Austrasia. The true rivals were Austrasia and Neustria, Burgundy being a semisubject land and more peaceful than the major powers.

At the turn of the seventh century the struggle was personalized in two women, the Visigothic princess Brunhilda, who was wife of Sigebert the king of Austrasia, and the low-born Fredegond, who was mistress of Hulperik king of Neustria. In 597 Fredegond died and Brunhilda seized almost all of Neustria and in effect was regent of France. The farsighted grandmother of Theuderic saw in his sons the tools by which she would rule his portion of the land, but two difficulties beset her. The first difficulty was that the sons of Theuderic had been born out of wedlock. The other difficulty was Columbanus, who had been striving mightily for the conversion of Theuderic, not his conversion to Christianity, for he was a nominal Christian, but his conversion to morality. Jonas may tell the story:

After Childebert died while still a young man, his two sons Theudebert and Theuderic reigned with the aid of their grandmother Brunhilda. Theuderic held the kingdom of Burgundy and Theudebert the rule of Austrasia. Theuderic congratulated himself that the blessed Columbanus dwelt within his territory. After many visits to him the man of God began to rebuke him because he involved himself in adulterous relations with concubines rather than enjoy the legitimate pleasures of marriage to an honorable queen of royal stock, adding that he should not appear, as he did, like a man emerging from a house of ill fame. When the king said that he would obey the bidding of the man of God and would end all illicit relations, the ancient serpent entered the mind of his grandmother Brunhilda, second Jezebel that she was, spurring her with the stings of pride against the man of God since she saw that Theuderic was obeying him. This was possible since she feared that if he abandoned his concubines and put a queen at the head of his house, she would lose her dignities and a portion of her honor.

It happened one day that the blessed Columbanus came to Brunhilda at her villa in Brocariacum [Bruyères-le-Châtel]. When she saw him enter the hall, she brought before the man of God the sons that Theuderic had by his adulterous relations. When he saw them he asked what they wished of him. Brunhilda said, "They are the sons of the king. Fortify them with your blessing." He replied, "Let it be known to you that they will never hold the royal sceptre, for they were begotten in a state of sin." In a fury she ordered him to leave. As the man of God left the royal hall and crossed the threshold, there was a crash and the whole house shook, terrifying all. But the wrath of that wretched woman it did not quell.

(Book I, ch. 18–19)

The above passage and what follows make it clear that Brunhilda feared the influence of Columbanus on Theuderic and the resulting lessening of her own influence. It is equally clear that Theuderic wanted no trouble with Columbanus, and even less, trouble with the God of Columbanus. Brunhilda, however, forced his hand and, after considerable harassment of the monastery at Luxeuil, Theuderic had Columbanus seized and brought to Besançon where, Jonas tells us, he brought the light of faith to his fellow prisoners, many of whom had been condemned to death. But there was both a leniency and a laxity in the entire treatment of the abbot and his fellow Irishmen that suggest at least the moderating hand of Theuderic, who seems to have had an honest respect and admiration for Columbanus. In any event, Columbanus was not condemned to death. He and the other monks of Luxeuil who were of Irish birth were condemned to deportation back to Ireland. Presently they were in the hands of the Burgundian soldiery and purportedly en route to Erin.

There are perplexing aspects to the entire business of Columbanus's exile. Why should Brunhilda, as the power behind Theuderic, have turned to Columbanus to give the blessing of the Church to the by-blows of her royal grandson? If any clergyman was appropriate for the purpose, and we prescind from judgment on the point, surely it was the bishop of Besançon. Two interpretations suggest themselves, not to the exclusion of other possibilities. One is that the prestige of Columbanus in Burgundy and neighboring Austrasia was so great that he and he alone had the universal respect needed to make the benison accepted. The other possibility that suggests itself is that time-serving clerics urged this consideration upon Brunhilda, thus contriving an adroit way of ridding themselves of a troublesome rival. They knew that the independent minded abbot would never compromise with the dictates of canon law, and hence would pay whatever penalty Brunhilda exacted. The penalty, however, gives rise to another question. Merovingian penalties did not take such mild and modern forms as deportation, and particularly deportation so explicit as a forced return to Ireland. In addition the penalty was imposed not merely on Columbanus but on all the monks of Luxeuil who were Irish by birth. The Gallo-Roman monks and the Frankish monks, if such there were, were not to be disturbed. May we infer that the moderate penalty reflects the moderating influence of the bishops over the decision of an imperious regent and her compliant grandson? May it reflect an episcopal desire to eliminate the Irish influence from Luxeuil and make the monastery compliant and Gallo-Roman? Or may there be a quite different explanation?

Columbanus was a great saint and great saints are capable of working great miracles. Ananias, for example, fell dead at the feet of St. Peter, and that was the sort of miracle the Merovingians understood most readily. Extreme caution is advisable when it comes to penalizing great saints, and motives other than respect for saintliness might hold the royal hand from resting too hard upon a saint so potent in miracle as Columbanus. The deportation order stood, however, and in 610 Columbanus and his Irish comrades, those who still survived, started the long journey that was to lead not to Ireland but to the foundation of the monastery at Lure and the magnificent abbey at St. Gallen, to initiate the conversion of Switzerland, and to bring Columbanus himself to Bobbio in Italy and, in the short time left him, to the task of converting the Lombards.

The Travels of Columbanus

In the pages of Jonas we can follow Columbanus and his Irish fellows on their long and intricate wanderings. Even more effectively, we can follow them on the map provided for the purpose by Daniel-Rops, whose knowledge of early French place names and his unsurpassed experience with early hagiography helped him to interpret, more effectively than an outlander could, the not always explicit Jonas. Columbanus, the other monks, and their guards started down the long and winding ways that led to Nantes and the seaway to Ireland. They had gone but a few miles when it was evident that one aged monk, Deicola, thought by some to have been the older brother of St. Gall, could not stand the pace. He bade Columbanus farewell, the guards looked the other way, and he entered the forest where it might be the will of God that he live in solitude as an anchorite. His companions watched him disappear, thinking him soon destined for unrecorded martyrdom by the elements or savage beasts, never suspecting the true will of God. The old man stumbling over roots and rocks was destined to start the chain of events that culminated in the building of the great monastery of Lure.

Columbanus and the others proceeded under guard through Auxerre and Nevers to Orleans, where Jonas records that Columbanus restored the sight of a blind man. From Orleans they proceeded to Tours where Columbanus spent the night praying before the tomb of St. Martin, and monks and guards alike were entertained with courteous hospitality by the bishop. From Tours they went to Nantes, where the ship presumably was waiting and the guards would be freed of the responsibility for the sort of custodianship which presents peculiar problems when the person in custody has the power of miracle.

From Nantes Columbanus wrote a long letter to the monks at Luxeuil. From start to finish the letter is an eloquent plea for harmony of spirit and the preservation of monastic discipline. One sentence in it expresses the essence of its thought: *"videte ut 'unum cor et anima una' sitis"* (See to it that you be 'of one heart and one soul'). The quotation is a paraphrase of Acts 4:32: "And the multitude of believers had but one heart and one soul: neither did any one say that aught of the things which he possessed, was his own; but all things were common unto them." The verse expresses the basic inspiration of monasticism. Columbanus was clearly disturbed over two problems: the question of obedience to whoever might be his successor as abbot, and the difficulty of preserving the monastic integrity of Luxeuil in the face of episcopal opposition, especially over the Easter issue. There were two obvious heirs to his position: Attala and Waldelenus. The monks should obey the person elevated, whichever he might be. As for Columbanus himself, his concern is entirely for those he has left at Luxeuil, not at all for himself. Then he proceeds to reveal that his own future is by no means the one ordained for him by Brunhilda and Theuderic, with or without episcopal prompting. Late in the letter he says, "Even as I am writing a messenger has come to say that the ship is ready for me in which I am to be borne against my will to my native land. But if I escape from it, no guard will bar my way, for they appear to wish me to escape. If, however, I am cast into the sea like Jonah, whose name in Hebrew is said to mean *dove*, say a prayer that in place of a whale some reliable rescuer with stout rowing arms may bring your Jonah safely back to the land he longs for." As things turned out, Columbanus and the others did escape without the aid of a whale, a miracle, or a rescuer, and much as Columbanus had predicted. Hardly had the ship left Nantes when a storm helped it run aground on a conveniently accessible sandbar and Columbanus and his fellows escaped comfortably and almost dryshod.

They now proceeded to Soissons, to the court of Clotaire II of Neustria. There was a logic in this, because Clotaire was the enemy of Brunhilda and Neustria was at odds with Burgundy. The king gave Columbanus a friendly welcome, as he always did to the monks of Luxeuil. The *peregrini* then proceeded to Metz, to the court of Theudebert II of Austrasia. Theudebert, in matters of general import, was under the ideological control of Brunhilda, but either he was free to deal with Columbanus as he chose or all that Brunhilda and perhaps the bishops desired had been achieved when Columbanus and his Irishmen were safely out of Luxeuil. In any event, Theudebert gave Columbanus a mission field in the lake district of northern Switzerland, at Tuggen where the Limmat River enters the Lake of Zurich. Excessive zeal in the smashing of idols led to resentment sufficiently substantial for a local priest working for the conversion of the resolutely pagan elements of the area to urge Columbanus and his followers to move on. They moved on, to Bregenz at the eastern end of Lake Constance where today Austria has a tiny corridor to the waters of the lake. Here they remained three years, working among the pagan Suevi and Alamanni with a limited measure of success.

Once more the specter of Merovingian politics loomed before them. Theuderic defeated Theudebert of Austrasia and subsequently had him killed. Now Theuderic and Brunhilda ruled all Austrasia, Bregenz included, and old animosities grew more menacing. These animosities were fed by complaints from the natives, who found that monks in a forest are detrimental to hunting. Columbanus was not one to be moved by threats from denizens of either Merovingian courts or Germanic woodlands, but there had grown steadily within him the conviction that his destiny lay in northern Italy. There Christendom was riven by the Catholic-Arian division while the Lombards, by and large, had little but the drying drops of baptismal water to remind them that they had changed from pagans to Christians. This was the mission field to which he now aspired.

This is a point at which to pause, that geographical implications may sink in. Columbanus has now made his way from Nantes, on the Bay of Biscay, to Soisson, northeast of Paris. From there he proceeded to Metz, on the Moselle. Jonas makes it clear that he then made his way to the Rhine, proceeding down the river in a barge sometimes propelled by the wind and sometimes by oars. Ultimately he reached Bregenz, at the western tip of Austria. The map already mentioned in Daniel-Rops's *The Church in the Dark Ages* (p. 215) is as accurate a tracing of his travels as is achievable. This map, translated into the distances on modern automobile highways, shows Columbanus traveling 934 miles. These miles were traveled sometimes on good roads the Romans had built, but even then traveled on foot. Sometimes they were traveled on crude forest trails. Sometimes they were river miles, miles hard won by weary men who tugged at cumbersome oars. They were miles that extended from the western coast of France to its border with modern Germany, and down the Rhine through what now are Coblenz and Mainz, Strasbourg and Basle, to Lake Constance and along that beautiful but endless stretch of water to Bregenz at its eastern tip. These miles were traveled by men of the Dark Ages but guided by a light next to inconceivable to most moderns who deem themselves enlightened. They were men of iron constitution, but their iron constitution was motivated by an invulnerable faith and an iron will. The world would not see their full like again until the same faith and will appeared in sixteenth-century France, and Gallic heirs to the task of Columbanus did their endless miles in the wilderness of North America and faced death by tortures at which the Merovingians would blanch.

The Parting with St. Gall

By the tungsten steel in the spirit of Columbanus the next episode in his life must be judged. Jonas does not record it, but it is in the Life of St. Gall of Walahfrid Strabo. It was now the fixed determination of Columbanus to proceed to northern Italy and enter the mission field among the Lombards. It was his fixed conviction as well that his monks should in obedience follow him. Gall, who had followed him from Bangor to Luxeuil, and from Luxeuil to Bregenz, staying with Columbanus when his aged brother Deicola had to drop out of the march and face a fearsome future in solitude near Lure, was too ill to leave Bregenz. Walahfrid Strabo tells what happened:

Columbanus began to address them in these words, ". . . God Whom we serve will send his angel to lead us to Agilulf, king of the Lombards, in whose realm aided by his clemency we shall find human feeling and a place of peace for our habitation." Then, when the time for departure was at hand, a sudden fever struck down St. Gall. Hurrying to the feet of the abbot, he said that he was severely stricken and could not make the journey proposed. The abbot, thinking that he was quailing at the exertion of a still longer journey, both from his love of the place where they were and in the light of the exertions already undergone, said to him, "I know, brother, that you suffer from the fatigue of the many exertions you have undergone for me; but this I enjoin upon you as I leave, that while I am alive never again will you presume to say Mass." (p. 291)

The story may be apocryphal, it is not in Jonas, and Walahfrid Strabo lived in the ninth century, long after the death of St. Gall. On the other hand, it was well within the rigidly unbending and even fanatical determination of Columbanus to follow his gleam wherever it led and to exact from the others unwavering obedience that he should place upon the most gifted of his followers the sternest injunction within his power to impose. One note of amelioration may be culled from Jonas: on his deathbed Columbanus sent his abbatial staff to Gall.

To conclude the incident, Gall threw himself on the mercy of a local priest named Willimar who received him kindly, gave him a dwelling, and appointed two priests to nurse him back to health. Walahfrid Strabo concludes his story with a series of exclamatory bursts: "Oh infirmity mightier than any human strength! O fever, to be celebrated with fervent praise! O weakness, to be ascribed to a happy health of mind! After the example of our Lord, Gall suffered for us that by his sacred preaching he might cure the illness in our soul. He was unable to go with his master that he might show us the way to truth. Truly long suffering and merciful is the Lord!" The justification for his rapturous exclamations exists in abundance, but must be deferred until we treat the career of St. Gall.

As for Columbanus, accompanied only by a monk named Attalus, he made his way south by Chur, to use contemporary place names, by the Italian lakes, to Milan and then to Pavia, capital of Lombardy, where King Agilulf reigned on friendly terms with the popes and, although by ancestry an Arian, was benign toward the orthodox Catholicism to which his beloved queen, the Bavarian Princess Theudelinda, was devoted.

The Monastery at Bobbio

Midway between Genoa and Piacenza, sufficiently withdrawn then, and indeed now, from centers of trade and politics, was an aged and decayed church that legend ascribed to St. Peter. Its locale was called Bobbio, and Agilulf gave the church and the site to Columbanus. Work of restoration began, with Columbanus shouldering his share of the lumber and the extra share that befitted an abbot and preeminently befitted Columbanus. The community was organized under the Rule of Columbanus, and although the Rule admitted some Benedictine modifications within a half century of its foundation, the Rule of Columbanus was observed in the monastery of Bobbio until the tenth century. The community at Bobbio, however, was recruited in northern Italy and, although as time went on important cultural links developed between Bobbio and monasteries in Ireland, Bobbio was always an Italian institution.

Although he left an indelible mark at Bobbio, and indeed in a major way affected the course of religion in northern Italy, the abbacy of Columbanus at Bobbio was brief. Expelled from Luxeuil in 610, he died at Bobbio in 615. When allowance is made for his intermediate visits to the courts of Neustria and Austrasia, his time in the Swiss lake country, and his stay at Bregenz, he could hardly have been at Bobbio for more than two or three years.

Northern Italy was in religious turmoil during his brief tenure. The Lombards, the Longobardi or long-beards, who had moved at first it would seem from Scandinavia, had made their way to Moravia and the middle Danube basin in the fifth century, and then had been driven west and south by pressure ultimately exerted by a race unknown and unseen far in the unprobed East, the Turks. In the mid-sixth century they were admitted to northern Italy as soldiers in the army of Justinian for the war against the Ostrogoths. They had received Christianity in the Arian form, a matter of little theological consequence to them since the doctrine of Arius which denied to the Second Person of the Trinity coequality and coeternity with the First was as far from pivotal in their thinking as its Catholic repudiation was in the thinking of the Franks. To the Arian Lombards the Christian God was more powerful than the pagan gods since his powers transcended the elements, a theology in which Arian Lombard and Catholic Frank saw eye to eye. The important point is that the religious structure among the Lombards had been erected by Arian missionaries, and this hierarchy Columbanus was dedicated to make tumble.

The situation was worsened by a cleavage in the Catholic ranks. In the fifth century treatises had been written by three theologians

whose names have proven to be writ on water: Theodore of Mopsu-
estia, Theodoret of Cyrus, and Ibas of Edessa. They were condemned
by the Council of Constantinople (553) on the grounds that they were
tainted by Nestorianism, the thesis that in Christ there were two
distinct persons, one divine and one human. The decree of condem-
nation was known as the Three Chapters. It was widely held that the
action of the council was speeded if not directed by political pressure
from Justinian, and Pope Vigilius (538–555) held out against the con-
demnation of the three theologians and their works. It was further
held that Vigilius himself gave way under pressure from Justinian.
Columbanus was not certain that there had not been a taint of Nestorianism in the thinking of Pope Vigilius himself. It was his ardent
wish that this taint be removed from the papacy, that the serious
resentment felt in northern Italy at the action of the council and the
resulting diminution of Catholic ranks in an area dominated by Arianism be terminated and the trend reversed. The result was a letter
to the reigning pope Boniface IV (608–615), a long letter, rambling,
rhetorical, only incidentally theological, but always hortatory. That
the Pope must clear the air by calling a synod and enunciating the
true Catholic doctrine in question is its constant message.

The Letter to Pope Boniface

"This is not presumption," declares Columbanus, "not when it is
clear that the enlightenment of the Church is in question. If anyone
raises an objection to the one who is speaking, let him consider not
who speaks but what he says. Why should a Christian *peregrinus*
keep silent when his neighbor the Arian has so long been clamor-
ing?" Columbanus is an Irishman, and the position of the Irish in the
Church is crystal clear. "All we Irish are disciples of Saints Peter and
Paul and all the disciples who wrote the sacred canons under the
inspiration of the Holy Spirit. We are dwellers at the end of the earth,
and we have no doctrine save that of the evangelists and the apostles.
There has never been a heretic, a Jew, or a schismatic among us. We
hold undiminished the Catholic faith as we first received it from you,
the true successors of the blessed apostles." These are the grounds on
which Columbanus feels confidence in his right to exhort the Holy
See. There is always the sad example of Vigilius to bear in mind. "Be
vigilant, I beg, Holy Father, be vigilant. Again I say it: be vigilant.

Vigilius perhaps was not vigilant, and they attribute to him the source of that scandal which they level against you. . . . A doleful and a mournful thing it is, if the Catholic faith is not held in the Holy See."

Late in the letter he spells out his own faith: "If as I have heard there are some who do not believe that there are two substances in Christ, they should be considered heretics, not Christians. Christ our Savior is true God, eternal and without beginning in time, and He is true man born in time without sin. In His divinity He is co-eternal with the Father; in His humanity He is younger than His mother. Although born in the flesh, He was never absent from Heaven. Though remaining one of the Trinity, He lived on earth. And so, if as I have been told it was written in the fifth synod that the one who worships two substances divides his prayers in two directions, he himself who wrote this is divided from the saints and from God. In terms of the unity of person in which the Divine Omnipotence chose to dwell in bodily form, we believe there is one Christ, we believe in His divinity and His humanity, because 'He Who so went down is no other than He who has gone up, high above all the heavens, to fill creation with His presence.' " Consequently he makes his plea to the Pope to remove from the name of the Church the charge of inconsistency, and the further charge "that it can be moved by any force from the solid rock of true faith for which so many martyrs preferred to shed their blood, choosing death rather than recantation." In closing he makes it clear that all northern Italy is disturbed, king, queen, and people alike, and no one profits but the Arian. "The king asks, the queen asks, all the people ask that as soon as possible all be united, that there soon be peace in our country, peace for our faith, and there be a single flock of Christ. King of kings, you follow Peter and the whole Church follows you. What is sweeter than peace after war? What is happier than the reunion of brothers long separated?" The letter ends with an eloquent prayer for himself, his fellow *peregrini*, and all the children of Christ, that they may merit eternal salvation.

There is more of the essential Columbanus in this letter than in anything else we have from his pen. It is the word of a soldier of Christ, ardent in his will for the complete triumph of the orthodox Catholic doctrine, impatient at hesitation in the papacy, endlessly jealous for the unblemished name of the seat of Peter, and very much aware that the Arian enemy would never be defeated while the orthodox forces were divided among themselves.

There is a corollary of importance implicit in this letter. The term *Celtic Church* is a commonplace and, properly employed, a useful one. It identifies the Church among the Celts of the British Isles and their foundations on the continent. Furthermore the Celtic Church has certain characteristics that set it apart from the Church in general: the primacy of abbots, the limitation of the role of bishops to pastoral concerns, the dating of Easter, and the fashion of the tonsure are the most important, or at least the best known. There have been those, however, whose ideological bias was of the nineteenth century rather than the seventh, who would see in this concept of a Celtic Church a Church substantially independent of Rome. There is not a vestige of evidence that Columbanus, or indeed any other Irish missionary working in the British Isles or on the continent in the Dark Ages was in fact or in intent other than a loyal son of Rome or considered his Church, for all its incidental divergences from the Roman model, other than an integral part of the universal Church of Rome. In this faith Columbanus lived, worked, suffered, and died.

The Last Days of Columbanus

Among the Merovingians the mills of the gods began to grind with greater speed than usual. Theuderic died at the age of twenty-six, worn out by debauchery. Clotaire II of Neustria defeated the forces of Brunhilda, killed the sons of Theuderic, and put Brunhilda to death in a fashion appalling even by Merovingian standards. Then, with that sudden swing from savagery to piety at which the Merovingians were so dexterous, he sent Eustasius, successor to Columbanus as abbot of Luxeuil, to Bobbio to plead for the return of Columbanus. Eustasius, devoted to his mentor, accepted with happiness the assignment which would bring about his own replacement. Columbanus received Eustasius with joy, tactfully declined the offer of Clotaire, exhorted Eustasius to exact at Luxeuil the virtue of holy obedience, wrote to the king beseeching royal aid for Luxeuil and then, being always Columbanus, rebuked him soundly for the bloody death of Brunhilda. Columbanus had lived, worked, and suffered at Luxeuil and places between it and Bobbio. There remained for him only what years of work at Bobbio the Lord might grant, and then death.

His days at Bobbio were to be very few, but they left their enduring mark both there and elsewhere in northern Italy. As time passed

Bobbio gave its name to a diocese that lasted until 1803 when it was seized and secularized by the soldiers of Napoleon. The diocese was reestablished by Pope Pius VII, and today Bobbio is a diocese of some seventy parishes. Like virtually all the monasteries of the period Bobbio became Benedictine in the mid-seventh century, but it held to the Rule of Columbanus until the tenth. In a modest way Bobbio became in the Middle Ages such a center of scholarship as St. Gallen preeminently was. Among its most notable possessions were the *Antiphonary of Bangor,* a literary and artistic link with Ireland, and the Bobbio Missal. Through the centuries "The Goth, the Christian, Time, War, Flood, and Fire" did their work. Today some books from Bobbio may be found in the Vatican, some others in the Ambrosian Library at Milan and the National Library at Turin. The traveler who takes the road up from Genoa or down from Piacenza will reach the River Trebbia at Bobbio and near it find the monastery now used as a school, the basilica which is now the parish church, and in a tomb in the crypt chapel the body of St. Columbanus.

Bibliographical Note

There exist ten letters by St. Columbanus and an eleventh of questionable authenticity. Six in prose concern his religious work; four are poems addressed to friends. The letters dealing with the Easter dating are the only contemporary documents that present the Celtic side of the question. Four minor works are attributed to Columbanus, seventeen sermons most of them on shaky grounds, and the celebrated Rule of Columbanus, the *Regula Monachorum.*

The first collected edition of his works appeared at Louvain in 1667. It was compiled by Patrick Fleming, an Irishman who was ordained a Franciscan in 1617 and sent abroad to gather manuscripts by Irish writers as part of a movement to make Louvain a center in exile for Irish culture. Father Fleming left the manuscript at Louvain in 1630 when he was sent to head the Irish Franciscan College at Prague. He was murdered the next year by a band of peasants inflamed by the hatred engendered in the Thirty Years War. The *Collectanea sacra seu S. Columbani Hiberni abbatis. . . .* appeared thirty-six years after his death. There is a modern edition, *Sancti Columbani Opera,* ed. and trans. G. S. M. Walker (Dublin, 1957). His works are also available in Migne, *Patriologiae cursus completus,*

Series secunda (Paris, 1850), vol. 80, col. 201–326. The letters are in W. Gundlach, ed., *MGH: Epistolae Merowingici et Karolini aevi* III (Berlin, 1892), pp. 159–90. The quotations from the letter to Pope Boniface are translated from this edition. *The Poems of Saint Columban* were edited and translated by Perry Fridy Kendig (Philadelphia, 1949). The Rule is in *The Irish Penitentials,* ed. Ludwig Bieler and D. A. Binchey (Dublin, 1963).

The contemporary life of Columbanus, on which all subsequent writing about him is based, is by Jonas of Bobbio, *Vita Sancti Columbani,* in Bruno Krusch, ed., *MGH: Scriptores Rerum Merowingicarum* IV (Hannover, 1902), pp. 1–52. Jonas's *Vita* has been translated by Dana C. Munro, *Life of St. Columban* (Philadelphia, 1899). The part which deals with Columbanus's relations with Brunhilda and Theuderic is incorporated into chapter 36, Book IV, of Fredegarius, *Chronicle, MGH: Scriptores Rerum Merowingicarum* II, pp. 18–168. The description of the *Chronicle* quoted in the text is from F. Funck-Brentano, *The National History of France: the Earliest Times,* trans. E. F. Buckley (London and New York, 1923, 1967), p. 267. See also H. Daniel-Rops, *The Church in the Dark Ages,* trans. Audrey Butler (London and New York, 1959), for the primitive view of the deity held by the Merovingians; for the quotation in the text, p. 197. The case for the bishops in the Merovingian age is presented in the excellent, philosophic Introduction by O. M. Dalton, trans., to *The History of the Franks by Gregory of Tours* (Oxford, 1927); see vol. I, p. 243. For the injunction addressed by Columbanus on leaving Gall, forbidding him to say Mass again while Columbanus lived, see Walahfrid Strabo, *Vita Sancti Galli* in Bruno Krusch, ed., *MGH: Scriptores Rerum Merowingicarum* IV, p. 291.

The following books about Columbanus are available in English: Clarence W. Bispham, *Columban: Saint, Monk and Missionary 539–615 A.D. Notes concerning his Life and Times* (New York, 1903); George Metlake, *The Life and Writings of St. Columban 545–615* (Philadelphia, 1914); Helena Concannon, *Life of St. Columban* (Dublin, 1915); and J. MacManus, *Saint Columban* (New York, 1962). Bispham presents a scholarly consideration of certain perplexing problems in the life and background of St. Columbanus. Metlake is a pseudonym for Johann J. Laux; his book was published in 1919 at Freiburg under the title *Der hl. Kolumban, sein Leben und seine Schriften.* The MacManus book is a pleasantly readable work addressed to those with a taste for hagiography. I have not seen Helena Concannon's book.

French scholarship has produced several important books about Columbanus. Eugene Martin, *Saint Columban (vers 540–615)* (Paris, 1905), is a well written and readable account of his life and works, including a good description of the Rule and a valuable last section on the monasteries founded under the influence of Luxeuil. The fourteen-hundredth anniversary of the birth of Columbanus elicited two works of primary importance, one from the pen of M. M. Dubois, *Saint Columban* (Paris, 1950), and one under his editorship, *Melanges Columbaniens* (Paris, 1951).

The following are important articles about Columbanus: Thomas J. Shahan, "Saint Columbanus at Luxeuil," *American Catholic Quarterly Review,* January 1902; Gaston Bonet-Maury, "S. Columban et la fondation des monasteres irlandaises en Brie au VII siècle," *Revue historique* LXXXII (1903), pp. 277–99; J. J. Dunn, "Irish Monks on the Continent: St. Columban, St. Gall," *Catholic University Bulletin* X (1904), pp. 307–28; and J. O'Carroll, "The Chronology of St. Columban," *Irish Theological Quarterly* XXIV (1957), pp. 76–95.

7

The Light from Luxeuil

COLUMBANUS struck the light at Luxeuil which shone long after his passing, illuminating darkened places throughout Burgundy, Austrasia, and Neustria, reaching south and west across the Loire into Aquitaine, and reaching north and west until it blended with the light from Wales that brightened Armorica. The light of Luxeuil penetrated what now is Belgium, touched the Rhine, and showed Switzerland the road to Christendom. By the most austere reckoning at least thirty-five monasteries were founded under the direct influence of Luxeuil, and Daniel-Rops estimates that some two hundred monasteries could have traced their ancestral lines ultimately to the foundation that Columbanus brought into being near the Vosges.

Once more we see illustrated the principle governing the history of Iona and Lindisfarne. Columba founded Iona, but it was the successors of Columba who brought Christianity from that holy island to most of Scotland. Aidan founded Lindisfarne, but it was those who followed him who brought the faith from Britain's other holy island to most of Anglo-Saxon England. So with Columbanus. He founded personally the initial monastery at Annegray, the great monastery at Luxeuil, and the satellite monastery at Fontaines. In his last years he founded Bobbio in Italy. All the others were the work of his successors.

The Companions of Columbanus

When Columbanus left Bangor twelve Irish apostles followed him. Fleming's edition of the works of Columbanus published at Louvain in 1667 presents the names of the twelve, gleaned from a source that seems no longer traceable. Three are commemorated in the monasteries that they founded: Gall, Deicola, and Sigisbert. Several other names from the list appear fitfully in the Lives of their fellows, notably Lua and Columbin. The rest are names and nothing more. Perhaps when Columbanus left Luxeuil for exile, he left some of his Irish compatriots behind among the seventeen followers in the tiny graveyard by the abbey. Perhaps some who started down the road of exile with him were more recent arrivals from Ireland, because the road from Bangor to Luxeuil stayed open and it is known that a number of aspirants took it. We know that Gall, Deicola, Ursicinus, and Sigisbert left him at various stages on the road to Bobbio, and that only Attalus was with him when he reached his destination. For the moment we may pass by Gall and Sigisbert, whose names belong to the religious history of Switzerland, and follow Deicola to his unsuspected and most unlikely destiny.

St. Deicola

We left Deicola aware, after only a few miles down the road from Luxeuil, that the journey into the unknown was beyond his dwindling strength. He asked and gained permission of Columbanus to leave the company, enter the forest, and make himself a hermitage for what days the Lord might grant him. Columbanus gave permission, embraced him, and Gall watched the man thought to be his elder brother push aside the boughs and enter the forest depths. At this point begins the legend of Deicola, which was written three centuries after his death by a monk from the Benedictine monastery of Murbach.

Deicola was without food or drink, and he passed the first night huddled beneath a tree. In the morning he struck the ground with his staff and a spring of water gushed forth. Refreshed, he pushed on until he met a swineherd. He told the swineherd that he was a monk seeking a place where he might build his cell. The swineherd suggested a marshy area called Lutra, since marshes ranked not far behind islands and promontories as sites for the cells of anchorites. The swineherd would be happy to show him the way, but could not leave his herd. Therefore Deicola planted his staff in the ground, a mesmerized herd formed a circle about it, and stayed mesmerized until the swineherd brought Deicola to the place where the town of Lure now stands. Here was a well, and Deicola made his cell beside it.

One day King Clotaire II was hunting in the forest. A huge and thoroughly terrified boar fled from him and sought refuge in the cell of Deicola, crouching at the feet of the saint. The hounds traced the boar to the cell but as they raced toward the entrance of the cell a supernatural force stopped them in their tracks. The huntsmen brought the king to observe the miracle. Learning that Deicola was a follower of Columbanus and a monk from Luxeuil, the king forgot the hunt, entered the cell, and asked Deicola how he and his followers fared in this wilderness. The saint told the king that he and those who had come to learn and pray with him were sustained by the fear of the Lord and the love of the Lord, and they needed no further riches. The king, however, gave them the entire revenue of the neighborhood of Lure and added to it the town of Bredana, its church and vineyard.

When Deicola came to Lure he discovered nearby a church dedicated to St. Martin. Each night he went there to pray, and angels opened the door for him. The local priest, who held his post by the powers of lay investiture assumed by Werfarius, the local noble, resented this intrusion of his property and resented even more the way the people were leaving his church to seek out Deicola in his isolated cell. The priest proceeded to barricade the church door with bushes and branches, but they posed no serious problem to the angelic doorkeepers. Therefore he appealed to Werfarius who ordered that Deicola be seized and punished, whereupon Werfarius sickened and speedily died. His widow sent for Deicola to seek his forgiveness. A weary Deicola arrived and hung his cloak upon a ray of sunshine beaming through the room. The widow threw herself at his feet, begged forgiveness for her departed husband, and gave to Deicola the Church of St. Martin and its endowment in land. With the revenues thus obtained from Clotaire and from the widow, the great monastery of Lure was built, a monastery destined to become one of the richest in France, to have abbots who were princes of the Holy Roman Empire, to be granted exemption from episcopal jurisdiction by the Holy See, to be linked in the fourteenth century with the abbey of Murbach where Deicola's biographer lived and worshiped, and so to endure as a living memorial to an aged Irish monk who

found the journey into exile too much for his failing powers, said
farewell to his master and his fellows, pushed aside the boughs and
entered the forest depths. His end was like his beginning. With the
monastery well established, he made its abbot a monk named Columbin who may have been one of the Bangor twelve, built a tiny oratory
dedicated to the Trinity, lived there in solitude until his death on
January 18, in the year 625 as it appears, and there was buried.

The legend of Deicola seems worth the telling as a fine example
of hagiography at its typical best. Furthermore, it is instructive to
match it with the biography of Deicola as the *Dictionary of National
Biography (DNB)* presents it, shorn of its fairy-tale qualities and yet
based as it had to be on the only original source of information that
we have. Deicola in *DNB* is a native of Leinster, he is known to the
French as Saint Desle and his name ("the servant of God") is a pious
bit of Latinizing worked upon the Irish name Dichul. He came from
Bangor with Columbanus, found the road to exile beyond his powers,
entered the wilderness, met the swineherd, found the little church,
aroused the ire of the local priest, escaped the wrath of the nobleman
by the latter's sudden death, was endowed by the widow who
deemed her husband's death a judgment, and built the monastery of
Lure. *DNB* has it that the endowment from Clotaire was a later
development, and adds a note that may have quite as much of the
fairy tale to it as anything in the pious pages written at Murbach. It
has Deicola travel to Rome, meet the pope, tell him of the rapacious
nature of the denizens of northern Burgundy, ask his personal protection, and return with some relics and a papal anathema against his
enemies after paying ten silver *solidi,* or the value of twenty cows
by Frankish law, for a charter to Lure.

The basic facts as the tenth-century monk records them and the
twentieth-century scholar views them are the same. There is little
danger that twentieth-century rationalists will be led into asphodel
fields of unquestioning faith by a tenth-century account of miraculous embellishments surrounding a set of solid deeds. There is a very
real danger, on the other hand, that they will throw out the baby with
the bath, discarding the solid core of fact so often at the heart of
legend. The fundamental facts about Deicola are above challenge,
and some of the corollaries to them are of substantial interest. His
career illustrates how instinctively the people turned to these Irish
monks, incredibly hard upon themselves but strangely kind to oth-

ers, preaching a religion pure and undefiled and different indeed from the institutional religion of the city and the court, where bishops were becoming civil functionaries and cynicism was corroding what once was strong and simple faith. Strip away the bushes and branches that guarded the door of St. Martin's Church and dismiss the angelic doorkeepers; there remains the conflict between the Irish monk and the Gallo-Roman priest, the one a man of God alone and the other Caesar's man of God. It was a conflict destined to mark the entire missionary movement that stemmed from Ireland, with form of tonsure and dating of Easter the surface issues in a struggle in which the real issues were far deeper. The fundamental facts are present in this tenth-century Life, as they often are beneath the most pietistic and imaginative embellishments hagiography can contrive.

Renewal in Besançon

Another development from Luxeuil of major importance came in Besançon. Besançon was the metropolis of the region in which Luxeuil and Lure were located, and a city of great antiquity and haughty bearing. In theory the bishop of Besançon was metropolitan of the area and Luxeuil was subject to him. It may be that the bishop of Besançon was among the episcopal opponents of Columbanus, but Jonas is silent on the point. In any case, Besançon was one of the earlier spiritual conquests from Luxeuil, and with conquest came spiritual regeneration.

The story begins with Waldelen, duke of upper Burgundy and resident at Besançon, and his wife Flavia, a woman of high birth and widely recognized sagacity and piety. They vowed that if they had a son they would dedicate him to the service of the Lord, and they asked Columbanus to pray to that end. He agreed to do so, stipulating that he baptize the baby and that in due time the child become a novice at Luxeuil. The son was born and was christened Donatus ("the one dedicated"). Columbanus acted as his godfather, and when old enough to be separated from his mother the boy was entered at Luxeuil. He was trained by Columbanus, remained at Luxeuil after his mentor was driven into exile, and after some thirty years in the monastery became bishop of Besançon.

There followed a surge of monastic building in Besançon and its environs. In Besançon itself Donatus built a monastery known as the

Monastery of the Palace or the Monastery of St. Paul. His mother, Flavia, now a widow, built with his assistance the convent for cloistered nuns called Jussanum or Joussamoutier (literally, the Joussa monastery), this also in the city. In both monasteries there was observed from the start a fusion of two monastic rules, those of Columbanus and Benedict. Donatus himself lived in the monastery of St. Paul and, bishop though he was, wore to the day of his death the habit of a monk.

When Duke Waldelen died, his younger son Ramelen succeeded to the title. His secular concerns did not stop him from showing that he had his share of the family piety. On the southern side of the Jura Mountains was the ancient abbey of Romainmoutier, the Roman monastery, so called because Pope Stephen II who once lived there insisted that such be its name. It had been founded by St. Romain de Condat and had enjoyed its hour of glory when it was the architectural model for churches built in the area between the Jura and the Alps. It had supported one of the great schools of Christian Gaul, but the Roman monastery had declined and almost fallen under the impact of the barbarian invasions. Ramelen rebuilt the monastery, staffed it with monks from Luxeuil, and Romainmoutier was once more a center of piety and learning, making its contribution, in a rugged area of wooded hills, to the spiritual and intellectual uplift of nominal Christians and unabashed barbarians, where room for uplift was ample.

The family contribution is not finished. Donatus had an uncle, Amalgar, who was also a duke in Burgundy. Amalgar sent his second son Waldelen, who bore the name of Donatus's father, to Luxeuil to be trained by Columbanus. When ready for the responsibility, Amalgar made his son Waldelen abbot at Beze, a monastery which he founded in the forest between the Saône and the Tille, about fifteen miles northeast of the modern city of Dijon. Assuming the post at an early age and aided mightily by his family connections and concomitant piety, Waldelen was abbot of Beze for fifty years and made it one of the most important abbeys in France. Amalgar also had a daughter, Adalsind, whom he made abbess of a convent at Bregille, on the right bank of the Doubs River opposite Besançon. It is said that local hostility forced her rather quickly to leave her post. As for Donatus, with whose birth the family's pious saga starts, he lived until 660 and was buried in one of the chapels of the abbey of St. Paul. There are still extant traces of the abbey in the courtyard of the Besançon library and Montalembert records that in his day the abbey of Joussamoutier was a military barracks. Protected by remoteness, always the safest guardian of these ancient monasteries, the original church of Romainmoutier still stands.

Thus within the span of one man's life, and within a generation after the death of Columbanus, there came into being five monasteries in Besançon and its environs, four of them new, one an ancient monastery restored. The deduction about the state of religion is obvious and unmistakable. There came from Luxeuil a revival of the spirit, it swept over the ancient city of Besançon, entered the palace of the bishop—who stayed a monk in heart and appearance for all his lofty title—found expression in a people eager for religion in their lives and for lives in which religion was the inner essence. Today in Besançon there is the Church of St. Donat which commemorates the son of Luxeuil who routed indifference and implanted fervor, gave life to a disspirited and indifferent Christian community, and was a true son of Columbanus and Luxeuil, one of the first of the Burgundians to catch fire from Ireland and one of the brightest lights that kindling ever produced.

St. Ursicinus

Well to the east of Besançon lie the Jura Mountains, forming today the boundary zone between France and Switzerland and extending into both countries. It is a region of pine forests, upland pastures, and deep and narrow valleys, with the Doubs River winding through its deepest cleft. The mountains are not of Alpine height, but the highest of them rise upward of a mile, and the highest one of all, Mont Chasseral, tops that mark. Here and there are towns with names that memorialize an ecclesiastical past: St. Imier, which was the abode of a Burgundian hermit; Moutier, the monastery town where the abbey of Bellelay once stood; and Delémont, which was the summer home of the prince-bishops of Basel in the Middle Ages. Ten miles or so west of Delémont on the banks of the Doubs River, down a narrow road that winds, soars, and tumbles on its way to Porrentruy, the very minor metropolis of the Ajoie district, is the hamlet of St. Ursanne. Its houses huddle together beneath its ramparts, and St. Ursanne still has the defenses to face whatever challenges the fourteenth century may offer. St. Ursanne perpetuates the name of Ursicinus, an Irish monk and hermit from Luxeuil.

Ursicinus was the companion of Columbanus, possibly from Bangor and certainly in exile from Luxeuil, until they reached this wild and remote area. Here Ursicinus, like Deicola before him, left his leader and plunged into the wilderness. At all times, at home and abroad, an Irish monastery was an unstable mixture of individualists, and today's obedient monk was tomorrow's separated anchorite. Ursicinus found his cell on a mountain top, somewhere near the Bielersee which the French call the Lake of Bienne. He lived on his mountain top, or more exactly existed there, until herdsmen found the wild, shaggy, emaciated, but to their direct and simple minds inspired prophet. They sought him out in numbers, and it is not impossible that Ursicinus is a name they gave him, "the bear-man," whose cell was a cave on the mountain top. The numbers increased, and Ursicinus accepted his destiny. He left the solitude of his mountain top, descended to the Doubs, and there he built a monastery and with it a hospital. Showing a capacity for organization not exactly predictable in a bear-man, he kept pack animals to bring the sick and their belongings to the hospital he conducted for them.

Ursicinus did his work and died. Meanwhile there had been a prodigious growth at Luxeuil. When Eustasius, successor to Columbanus, died in 629, there were several hundred monks in residence. Under Waldebert, the third abbot, the number increased until more than six hundred monks lived, worked, and worshiped at the three monasteries in the Luxeuil group. The number was far too large, and as Abbé Martin puts it in his life of Columbanus, the hive had to swarm. Waldebert sent Germain, an erstwhile nobleman of Treves turned monk, with a large group from Luxeuil to expand the monastery on the Doubs. Beyond lay a broader field to enter. Gondoin, duke of Alsatia, had given Luxeuil a valley in Raurasia. At Delémont one is on the Aare River, in the Birs Valley through which the Aare follows a winding course northeastward to the Rhine at Basel. The valley was populated by a recently evangelized people called the Warasques. Germain led part of his contingent from the monastery which Ursicinus had founded through a narrow defile into the Birs Valley. Here he founded the monastery called Moutier-Grandval. The valley itself was later called le Val de Moutier, Monastery Valley, and since it was located in the diocese of Basel, the sons of Columbanus had reached the Rhine. Grandval formed a union with the monastery which, for the sake of simplicity, may be called St. Ursanne in accordance with the ancient Irish tradition.

St. Germain

St. Germain was the first martyr to come from Luxeuil. The benevolent Gondoin passed to his fathers, and the duke of Alsatia who succeeded him was hostile to the monks, sent his Alamans to sack Grandval, and in the course of their attack they murdered Germain. His bones rest in the church of St. Ursanne. St. Ursanne, like Lure, was a somewhat accidental by-product of the exile of Columbanus, and Grandval was the only monastery ever founded directly from Luxeuil itself. After the fashion of Lindisfarne rather than the fashion of Iona, Luxeuil exacted no obedience from either St. Ursanne or Grandval.

Germain, the nobleman of Treves turned monk, was far from the only member of his caste to turn from the dreary, meaningless wars of the Merovingians to the service of the Lord. Indeed the generalization that primacy in the abbey went to blood and family quite as truly as it did in the castle stands examination fairly well, a fact not surprising in an age when the intellectual preparation essential for the exercise of religious authority was all but inseparable from family background. The exceptions are rare, obvious, and even startling. Another of Germain's sort was Vandregisil, born near Verdun and closely related to Pepin of Landen, mayor of the palace, and in effect ruler of both Neustria and Austrasia under King Dagobert I. When we come to Vandregisil and Pepin of Landen, we have passed beyond the reign of Clotaire II, friend to all from Luxeuil. Dagobert was his son and heir, but in his youthful days he was under the tutelage of Pepin, founder of the Carolingian line.

Vandregisil

Vandregisil became Count of the Palace, a post partly judicial and partly fiscal as he judged cases referred to the king and collected the royal revenues. His parents arranged for him an appropriate marriage, he rejected it, and went to live as an anchorite on the banks of the Meuse. Dagobert interpreted this as avoidance of military service, and sent peremptorily for Vandregisil. As the noble hermit approached the castle, he saw a poor man struggling to right an overturned cart. Vandregisil plunged into the mud with him, got the cart back on the road, and entered the royal presence dripping. Dagobert, who recognized obedience to the law of charity when he saw it and was astute enough in the ways of contemporary clerics to deem it more the attribute of a hermit than of a bishop, freed Vandregisil from all secular service and sent him back to his cell.

He did not remain there long. His true call was to the monastery and not the river bank. He went to the monastery which Ursicinus had constructed, and there at the first remove came under the influence of Luxeuil and Columbanus. It is certain that he made a pilgrimage to Luxeuil. What is intriguing is the possibility that he also made a pilgrimage to Bobbio—long after the death of Columbanus, it should be added. There are two Lives of Vandregisil, one by a contemporary and the other a curious affair padded with passages from a Life of Columbanus. Both are in the Bollandist *Annals*. The first Life states that Vandregisil was carried, in Kenney's paraphrase (p. 491), "in spirit by an angel to Bobbio and given a view of the monastery, as a result of which he renounced the world; he practised austerities similar to those of the Irish saints and wished to pay a visit to Ireland. . . ." Although most books that treat of Vandregisil state that he visited Bobbio, it is more prudent to consider it a visit in a vision, an occurrence not infrequent in the Age of the Saints.

From St. Ursanne he went to Romainmoutier and from there to Rouen, where Bishop Ouen ordained him a priest and gave him an area in which to build a monastery. The monastery of Fontenelle which he built is on the right bank of the Seine, near Caudebec-en-Caux in the diocese of Rouen, midway between Rouen and Le Havre on the winding, secondary road that parallels all the leisurely curves of the river. The foundation year was 649. The region of Caux was at best nominally Christian, but actually sunk in a murky barbarism. It provided a mission field admirably complete from the viewpoint of the work that needed to be done but sadly deficient in grounds for optimism by those who would do it. Here St. Wandrille, to slip into the French form of Vandregisil, the name that still is honored at the abbey which he founded, labored until his death in 668. The work was hard, the rewards were slow in coming, but the work succeeded and the rewards came. In the two decades given him St. Wandrille and the three hundred monks under him added to Christendom the people of the Seine valley, and thus the light of Luxeuil which Columbanus kindled illuminated Normandy.

The later history of the abbey of Fontenelle has many chapters of interest, and at least the chapter titles may be mentioned. It flourished through the Middle Ages and from it developed other foundations of importance in religious history. The truly celebrated one is Mont-Saint-Michel, founded from Fontenelle in 965. Fontenelle survived the Normans with some difficulty and the French Revolution with great difficulty. It was sold in 1791 and partially dismantled. In the nineteenth century it fell into the hands of an ideological descendant of the seventh-century barbarians of the region. He tore down as much of the structure as he needed for paving blocks for his driveway. It is more pleasantly recorded that an Englishman whose name seems now beyond recapture bought as many of the stones as he could and set up a miniature Fontenelle in his English country park. In 1894 the diocese of Rouen acquired what was left of Fontenelle, rebuilt it, and staffed it with Benedictine monks. For a time they had as a house guest Maurice Maeterlinck, who found that this somber memorial to an ancient age set the proper atmosphere for writing dark mysteries of love and death. Even in its present state it is capable of giving birth to monastic offspring. As recently as 1912 out of Fontenelle was founded the monastery of St. Benoit-du-Lac in the Province of Quebec.

Philibert

Inseparable from the names of Vandregisil and the monastery of Fontenelle are the names of Philibert and the monastery of Jumièges, although their actual lifelines had few intersections. Philibert also was of noble birth and a Gascon. He was brought up at the court of Dagobert I, but at the age of twenty he entered the monastery of Rebais, a foundation of Bishop Ouen. At Rebais Philibert came under the influence of Luxeuil, the Rule of Columbanus being observed there and the monastery headed by Abbot Agile, a Luxeuil alumnus. He remained at Rebais for at least ten years, succeeding Agile as abbot but shortly afterwards resigning the post to undertake the study of monastic methods at Luxeuil and Bobbio. The inference is obvious: Columbanus, now dead for twenty-five years, was still a living influence at his two monasteries and it was that influence and its functioning that Philibert undertook to study.

Returning to France, in 654 he founded the monastery of Jumièges on a tract of land granted him by King Clovis II and his pious queen Bathild. He dedicated an abbey altar to St. Columbanus and proceeded to build at Jumièges a port of entry for merchandise coming up the Seine from England and Ireland, with corn and cattle imported from the British Isles and clothing and shoes traded for them. It is recorded that the monks of Jumièges used to catch porpoises and make candles from their oil with which to light their vigils. Furthermore, in anticipation of one of the supreme charities of the Middle Ages, they outfitted boats and sailed great distances to redeem slaves and captives. The monastery so thrived that within the lengthy rule of Philibert it came to be populated by 2400 residents, 900 of them monks. Before he died in 685 Philibert restored the monastery of Quinçay near Poitiers and built two convents for nuns at Pavilly and Montévilliers. His last achievement was to build the monastery of Noirmoutier on an island near the mouth of the Loire. He died at Noirmoutier and his relics, after peregrinations forced by the unsettled times, finally came to rest at the Church of St. Valerian in Tournus, where they still remain. As for his primary monastery, Jumièges, the Rule of Columbanus was not replaced by the Rule of Benedict until the early ninth century. The abbey was obliterated and rebuilt several times, had a period of great prosperity and influence in the twelfth and thirteenth centuries, and then was abolished during the French Revolution. Today Jumièges is an imposing set of medieval ruins at the end of a bulbous peninsula created by one of the more leisurely loops of the River Seine, closer to Rouen than Fontenelle is and off the same sinuous river road. Jumièges was a seat of learning in the Middle Ages, and still makes its contribution to knowledge of French antiquities, since the monastic library is the nucleus of the city library of Rouen.

German Monasticism

With Fontenelle and Jumièges a new chapter opens in the history of Luxeuil and the Irish monasticism in Europe of which it was the fountainhead. There was something instinctively centrifugal about the Irish monks, and it was at once the source of spiritual strength and temporal weakness. Their instinct was for the remote, the hard of access, the place of seclusion far from the city and the court. Their very monasticism itself was unstable, with the monk having the instinct of the anchorite, seeking at least from time to time, and often permanently, the solitary cell. Deicola plunging into the forest and Ursicinus seeking out the mountain top were in the ancient Irish tradition. Such men were personal inspirations with the status of major prophets and their religion was pure and undefiled, but it had little in common with the institutional Church beyond the common faith. It is entirely consistent with the thinking of the Irish monks who created them that such monasteries as Annegray, Lure, St. Ursanne, and to a degree Luxeuil itself, be deep in the forests and the mountains.

Then, in France as in England, there came the second stage in which the pupils of the Irish were the Franks, the Burgundians, and the Alamanni, as in England they were the Angles and the Saxons. Religion was revivified, a new dedication to God's service born, an infusion of idealism and determination given the tired Church of the Gallo-Romans, but the converts were Germans and not Celts, and they had a different set of attitudes and indeed of virtues. Furthermore, the converts who headed the revival were of the nobility, men bred to the court and to the city, and one might add men with an instinct for organization and rule which the Irish lacked. The Rule of Columbanus was a rule for saints living in as nearly complete disregard for flesh and blood as flesh and blood can stand. It was the Rule adopted by the new Frankish monasteries, to be sure, but just as human nature demanded that it be modified to the sensible and attainable Rule of Benedict, so Germanic nature insured that cohesiveness prevail in the monasteries and that they be located close to court and city, close to the people they would serve. An unintended secondary reaction, but one of the results of conversion, was to make the German prince more at home in the city, less given to the bosky dells and sylvan glades than his pagan forebears. Thus Fontenelles and Jumièges are in the valley of the Seine, on the high road from Paris to the sea, in well-populated Normandy. The fountainhead of inspiration is still Luxeuil, the universally revered mentor is still Columbanus, but Germanic efficiency looms larger, Celtic asceticism smaller, in the newer monasteries.

St. Ouen

We have seen that behind both Fontenelles and Jumièges was the bishop of Rouen, whose name probably was Dado, Gallicized to Ouen, Latinized to Audoenus, and then re-Gallicized back to Audoen. Since the church which bears his name in Rouen is the Church of St. Ouen, we select this from the four possibilities as the name to be applied to the nobleman born at Sanci near Soissons about 609, blessed with his brothers in their childhood by the traveling Columbanus, educated at the monastery of St. Medard, and then emerging as a figure at the court of Dagobert. In Ouen we see foreshadowed the person who in the Middle Ages would be a prince-bishop. Ouen became chancellor at the court of Dagobert and keeper of the royal seal. Then one by one the three brothers, sons of Autharis of the high Frankish nobility, withdrew from the active life to the contemplative, but brought with them the sense of power and position their birth and court position gave them.

The first to leave was Adon. He left to found the monastery of Jouarre, high on a bluff above the River Marne. Beside it was a convent for nuns, and in both the Rule of Columbanus was observed. Then Radon the second brother withdrew and founded the monastery of Reuil, also on the Marne. The last of the three to leave was Ouen, and by a little tributary of the Morin River in La Brie called Rebais he built the monastery that bears that name. The three monasteries formed a triangle based on the Marne and extending to the Morin, with Rebais not far from Meaux. Ouen was allowed the contemplative life for a very short period, as Dagobert soon recalled him to court. He returned, performed the service exacted, and then himself exacted something of true substance from the king. He was made bishop of Rouen, with the proviso that no administrative, judicial, or ecclesiastical official could be appointed in the diocese of Rouen without his permission.

The care he took of Rebais is indicative both of the way he looked to Luxeuil for inspiration, and the practical methods he would take to make inspiration reality. One of the most important figures at Luxeuil was named Agilus. His father had obtained from the king of Burgundy the grant of land at Luxeuil for Columbanus. He had been blessed as a child by Columbanus and later educated by him at Luxeuil. When Columbanus was exiled from Luxeuil, the monks sent

Agilus to plead with Brunhilda and the king for a reprieve. He was received with courtesy but denied his request. Agilus performed missionary service to the Warasques and the Bavarians, and so substantial was his reputation that the dioceses of Metz, Langres, and Besançon sought him as bishop. Ouen, however, had him marked for Rebais and so he left Luxeuil accompanied by the time-sanctified twelve disciples. The company grew to over eighty before it reached Rebais, as some eighty noblemen from the royal retinue joined the traveling ranks. One was a young aristocrat named Philibert. For years Agilus, whom the French still know as St. Agile, ruled Rebais and it is recorded that the second wave of Irish missionaries crested in his period and nearly swamped the monastery, all but exhausting its resources.

As for Bishop Ouen, his life continued to be divided between diocesan administration, the extension of monastic construction in the Rouen area, and service to the king. Just as the light from Luxeuil kindled a new fervor at Besançon, so it did at Rouen. When Ouen wrote the Life of his friend Eligius, who founded the monastery of Solignac, he said of the period before the influence of Luxeuil was felt: "Monasteries in Gaul were not so numerous then nor under any systematic discipline, but everywhere they were secular in spirit, 'in the malice of the old leaven.'" The contrast was impressive, both in his testimony to the achievements of his friend Eligius and implicitly, in what he himself did at Rebais and elsewhere, and what he aided Vandregisil and Philibert to do at Fontenelles and Jumièges. He died on August 24, 684, on his way back from Cologne where he had negotiated a peace between Neustria and Austrasia. His body was brought back to Rouen, where it now rests in the Church of Saint-Ouen beneath the 375-foot central tower, which is one of the loftiest in France.

Fontenelle and Jumièges are in Normandy; Jouarre, Reuil, and Rebais are in the Île de France; and Solignac is deep in the heart of France, near Limoges. The light from Luxeuil was penetrating the great, open, populated parts of France. Furthermore, the bishoprics of France were coming into the hands of men either trained at Luxeuil or trained in the Luxeuil tradition. In addition to Donatus at Besançon and Ouen at Rouen, Chagnoald, who was vicar to Eustasius at Luxeuil, became bishop of Laon; Acharius, who had been a monk at Luxeuil, was successively bishop of Vermand, Noyon, and Tournai;

Omer passed from the monastery of Luxeuil to become bishop of Boulogne and Therouanne; Burgundofaro, brother of Chagnoald, was bishop of Meaux. The institutional Church was gradually passing from the old, decadent Gallo-Roman hands into the hands of men trained at Luxeuil or in the tradition of Luxeuil. The Irish conquest of the Frankish Church, if epigrammatic succinctness may for the moment replace literal truth, was completed within a half century of the death of Columbanus.

From Luxeuil and the genius who was its founder came a new spirit of fervor that slowly won its way into the hearts of half-Christians, made some of them true followers of the Crucified and then, by the sort of cross-fertilization that works in human life when the best of differing peoples are blended in a common cause, Celtic asceticism and fervor were regularized and disciplined by Germanic efficiency and thoroughness. There was a monk of Luxeuil, not previously mentioned, named Bercharius. Before his death in 685 he founded two monasteries, Hautvilliers in the diocese of Reims and Montierender in the diocese of Châlon-sur-Marne. Many years after he died an abbot of Montierender wrote his life and made a generalized statement that stands the test of research: "And now what place, what city, does not rejoice in having for its ruler a bishop or an abbot trained in the discipline of that holy man [Columbanus]? For it is certain that by the virtue of his authority, almost the whole of the land of the Franks has been for the first time properly furnished with regular institutions."

We have spoken of Columbanian monasteries in the Île de France, in Normandy, and deep in Limousin. A chain of monasteries also came into being north and east of Luxeuil, not only in the Île de France but in Champagne, Alsace and Lorraine, and Picardy. Then, reinforced by a later wave of Irish missionaries centered at Péronne, east of Amiens, the chain was extended into what today is Belgium. We turn our attention now to the monasteries of ancient Picardy and the regions east and south; later to Péronne and its extensions.

Burgundofara

During that part of his journey in exile which brought Columbanus from the court of Neustria to that of Austrasia he visited the home of a nobleman named Agneric. Agneric's son Chagnoald had been a monk at Luxeuil amd had accompanied Columbanus on his journey into exile and so to his father's house. Agneric asked Columbanus to bless his little daughter Fara, who is known in the ecclesiastical history of France as Burgundofara, the noble baroness of Burgundy. Time passed, the child grew, and Agneric repented letting Columbanus dedicate her to religion. Instead she would marry the man of his choice. The girl sickened to the point of death when Eustasius, now successor to Columbanus at Luxeuil, arrived returning from a mission to Rome. The day of Columbanus had passed, but the day of Eustasius was at high noon and a formidable day to those who feared the Lord and his anointed. Eustasius demanded that Agneric abide by his decision and Agneric agreed. However, it was a well-established principle in the Merovingian period that the fear of the Lord departed when his anointed departed. Hardly was Eustasius gone when Agneric changed his mind, whereupon Fara fled taking refuge in a cathedral. An outraged Agneric sent some more than diffident retainers to violate sanctuary by dragging Fara forth. She resisted their not necessarily wholehearted tugs by clinging to the altar until Eustasius returned, won her finally from her father, and extracted in addition a grant of land in La Brie. Here, probably in 627, the monastery of Faramoutier ("Fara's monastery") was erected. For forty years Burgundofara was its abbess, many women of the Frankish nobility became nuns there, the Rule of Columbanus was observed, and to this day in the diocese of Meaux, some twenty-five miles east of Paris and close to the town of Coulommiers, there remains the minor pontifical cloister of Faramoutier, restored in 1931 by Bishop Gaillard of Meaux and staffed by Benedictine nuns.

Once more we are dealing with a family of the nobility in which dedication to religion replaced pride of worldly position. As already stated, Fara's older brother Chagnoald ultimately became bishop of Laon. A second brother whose name is not known but who is identified as Burgundofaro, "noble baron of Burgundy," became bishop of Meaux. A curious story is told of St. Faron, as the ninth-century bishop of Meaux who wrote his life calls Burgundofaro. Faron was a married man who separated from his wife, was ordained a priest, and promptly consecrated a bishop. The wife became a nun. Faron, as a monk, wore the tonsure, but nuns did not wear the tonsure. Faron wished to see his wife again and she, alarmed that the sight of her would turn his mind away from his religious calling, had herself given the symbol of the religious vow, the tonsure. Faron saw his wife, and saw the tonsure as well. Horrified of the impulse which made him desire once more to see her, he returned at once to his bishop's palace and buried himself in good works. Bishop Faron used his ample patrimony to establish monasteries, and many Angles and Saxons came from England to enter them. Quite as important, many Irish monks of the second wave of missionary activity came, were received by Bishop Faron, and got their feet planted on French soil before proceeding on to Péronne and their destiny which lay beyond.

Amatus

There is a holy mountain in the southern Vosges, near the town of Remiremont, in what once was the diocese of Toul and now is the diocese of Saint-Dié. "Saint Mont" was the site of the largest monastery for women ever to develop in Christian Gaul. It was at first a double monastery allied with Luxeuil, observing the Rule of Columbanus and observing as well a piece of ritual rare in any place or age, the continuous chanting of the Holy Office by alternating choirs. It was founded by two noblemen, one Gallo-Roman and one probably Frankish, who had been monks at Luxeuil.

Amatus, or Amé, was the Gallo-Roman. Placed as a child in the monastery of Agaune, near the source of the Rhine, he lived as a South Germanic John the Baptist, always barefooted, clad in a sheep's skin, his diet barley bread and water. The barley he grew and ground himself. His monastic home was Agaune, his retreat a cave high up on a crag. Eustasius, returning from his fruitless attempt to induce Columbanus to return to Luxeuil, stopped at Agaune, met Amatus, and enlisted him for Luxeuil. He went to the parent monastery with Eustasius and then was sent on a mission to Austrasia. On the mission he met Romaric, the presumptively Frankish nobleman.

Amatus won Romaric to religion. The convert gave all his land to the poor except the castle called Castrum Habendi, site of an ancient Roman fort. Further, he freed his serfs and proceeded to Luxeuil to become a monk. Some years passed, and Amatus and Romaric won permission of Eustasius to leave Luxeuil and found a monastery at Castrum Habendi. They did so, and built as well seven chapels on the side of the hill which Castrum Habendi crowned. First Amatus was abbot, then Romaric. The abbey, called Monasterium Hebendense in the oldest manuscripts, came to be called Remiremont, "Romaric's Mountain" *(Romarici Mons)*.

Remiremont was a favorite benefaction for Clotaire II and, perhaps consequently, for the wealthy nobility of Austrasia. From the start of this double monastery it was primarily a woman's world and although ruled by an abbot, the abbess of the woman's monastery was a person of prime importance. The importance of the first abbess was not lessened by the fact that she was granddaughter of Romaric, a married man before he became a monk. This granddaughter has her own story, not without interest, and indeed of some value in establishing the fact that Remiremont was indeed Romaric's Mountain. Romaric's eldest daughter had married without his consent. She sent her firstborn to her father in the hope of winning forgiveness. He kept the child, had her reared in the abbey, made her a nun and ultimately an abbess, and kept his grudge. She sent her second child, a boy. He kept the child and in due time made him a monk. Ultimately Romaric died, and presumably his daughter inherited his name. His other two daughters never faced parental displeasure, since they became nuns of their own free will. One may add the grace note, if such it be, that Remiremont became not only the largest but the lordliest of all the nunneries of France, with its abbess a princess of the Holy Roman Empire. One spoke of the ladies of Remiremont, the chambermaids of Epinal, and the laundresses of Poussey, and did so although even Poussey required proof of appropriate family connections for admission. The suppression of Remiremont during the French Revolution is not surprising. Today the Holy Mountain of Romaric is the nucleus of the town of Remiremont about twelve miles northeast of Luxeuil, on the main highway from Mulhouse to Nancy.

Walaricus

One of the most romantic figures ever to emerge from Luxeuil was a shepherd of Auvergne named Walaricus. Inspired by the Holy Spirit and fortified by the dogged determination of underprivileged intelligence, he asked a teacher of the area to write out the alphabet for him. He learned it, learned the sounds of the letters, decoded written words on phonetic principles, taught himself to read, and ultimately read the entire Psalter. He then presented himself to Columbanus at Luxeuil, who made him gardener of the abbey. It is recorded that the fragrance of flowers always accompanied him, and that Columbanus said to him, "It is you, my well beloved, who are the true abbot and lord of this monastery." After Columbanus was exiled, Walaricus obtained permission of Eustasius to enter the missionary field. He went to the land of the Salian Franks and, in 611, Clotaire II, invariably the benefactor of anyone from Luxeuil, gave him Leuconaus, a headland near the mouth of the Somme, for his monastery.

The Salian Franks were a recalcitrant set of quasi-Christians with a pronounced penchant for either paganism or irreligion. Walaricus made slow and painful progress, and it is part of the record that monks who labored on the easier and more fruitful plains belittled this earnest worker on the rugged, storm-wracked headlands of the Channel. Yet Walaricus labored on, and gradually the abbey called Leucone became a sort of small and modest Luxeuil for that part of Picardy south of Calais and west of what is now the Belgian border. With the passage of time Leucone prepared the way for the work in Belgium and beyond, which once more, as in France, would be done in no small measure by Irish hands. As for Walaricus, his fame waxed and his name changed. As St. Valéry he was buried at St. Bertin, and his remains later transferred to Leucone which was destined to become, as the town of St. Valéry-sur-Somme, one of the largest Channel ports in the Middle Ages. Today it is a tiny place on a promontory between the Somme and the sea, with abrupt cliffs on each side except the south, a fit place for the ruins of an ancient abbey and a proper memorial for the self-taught gardener of Luxeuil, St. Valéry, whose nobility was of the heart and not the heritage.

Omer and Roding

Two other monasteries on which the light shone from Luxeuil should be mentioned before we close, St. Bertin and Beaulieu, the former about fifty miles west of Belgium and the latter about twenty. The founder of St. Bertin was St. Omer of Thérouanne, whose name in its pristine form was Otmar, Latinized to Audomarus, and whose birthplace, Coutances, is far to the west in Normandy.

His mother died when he was a young man, and thereupon both

Omer and his father became monks at Luxeuil. Omer remained at Luxeuil some twenty years. About 640 or a bit earlier, he became bishop of Thérouanne and promptly elicited help from Luxeuil in the task of winning back to Christianity the natives of his diocese, which might be identified approximately with the modern diocese of Arras. The men sent were named Mommelinus, Bertinus, and Ebertramnus. It took twenty years of vigorous missionary work before Omer felt certain enough of his recaptured territory to undertake the building of a monastery. A monastery was built near Sithiu, Mommelinus was made abbot, and then a providential grant of land gave Omer and his associates a better site, an island in the River Aa. Here was built the second monastery of Sithiu. Mommelinus then was elevated to the bishopric of Noyon-Tournai, and Bertinus succeeded him as abbot. When in the course of time Sithiu became a Benedictine abbey, it was rechristened to bear the name of Bertin, its last Columbanian abbot. The abbey prospered and in the Middle Ages was one of the great monasteries of France with a school of European renown, one of the greatest manuscript collections of France, and a favored place for tournaments and the weddings of the nobility. The monastery has perpetuated the name of Bertinus; the city that grew between the river and the hill on which the associated Church of Sainte-Marie stands perpetuates the name of St. Omer.

The annals of the other monastery, Beaulieu, are brief. To be exact, they occupy six pages in the Bollandist record. Beaulieu stood in the Argonne Forest, the wooded area between France and Belgium vividly remembered by the dwindling generation that fought the First World War. It was erected by St. Roding, also known as Chrauding which has a Germanic ring, and as Rouin, the ring of which is Gallic. The truth seems to be that he was an Irishman, a companion of Columbanus. His name is not on Patrick Fleming's list of the original twelve, but it is known that many Irish monks came to Luxeuil after its foundation. The fact that he sought out the remote fastnesses of the Argonne was definitely in the Irish pattern, but beyond that little can be said of Roding or of Beaulieu.

Irish Monk and Frankish Monk

The story of Luxeuil and its influence is far from complete, but the reader has surely reached, and not impossibly passed, the point of satiety. The entire north of France, from Armorica across the face of the land to Picardy and the Belgian border beyond, down through the rugged foothills and front ranges of the Alps on both sides of what today is the border of Switzerland, through the Île de France and deep into Limousin to the south there were monasteries that owed their existence directly or indirectly to Luxeuil. Many of them are mentioned here, and a longer but far from complete list is tabulated in the bibliographical note to this chapter. In every one of them the Rule of Columbanus was observed until the day the milder, more practical Rule of Benedict supplanted it. In every one of them St. Columbanus was an inspiring presence.

There are hallmarks that distinguish the Irish and the Frankish foundations. As in England and Scotland and, as we shall presently see, in the Low Countries and Switzerland, the Irish were the pioneers. Theirs was the inspiration, the fervor, the willingness to plunge into the forests and climb over the mountains, to carry the cross to places where it had been forgotten or never known. The Irish monastery was typically located in a remote area and became a focal point to which the natives were drawn in search of a life and a set of values better than they had known. However, the instinct of the monk and the instinct of the solitary were inseparable in the Irish. The isolation of an Irish monastery was not isolation enough, as the typical Irish monk withdrew from time to time to the absolute solitude of a mountain top, a deserted island, or a bit of solid ground deep in the marshes. There is a great inspiration in the Irish rejection of this world and its values, an inspiration that commands profound respect, but from the missionary viewpoint there are limitations as well. Solitaries are not officers in the army of Christ.

In France as in England and Scotland, the day came when the converted became the converters and abbots were Franks and not Irishmen. As we have said before, this is the desired end of missionary work, which to be successful must be self-liquidating. But the Franks brought a different attitude and what is at least as important, a different instinct, to monastic life. They had a cohesiveness foreign to the Celt but native to the German. A typical Frankish monastery was liberally endowed by the benevolent among the nobility and it stood where people lived and naturally congregated. The Irish monks showed the way, and the Frankish monks consolidated the positions the Irish reached. Each group did its work, each complemented the other, each was vital to the welfare of the land.

Each was vital to the welfare of the land. The Merovingian age was a barbarous age in which passions were bestial and ill-controlled, and violence was the pattern of existence. A monastery was an island of calm, protected by the walls of the ancient Roman fortress within which it stood but protected even more by the spirit that reigned within it. Here was civilization's fortress, here morality found a refuge, and here there was sanctuary for stricken people. From the monastery the arts of peace were pursued: fields were plowed, fertilized, planted, and harvested; woodlands were cleared and marshes drained; roads were hammered flat and passable, with boulders rolled away and tree roots hacked apart. Even more than the work itself was the spirit of the work to be wondered at. No one paid the monks to do it, no one forced them to do it. One can picture a Gallo-Roman, educated in his youth and then beaten by what life had done to him, watching them work and remembering a line from old Tertullian: "See how these Christians love one another." One can picture a Frank, watching with wide blue eyes through tangled yellow hair as these men, some of them his own people, labored for others, dimly sensing in his still barbaric mind that there are values higher than his own, and feeling born within him a desire to know more about such values. The monks preached humility, self-denial, brotherly love, service to humanity, but infinitely more important, they lived it. The army of Rome could not defeat the Franks, but the army of Christ could, and it was defeat in the name of Christ that was victory for the Franks. As the Merovingian age yielded to the Carolingian, barbarism very slowly yielded to civilization, and the Franks with painful slowness became Frenchmen and Germans. Rome again had conquered, but the Rome that is universal.

Put in secular terms, each monastery in France was a fortress of civilization and the environs of each monastery its conquered territory. Over each monastery, Frankish and Irish alike, was the inspiring presence of St. Columbanus whose Rule each monastery followed, by whose example each monastery was inspired, and whose primacy each monastery recognized; St. Columbanus whom his French biographer properly calls *"le patriarche de la famille monastique."* In the long and glorious history of Irish missionary work, which is as old as Columba and is not finished yet, the greatest single figure is Columbanus.

Bibliographical Note

The concept of a multiple volume martyrology of the saints and martyrs in the form of a huge calendar, with each saint's life presented under his feast day, was that of a Jesuit priest, Father Heribert Rosweyd. He died in 1629 before the plan could be carried out. It was picked up by another Belgian Jesuit, Father John Bolland, who undertook an exhaustive search in the libraries of Europe. The first two volumes, presenting the January saints, appeared in 1643. Bolland died shortly after its appearance, and his work was carried on by a group of Belgian Jesuits known collectively as the Bollandists. It took a century and a half for the work to be carried through the middle of October. The original edition in sixty-seven folio volumes was published at Antwerp (1643–1770), with later editions at Brussels (1780–1786) and Tongerloo (1794). In 1794 the Bollandists were dispersed and their manuscripts largely destroyed when the French invaded the Low Countries. In 1837 three Jesuit fathers resumed the work and in 1863–1867 the final six volumes were published at Paris and Rome, and the original volumes reprinted.

The other great collection of saints' lives is limited to members of the Benedictine order and precursors of it who lived under the Rule of Columbanus. It was the work of the historian Jean Mabillon (1632–1707) whose *Acta Sanctorum ordinis S. Benedicti in saeculorum classes distributa* appeared in nine volumes in 1668–1701. A tenth volume was published posthumously in 1713 and an eleventh, the work of others, in 1739.

Lives of the following saints are in both the Bollandist *Acta* and the Mabillon *Acta:* Agilus, Burgundofaro, Omer, Philibert, Roding, Walaricus (Valéry), and Wandregisil (Vandrille). Lives of the following are in the Bollandist *Acta* but not in Mabillon: Amatus, Deicola, and Ouen. The Life of Romaric is in Mabillon but not in the Bollandist collection.

Lives of the following are in *MGH: Scriptores Rerum Merowingicarum* V: Burgundofaro, Omer, Ouen, Philibert, and Wandregisil. Walaricus is in vol. IV. The Life of Deicola is also in John Colgan, *Acta Sanctorum veteris et maioris Scotiae seu Hiberniae, sanctorum insulae* (Louvain, 1645; reprinted Dublin, 1948), pp. 115–77. The Life of Ouen was translated by E. Vacandard, *Vie de S. Ouen, evêque de Rouen* (Paris, 1902). One of the monuments of French historical writing, Charles Forbes Count of Montalembert, *Les Moines d'Occident depuis St. Benoît jusqu'à St. Bernard* (Paris, 1860–77), traces the lives and achievements of all the Columbanian monks treated in this chapter, with an extensive passage devoted to Columbanus himself; vol. II, livre ix, "Saint Columban et les Irlandais en Gaule"; vol. III, livre xi, "Saint Columba, Apôtre de la Calédonie." It is available in English translation by an unidentified hand, *Monks of the West* (Boston, n.d.) and also with translator not identified, *The Monks of the West from St. Benedict to St. Bernard* (7 vols., Edinburgh, 1861–1879).

The following are among the more important monasteries founded in France and the Swiss border country under the influence of Columbanus and observing in their earlier years the Rule of Columbanus. Some are located by approximate highway distances from major French or Swiss cities.

Monastery	Founder	Location
Annegray	Columbanus	Near Luxeuil
Beaulieu	Roding	Argonne Forest, 20 mi. W of Belgian border
Beze	Waldelen	15 mi. NE of Dijon
Chelles	Bathilda	E suburb of Paris
Corbie	Bathilda	Near Amiens
Faremoutiers	Burgundofara	Near Coulommiers, 25 mi. E of Paris
Fontaines	Columbanus	Near Luxeuil
Fontenelle	Wandregisil	River Seine, midway between Rouen and Le Havre
Grandval	Walbert	SW of Basel and NE of Delémont, in Switzerland
Hautvilliers	Bercharius	Diocese of Reims
Jouarre	Adon	River Marne, 30 mi. E of Paris
Jumièges	Philibert	River Seine, W of Rouen
Joussamoutier	Donatus	Besançon
Laon	Chagnoald	Laon; 80 mi. NE of Paris
Leucone (St. Valéry)	Walaricus	Mouth of River Somme
Lure	Deicola	10 mi. SE of Luxeuil
Luxeuil	Columbanus	50 mi. N of Besançon
Meaux	Burgundofaro	Meaux; 25 mi. E of Paris
Montierender	Bercharius	Diocese of Châlon-sur-Marne
Noirmoutier	Philibert	Island near mouth of Loire River
Noyon	Achaire and Eloi	Noyon; 50 mi. NE of Paris
Pentale	Gerner	Near Rouen
Rebais	Agile and Ouen	Near Meaux; 40 mi. E of Paris

Monastery	Founder	Location
Remiremont	Amatus and Romaric	12 mi. NE of Luxeuil
Reuil	Radon	River Marne, 30 mi. E of Paris
Romain-Moutier	Ramelen (restorer)	Near Vallorbe in Switzerland; 25 mi NW of Lausanne
St. Paul	Donatus	Besançon
St. Ursanne	Ursicinus	30 mi. SW of Basel; in Switzerland
Solignac	Eligius	Near Limoges
Sithiu (St. Bertin)	Omer	Island in River Aa at St. Omer; 50 mi. W of Belgian border

8

Péronne of the Irish
and the Mission to Belgium

SOME eighty-five miles north of Paris is the town of Péronne. It is
a quiet, unassuming place, deemed worthy of only moderate
consideration by even the assiduous compilers of the Michelin Guide.
The village church would seem to be the fifth in line of descent from
the church built at Péronne in the seventh century. The first was
destroyed by fire in the twelfth century and the second by lightning
not long after. The third fell victim to the French Revolutionists and
the fourth to the nemesis of fire in 1807. Yet despite the wrath of the
elements, the vandals, and the iconoclasts the essence of Péronne
and its church remains untouched, and on January 16 each year what
gives them their quiet and unassuming immortality manifests itself.
It is the start of the novena of thanksgiving to Saint-Furçy which has
been a Péronne tradition since 1536, when the saint in heaven and
a brave woman on earth named Marie Fourée saved the town from
capture and preserved undiminished the proud boast on the town
seal, *Urbs nescia vinci*, "The city that has never known defeat." On
that day it has been the tradition for an ox cart to pass through the
Porte de Bretagne, "Gate of the Britons," and the British quarter, the
Faubourg Bretagne, on its journey from the church through the
streets of the town. It carries the relics of Saint-Furçy and, after the
ancient tradition which puts in the graven hands of a monastic founder a model of his abbey, beside his remains is a model of the abbey
of Péronne. There has followed by tradition nine days of Masses at
which the Office of Saint-Furçy is recited.

Thus the twentieth-century Péronne has remembered the man in
whose honor it was built in the mid-seventh century, and the tradi-

tion which makes it unique among all the cities and towns of France. Only Péronne is remembered for the members of a foreign race, not conquerors but apostles, not hated intruders but revered visitants, who for two centuries gave the town its universally accepted name, Peronna Scottorum, "Péronne of the Irish." It is with Péronne and its influence, Irish but not in the immediate tradition of Columbanus and Luxeuil, with which we now concern ourselves and with the reason that the Irish *Annals of the Four Masters* calls Péronne *Cathair Fursa*, "Fursa's Camp."

Fursa (Latinized to Fursaeus, Anglicized to Fursey, and Gallicized to Furçy) was of the Irish nobility. One may abstract from his pedigree, fearsome to those unskilled in the tortuosities of ancient Irish genealogies, the fact that his father was named Fintan and that Fursa was of the Munster nobility on his father's side and the Connacht nobility on his mother's. An irascible father-in-law sent Fintan and his bride into exile. They sought refuge with Fintan's uncle, Brendan, abbot of a monastery located on Inisquin, an island in Lough Corrib, a large lake north of Galway, and there Fursa was born, baptized, and, after a childhood in Munster, educated and made a monk. There followed the pattern so familiar in the history of Irish monasticism. Fursa left the monastery and built his hermit's cell by the shore of the lake. Students sought him out and a tiny religious group came into being. It grew and the erection of a monastery became a necessity. The monastery was built and called Killfursa, "Fursa's church."

Margaret Stokes, whose search through western Europe for traces of the Irish saints brought her to Lough Corrib, found near the village of Cong, at the northern end of the lake, the foundations of a cell, part of the east wall and a south window which she identified with the hermitage of Fursa. There are other ruins not far distant believed by her to be the remains of Killfursa. Near Kilronan on the Aran island of Inishmore there is another ecclesiastical memorial to Fursa, the Teampall an Cheathair Alain, "Church of the Four Saints." The saints are Fursa, Conall, Berchan, and Fursa's mentor, Brendan.

For years Fursa preached and worshiped, and ever-increasing crowds sought him out. Once more there is evidenced that other phenomenon so characteristic of the Irish saints, their desire to seek seclusion. We have seen the pattern develop at Iona and Lindisfarne, Annegray and Luxeuil, Lure and St. Ursanne. After the fashion of Columba and Aidan, Columbanus, Deicola, and Ursicinus, Fursa started out from his now populous monastery back to the secluded quiet of Munster. There came to him the series of visions which made his name one of the best known in Europe of the Dark and Early Middle Ages.

Fursa's Visions

Fursa fell ill on his way to his father's house in Munster. In the course of his illness he seemed to have been carried to the heavens by angels. In the first vision he was in the angelic company from early evening until the cock crowed. In this vision he saw as living realities the soul of man in the state of sin and the soul restored to divine grace by repentance. The angels admonished Fursa to be more diligent in preaching the gospel of repentance and reform. Three nights later he had another vision. Once more the angels bore him to the celestial realms where he saw burning the four deadly fires: falsehood, lust, strife, and impiety. Angels and demons fought for the soul of Fursa. Fursa had never committed the deadly sins himself, but he had accepted gifts from sinners and he had loved this world too much, and so the demons had a beachhead. His soul was saved, however, and the demons fled from the conquering angels. Then he saw the marshalled saints of heaven, among them Beoan, and Meldan who had been his abbot in his novice days at the island monastery of Inisquin. In this vision he was aware that the Lord was just as wrathful at clerics who were neglectful of their duty as he was at secular rulers who led sinful lives. There were doctors of the Church who neglected their divine studies and the duties of their station, were wrapped up in matters of this life, and avid of popular acclaim. The Lord held them in abhorrence. Fursa was told never to hold himself aloof from the needs of other humans, but not always to live in the public gaze. He was warned against the vices of the spirit, which are pride, avarice, envy, falsehood, and blasphemy, as well as the vices of the body, gluttony and lust. He was told to bring to both the clergy and the secular rulers of Ireland this solemn message: abandon your vices, repent, and labor for the salvation of souls.

For ten years Fursa went about Ireland, preaching the word, telling of his visions, and urging penance upon master and man alike. If Bede is accurate on the point, it was the very success of his mission that led Fursa to turn to the mission field of East Anglia, as already mentioned in chapter five. Bede says (III, 19), "After having announced the word of God to all during many years in Ireland, he could no longer bear the crowds that thronged around him; and abandoning all that he seemed to possess, he at last abandoned his own country."

The great importance of Fursa in the developing story of Irish monasticism arises more from his visions than from his achievements. It is not necessarily the rationalistic and scientific course to dismiss them out of hand as figments of the fevered imagination. One recalls what Samuel Taylor Coleridge had to say about the composition of his magical "Kubla Khan," which generations of school masters have comfortably classified as "product of an opium dream." Coleridge says that being in ill health and taking "an anodyne," and then reading *Purchas's Pilgrimage* and proceeding to fall asleep;

The Author continued for about three hours in a profound sleep, at least of the external senses, during which time he has the most vivid confidence, that he could not have composed less than from two to three hundred lines; if that indeed can be called composition in which all the images rose up before him as *things,* with a parallel production of the correspondent expressions, without any sensation or consciousness of effort. On awaking he appeared to himself to have a distinct recollection of the whole, and taking his pen, ink, and paper, instantly and eagerly wrote down the lines that are here preserved.

Coleridge composed "Kubla Khan" at a time when his poetic powers were at their peak and he had worked with an unremitting application for weeks on end at poetic composition. The euphoria arising from the taking of laudanum after a long period of abstention and the consequent suffering from withdrawal symptoms gave to a poetic genius at the peak of his creative power precisely the right conditions for the composition of a poem "in which all the images rose up before him as things." The result is a poem of magical beauty, but it was not produced by magic.

One submits that the most probable explanation of the composition of "Kubla Khan" is the most probable explanation of the visions of Fursa. For years he had lived, breathed, and had his being in the contemplation of time and eternity, vice and virtue, damnation and salvation. For years he had preached the gospel of salvation to the people, interpreting reality in terms of virtue, salvation, eternity, and in terms as well of vice, damnation, eternity. Is it not possible that such a man, his head light with a raging fever and disoriented by the fight his body was waging with disease, might have exactly such an experience as Coleridge records, and see all that he lived and labored for appear in pageant form before his inward eye, with all the images arising before him as things, and thus, like the man St. Paul knew, be carried into heaven and see things it is not given man in mortality to see? *Visiones* is merely the Latin word for the experience, and the psychologist may substitute another from his professional vocabulary. There is a defensible sense in which the visions of Fursa may well have been real.

Elements in the visions substantiate this thesis. A "vision" is usually static and statuesque. Fursa's visions were dynamic and to a degree even analytic. He records a vision of the dark night of the soul, and then the radiant dawn of salvation. But this was for Fursa a lesson as well as a vision. It was his solemn responsibility to preach the doctrine of repentance and redemption, as well as to live it. As a priest, he had responsibility for souls other than his own. The visions include an analysis of the deadly sins, and the magisterial warning of the dangers of association: the man innocent of the direct sin may be contaminated by willingly accepted association with the sinner. Fursa had accepted gifts from sinners, and that was guilt by contamination. What Fursa had done in a degree that might endanger his soul but not damn it, other clerics had done to a degree that made them abominable in the sight of the Lord. One recalls Columbanus and his contempt for the institutional Church of Gaul and its administrative heads. The typical Irish monk was very much the reformer, and the Christianity of the solitary cell and its life of austerity, calculated to the last inch before the breaking point, was in a contrast with the lives of city bishops in episcopal palaces, even as such palaces may have been in the seventh century, that could neither be misunderstood nor disregarded.

Thus the visions of Fursa may have been a reality conjured out of a fever-wracked mind, not merely of what the shivering victim of disease had preached but of certain secret convictions he had entertained about life in the formal Church about him. Whatever their source, their explanation, and their significance, for ten years Fursa preached through Ireland the lessons he had brought back from eternity those nights when he left the body and time, and ventured into eternity where he saw the final truth. Everywhere he was known, sought out, and venerated as one who had crossed the infinite gulf and returned with the wisdom that abides beyond. Twentieth-century psychological subtleties did not bother the seventh century; people then accepted Fursa as a mortal man who had seen eternity. His Life was written in all probability in the seventh century, not long after his death, and it exists in a great number of manuscripts, evidence to its widespread popularity. Bede abridged it in his Book III, and his account of the visions made them even more widely known. Thus Fursa was unique among the Irish monks who restored the Word to a western Europe lapsed in seventh century darkness. All preached Christ's lore, but Fursa alone had heard it from angelic lips.

Fursa Leaves Ireland

After the ten years of preaching in Ireland which followed his visions, Fursa, his brothers Foillan and Ultan, and a few other companions retired for a time to an unidentified island and passed from there through Wales and ultimately into East Anglia. King Sigebert received them with kindness and gave them land for a monastery at a site called Cnobheresburg, now Burgh Castle, in Suffolk. The monastery was built, but Fursa did not remain long at his foundation. He left for the continent, Foillan remained at Burgh Castle, and Ultan followed tradition and built himself a hermitage. Only after the inevitable Penda of Mercia had invaded East Anglia and killed Sigebert, as well as his successor Ecgric and King Anna, did Foillan and Ultan leave for Gaul.

Fursa landed on the banks of the Somme and proceeded inland. The Life of St. Fursa has it that the Irish saint made a fast friend in Duke Haymon of Mazerolles by taking the body of his dead son to a quiet cell for the night, praying over the corpse, and in the morning returning a live and healthy child to his father. Haymon, understandably, would have had Fursa stay at Mazerolles the rest of his days and so offered him a perpetual inheritance, but he was now determined upon a visit to Rome. He continued on his way until he reached the court of King Clovis II and met his potent Mayor of the Palace, Erchinoald. The latter won from Fursa the promise to remain in the kingdom and gave him for a monastery a piece of land of Fursa's selection at Lagny on the Marne, some twenty miles east of Paris.

The year was probably 644 when Fursa built his monastery, which grew with great rapidity as monks flocked from Ireland to join the man who had seen eternity. Three of them may be named: Aemilian, Eloquius, and Mimbolinus. They were, in order, the successors of Fursa as abbots of Lagny, and after their names there is a silence. The monastery of Lagny had a further existence, and indeed the abbey church is today the parish church of Lagny. The surmise that for a time the monastery was abandoned and then reinstituted may well be correct.

The further annals of Fursa are brief. With Lagny in the safe hands of Aemilian, he determined on a visit to Burgh Castle. He had reached the castle of Duke Haymon at Mazerolles on the return trip when he sickened and died. The year of his death was probably 650. Fursa, however, was not a man whose destiny lay in any conventional sense in time and place. His visions of immortality had made him the most celebrated Irish monk of the century next to the great Columbanus, and he was to give in death a modest immortality to a place he had never seen.

The Belgian Mission

Erchinoald had built a church at Péronne dedicated to the Twelve Apostles. When Fursa died, Erchinoald had his body removed from Mazerolles over the passionate protest of Duke Haymon and brought to the Mons Cygnorum, "Mount of Swans," at Péronne on the summit of which the church stood. The Twelve Apostles were quietly forgotten and the apostle from Ireland took their place. It became the Church of St. Furçy and such it is today. It also became the focal point for the second wave of missionary activity from Ireland, the wave that was to sweep over Picardy and Belgium, and possibly lap the shores of the Netherlands. What Iona was to Scotland, Lindisfarne to northern England, and Luxeuil to France, Péronne in a more modest fashion was to the Low Countries. Like Iona, which was always Irish, Péronne was Perrona Scottorum, "Péronne of the Irish," and such it continued to be for centuries. The light which was flickering dimly among the Franks of the Low Countries and had hardly been kindled among the Frisians was to be brought to steady radiance from Péronne and monasteries allied with it, and once again many of the light-bearers were Irish.

The earliest of these Irish bearers of light to the Low Countries were the two brothers of Fursa, Foillan and Ultan. As we have seen, they remained behind at Burgh Castle after Fursa left for the continent. The attack by Penda and the death of the East Anglian kings convinced them that they should follow the footsteps of their brother, at a date that cannot be determined but after the death of Fursa. With the monks who accompanied them from England they went directly to Péronne where the remains of Fursa were already enshrined. There is a strong possibility that there was an inducement to emigrate very different indeed from the sort of inducement the shadow of Penda represented. The third Life of Foillan refers to one Madelgar who inspired many Irish monks to emigrate for the sake of Christ. We are told that Madelgar was an Irish soldier who served in the army of the Franks. He was sent by the wife of Pepin to enlist Irish monks for service in the Belgian mission. Hearing of Fursa, Madelgar went to Burgh Castle, was profoundly impressed, induced Fursa to return to Gaul with him, and with Fursa went Foillan and Ultan together with the already mentioned Eloquius and Mimbolinus. The details of this version of the Fursa story conflict with details well established elsewhere, but the general outline of the story is undoubtedly true. Irish monks were indeed enlisted for the Belgian mission, and by the wife of Pepin.

She was St. Iduberga, known also as Ida and Itta. Daughter of a Count of Aquitaine, she was married to Pepin of Landen, mayor of the palace and ancestor of the Carolingian line. After the death of her husband she devoted herself with unremitting vigor, and the use of the means available to one in her position, to the conversion of the Franks in what today is Belgium. In 640 she founded an abbey at Nivelles in Belgium, endowed it with her entire property, and enlisted nuns from Ireland to staff it. Five years before her death, which occurred in 652, she arranged that her daughter Gertrude should succeed her as abbess. Gertrude outlived her mother by only a few years but in that time she strengthened the establishment, which was a double monastery from the start, with both monks and nuns under the authority of the abbess. The Rule at Nivelles is described as "Irish," and since the nuns were in the first instance enlisted from Ireland this probably indicates an adherence to the Rule ordinarily observed in Irish nunneries rather than to the specific Rule of Columbanus.

At the invitation of Gertrude, Foillan and Ultan came to Nivelles.

It was her thought that they would give instruction, in music specifically, and in other branches of learning in general to the members of the community. Irish preeminence in sacred music was generally accepted on the continent, and Irish learning universally respected. More came out of the invitation than Gertrude had anticipated. St. Gertrude of Nivelles died in 655 and thereafter shared with St. Patrick the festal day, March 17. Foillan succeeded her as abbot. Before Gertrude died, Foillan and Ultan, with her assistance, erected a monastery at Fosse, not far from Nivelles, which is some twenty miles south of Brussels and quite near Waterloo. Foillan's period as abbot was measured in months. While traveling through Hainault on October 31, 655, he and his three companions were murdered by robbers. Their bodies were not discovered until the following January. Thereafter January 16 was observed at Nivelles and Fosse as the feast of the Invention ("Finding") of St. Foillan. As for Ultan, his annals are not only brief but extremely confused. It seems true that he served as abbot at Fosse. Some years later he is recorded as abbot of Péronne. We have three Lives of Fursa and three Lives of Foillan, but there is no Life of Ultan, and thus he is an appendage to the biographies of his brothers. The surmise seems safe that he not only outlived them but ultimately became abbot at Péronne. The certainty is that the Belgian mission was opened by Irish nuns and monks under the guidance of St. Iduberga, and that although Fursa was a guiding inspiration to those who worked in this distant field, foremost among the actual workers were his brothers Foillan and Ultan.

Franks and Frisians

At this point we face the danger inevitable in a study of one aspect of a subject as many faceted as the spread of Christianity. Our concern is the part that Ireland played, direct and indirect, in the conversions that took place in the sixth through the eighth centuries. Important as it is in the total mosaic, it is not the mosaic itself. The problem of tracing the conversion of the Low Countries both illustrates the danger and flies its own danger signals. Irish monks did much, but not everything. In the Low Countries, their part in the work was important but minor. It may be helpful to delineate it if we consider what the Low Countries themselves were in the seventh century.

At the start of the century the Franks ruled the area about Tournai and Cambrai but little else. The Frisians were both isolated and unchallenged in the north and along the North Sea coast, and the Rhine delta was untouched by the Franks. The conversion of the Frisians was the work of Anglo-Saxon monks, but a work performed with Frankish assistance, and the spread of Frankish political influence was as much a component as the spread of the faith. Pepin II defeated the Frisian king in 689 and had the Anglo-Saxon missionary Willibrord ordained bishop of a see created for him at Utrecht. The see had only the vaguest of boundaries but through it the conversion of the Frisians proceeded. Its most important figure was the Anglo-Saxon bishop, his chief coadjutors were from England and, being amenable to Frankish influence, he welcomed Frankish monks to his see. There is no evidence of an Irish hand in the Frisian mission, except in the oblique sense that Anglo-Saxon monks had become such ultimately out of Lindisfarne and what it represented. There is evidence of an Irish hand in the mission to the southern part of the Low Countries, and this is the evidence more difficult to assess. We have already seen that Fursa's brothers, Foillan and Ultan, were very early in the field, but we have also seen that they were called there by the pious wife of Pepin of Landen and his daughter. There can be no question whatever that the true apostle of Belgium was not an Irishman but a Frank.

St. Amand

St. Amand (Latin, Amandus) was born in Aquitaine, educated at the insular monastery of Yeu, received the tonsure at Tours, and proceeded for a time to live the life of a recluse. Taking the vow of *peregrinatio*, life of an exile in the name of Christ, he went to Rome, was consecrated a bishop without fixed see, and proceeded to the pagan north. In 639 or thereabouts he founded a monastery at Elnone, southeast of Lille and on the French side of the Belgian border. Even at this remote northern outpost the influence of Columbanus could be felt, as his biographer Jonas of Bobbio, ranging far afield in obedience to the calling of the peregrine, came to Elnone and for a time was its abbot. Amand himself proceeded to Ghent where he founded the abbey of St. Pierre on Mt. Blandin and the abbey of St. Bavon at the confluence of the Schelde and Lys rivers. Amand's biographer further ascribes to Amand the foundation of the already mentioned monastery at Nivelles, which is certainly an error, as well as the one at Barisis-au-Bois and possibly those at four other Belgian communities. Made bishop of Tongres against his will, he managed after three years to transfer the pallium to a more willing wearer and to return to Elnone. He died there, probably in 679.

Today there remain a church tower and entrance lodge, all that is left of the grandiose seventeenth-century reconstruction of the abbey, but it stands in the village of Saint-Amand and is called the abbey of Saint-Amand-les-Eaux. In the hundred years between 625 and 725, when the conversion of what today is Belgium was proceeding in the main from the twenty-five monasteries built during the period, no name ranks with that of St. Amand. Like Willibrord who labored farther north, and Boniface who came later as an apostle to the Germans, the spirit that inspired Irish monasticism was in his heart and some of its forms were present in his foundations, but the Irish contribution in the Low Countries was ancillary to that of missionaries of other stocks. The spirit they all shared, however, was the spirit of a revived, purified, idealistic, dedicated Christianity that was not of any one race or nation.

The Irish and Belgian Monasticism

It is not that the Irish missionaries to the Low Countries were necessarily few in number. As Kenney puts it (p. 501): "Many other Irish monks besides Foillan and his brother Ultan were laboring, then and later, among the Belgic people. In the case of the majority, however, the traditions are obscure and fabulous." A few names can be extracted from the mazes of fable. There is reason to believe that the Celestine who became abbot of St. Amand's foundation of Saint-Pierre on Mt. Blandin in Ghent was an Irishman. There are two others, seemingly reliable flesh and blood but with careers so nearly parallel as to make one wonder if there were two or only one. There was St. Livin, said to have been an archbishop in Ireland, who renounced mitre and native land, came to evangelize Brabant, and suffered martyrdom—at Hautem by one account, at Ghent by another. There was St. Rombaut, son of an Irish king and archbishop of Dublin, who had a vision of an angel who showed him the martyr's crown. He followed the vision to Mechelen (Malines) where he founded an abbey. He was martyred there about the year 775, and today is patron saint of the city and the see.

There is evidence of the Irish influence, even if it can be associated with no individual name beyond the remote but all-embracing name of Columbanus, in the relative independence enjoyed by Belgian monasteries of the seventh and eighth centuries. They were far less under diocesan jurisdiction than monasteries that followed the Benedictine pattern of government, even though for the most part they would appear to have followed the Rule of Benedict. Even in the seventh century several of them were granted "charters of liberty." Also characteristically Irish was the relationship of the abbot, administrative head of the monastery, and the bishop associated with the monastery but doing missionary work in the field. Finally there was the mark most characteristically Irish of all, the instinct for the hermitage, the centrifugal force that seemed to operate in Irish monasteries drawing monks from the cloister to the wilderness, sometimes for limited periods of time and sometimes for the rest of their days.

It is sound and reasonable to read with the utmost caution the names of the thirty-nine Irish saints who labored in the mission field of Belgium in the seventh century, according to the list compiled by Nicholas Vernulaeus, professor at the University of Louvain in 1639. What names can be rescued from the all but engulfing oblivion of the remote seventh century in the distant reaches of the Low Countries were rescued over three quarters of a century ago by the German scholar Ludwig Traube. Traube appropriately called his article "A Contribution to the History of Tradition" *(Ein Beitrag zur Überlieferungsgeschichte)*. It was that, and a valuable contribution to the Irish paleography of the Middle Ages as well.

Some names emerge with reliable clarity. There is the name of Cellanus, abbot of Péronne and correspondent of Aldhelm, who presided over the abbey at the end of the seventh century and died there in 706. There is Goban, a disciple of Fursa and a figure at Péronne, who is also mentioned by Bede (III, 19). There is the slightly shadowy figure of Madelgisil, who became a hermit in Ponthieu and died about 685. There is the more shadowy name of Etton, whose modest place in the record rests upon the fact that he became a hermit near Dompierre. Then there is Adalgisus, indeed shrouded in darkness, whose Life is a recast version of one of the Lives of Fursa, written one imagines on the thesis that the life of one holy man is very much like the life of another and what one does not know about one's subject can be supplied by another on the principle of interchangeable parts. Clear and shadowy alike, all were Irish monks and all were connected with Péronne. The fact is incontestable that from its foundation through the eighth century and into the ninth Péronne was an Irish monastery, headed by Irish abbots and peopled by Irish monks, and that from Péronne there proceeded the conversion of those Franks who lived in what now is Belgium and possibly the adjacent parts of the Netherlands. Some names have survived, others have not, and there can be no serious question that the unknown names vastly outnumber the known. Unquestionably the apostle of Belgium is St. Amand, and unquestionably the conversion of Belgium was in very large measure the work of Christian Franks. But by their side labored Irish monks, some shadowy figures and some totally forgotten, whose headquarters was Péronne and who worked out of Péronne as their countrymen worked out of Iona, Lindisfarne, and Luxeuil. By the end of the eighth century their work was completed and what today is Belgium was the permanent part of Christendom that on the whole its history has proved it to be.

Bibliographical Note

There are two early Lives of St. Fursa and an appendage to the first called *Virtutes Fursei.* Bruno Krusch, who edited the first Life and the *Virtutes* for *MGH* dates the Life to the seventh century and thinks it written shortly after Fursa's death, and the *Virtutes,* which is an account of Fursa's miracles, to the early ninth century. The second Life is by two monks named Serlo and Rotbertus, written at an unknown date. It has an epistolary Preface by Arnuf, abbot of Lagny, who died in 1106. The extremely popular account of Fursa's visions, which loom large in the Lives, is present in condensed form in Bede, *Ecclesiastical History,* III, 19. There is also an Irish Life of Fursa.

Vita prima and *Virtutes Fursei,* ed. Bruno Krusch, *MGH: Scriptores Rerum Merowingicarum* IV (Hannover, 1902), pp. 423–49. *Vita secunda,* in Bollandist *Annales,* 1863 ed., pp. 408–18. The Irish Life, ed. and trans. by Whitley Stokes, *Revue Celtique* XXV (1904), pp. 385–404.

Information about Fursa is contained in Louis H. Dahl, *The Roman Camp and the Irish Saint at Burgh Castle* (London, 1913); Dom Louis Gougaud, O.S.B., *Gaelic Pioneers of Christianity: The Work and Influence of Irish Monks and Saints in Continental Europe (VIth–XIIth Cent.)*, trans. Victor Collins (Dublin, 1923); and Joseph P. Fuhrmann, *Irish Medieval Monasteries on the Continent* (Washington, D.C., 1927). For Fursa's Irish period, see Margaret M. Stokes, *Three Months in the Forests of France in Search of Vestiges of Irish Saints* (London, 1895), pp. 134 ff.

The definitive study of Péronne and its part in the conversion of northern France and Belgium is Ludwig Traube, "Peronna Scottorum: Ein Beitrag zur Überlieferungsgeschichte und zur Palaeographie des Mittelalters," in *Sitzungsberichte* IV, Munich Academy, 1900. See also Fuhrmann, Part I chapter one.

The earliest account of Foillan, limited to a description of his death and burial, is in the *Additamentum Nivialense de Fuilano,* added to the *Vita prima* of Fursa in some MSS and available in *MGH: SRM* IV, pp. 449–51. There are also three early Lives of Foillan, all published in the Bollandist *Annales,* Oct. XIII (1883), pp. 381–95.

There is an early Life of St. Iduberga; see *Annales,* March II (1883), pp. 594–600. See also E. de Moreau, *Histoire de l'eglise en Belgique,* (2nd ed., Brussels, 1945), vol. I. There is a seventh-century Life of St. Gertrude most readily accessible in *MGH: SRM* II, pp. 447–74.

A Life of St. Amand, dating in the opinion of Krusch to the eighth century, is in *MGH: SRM* V, pp. 428–49. It is also in the *Annales,* 1949 ed., LXVII, pp. 447–64. For modern appraisals of his work, see E. de Moreau, *S. Amand, le principal evangelisateur de la Belgique* (Brussels, 1942), and *Histoire de l'eglise en Belgique,* I, pp. 78–92.

Livin and Rombaut are names from the list of Nicholas Vernulaeus, whose *De propagatione fidei christianae in Belgio per sanctos ex Hibernia viros* was published at Louvain in 1639 as part of the scholarly project in Irish ecclesiastical literature and history which produced Patrick Fleming's collected Works of Columbanus. Celestine as an Irish abbot of St. Amand's foundation of Saint-Pierre in Ghent stands on firm grounds. See *Fundatio monasterii Blandiniensis* in *MGH: Scriptores* XV (1887), p. 623.

Coleridge's description of the circumstances under which he composed "Kubla Khan" may be found, *inter alia,* in his *Complete Poetical Works* (Oxford, 1912), vol. I, p. 295.

9

St. Gall
and the Mission to Switzerland

WHEN Switzerland first begins to emerge from the mists of pre-
history and to take shape on the opening pages of Caesar's
Gallic War, it is part of the Celtic world. The Roman *provincia* in
Gaul, far larger than modern Provençe which perpetuates its name,
was tangent to it at Geneva. Caesar's first encounter with Gauls was
with what today we might term a Swiss tribe, the Helvetii, who had
in view a more comfortable and prosperous home than the great
sloping hillside above Lake Geneva afforded. Caesar decreed otherwise, and made effective his decree. Thereafter his bellicose concern
was with Celtic tribes of what today are France, the Low Countries,
and England. Mountain fastnesses make secure retreats but not bases
where major assaults are staged. Switzerland was no menace to
Rome and when Switzerland became part of Rome, it was Rome of
the Cross to which it belonged in a truer sense than it ever belonged
to Rome of the fasces.

The first, almost obliterated traces of Christianity in Switzerland
resemble the traces faintly discernible in England. A fourth-century
fibula with a Christian symbol has been found in Basel; a fourth-
century chapel has been unearthed in Agaune, and there are fragments of an early fifth-century altar in Geneva. There was a bishop
in Chur by the mid-fifth century and a bishopric centered at Windisch somewhat later. As in Britain, tiny chapels have been found in
Roman fortifications. The evidence is too fragmentary to support a
history of early Christianity in Switzerland, but clear enough to

prove that Christianity was well established among the Gallo-Romans of Switzerland by 500.

As a result of the invasions, Switzerland came to have two quite distinct Germanic populations, the Burgundians in the west and the Alamanni in the central portion. The Burgundians were initially Arian in their Christianity but, largely under the influence of Luxeuil, were won to orthodoxy. This we have already seen, as we have seen the establishment of monasteries on what now is the Swiss side of the French-Swiss border. From these monasteries, stemming in the main from Luxeuil, monks carried the orthodox Gospel to the Burgundians and any Franks who made their way into what is now west Switzerland.

The invasion of Switzerland by the Alamanni was more accurately a retreat. Defeated by the Franks under Clovis in the closing years of the fifth century, the Alamanni gradually filtered into central Switzerland. Like the Franks, they were men of the fields and the woods. In central Switzerland as in Gaul, the Gallo-Romans continued to hold the towns, and Christianity became distinctly a town religion, defended by the same walls that defended the town itself. Windisch continued to be a see as did Avenches, although as the Alamanni extended their domain westward, the latter was transferred to Lausanne. After the Alamanni had reached as far west as Lake Geneva, they turned south and pushed down into Vaud, incidentally destroying Romainmoutier as part of the push.

Meanwhile the Gallo-Roman hold on the towns became increasingly precarious, Christianity very much more beleaguered, and the Gallo-Romans increasingly forced south and east into Graübunden. They are still in this ruggedly mountainous, thinly populated, and—thanks to the ski—increasingly fashionable southeast of Switzerland, speaking Rhaeto-Romansh which perpetuates more accurately than any other Romance tongue the tonal nuances of spoken Latin and its vocabulary. Thus at the start of the seventh century Switzerland was divided into three parts, even as it is today, but not quite the same parts. There was the Burgundian part in the west, corresponding loosely with French-speaking Switzerland today. There was the Alamanni part which occupied central Switzerland down to the high Alps, and might be equated again quite loosely with German-speaking Switzerland today. Finally there was the Gallo-Roman part deep in the mountain valleys and the rugged uplands of Graübunden, where displaced sons and adopted sons of Rome spoke Rhaeto-Romansh and were guarded by the soaring bastions of the Grisons, abiding in solitude and remoteness until the hour had come for them to carry bags and wait on table at Davos, Klosters, and St. Moritz. The Burgundians were Arians in the process of conversion to Catholicism, the Gallo-Romans were orthodox Catholics, but the Alamanni were pagans. The last were the people whose slow and painful conversion St. Gall would undertake, after Columbanus left him in anger at Bregenz with the stern command never again to celebrate Mass while his mentor lived.

St. Gall and St. Columbanus

We return, then, to Gall, the companion of Columbanus at Bangor, the comrade of his wanderings, his mainstay at Luxeuil, the monk who had learned to speak German and could interpret for him in his dealings with the Suevi and Alamanni by the shores of Lake Constance, and the man from whom he parted in anger according to Gall's biographer but whom he forgave on his deathbed as shown by the gift of his abbatial staff. Gall was an Irishman of noble stock whose mother is said, with something less than probability, to have been queen of Hungary. He was educated at Bangor and was an ordained priest before he left with Columbanus for the continent. Two disparate enthusiasms are attributed to him, iconoclasm and fishing, and each got him into trouble.

The abbey of Luxeuil was on the River Breuchin, named for the Celtic water goddess, Brixia, and so presumably a promising place for an Irish monk to cast a net. Columbanus urged Gall to try his luck on the Breuchin but Gall perversely decided to fish the River Ognon. He could see the fish approaching his net and then turn back as though at a wall, and all day he caught nothing. He told his misfortune to Columbanus and was promptly ordered to fish the Breuchin as he had been told. He did so, and the nets nearly burst with the catch. The rationalist may interpret the tale as evidence of Columbanus's instinct for where they were biting, and the devout as further evidence of Columbanus's miraculous powers, but neither can avoid the lesson that obedience in a monk is a necessary virtue. As for the truth of the story, since Gall told it years later to Jonas, who put it into his Life of Columbanus, it would be impious to doubt it.

The matter of iconoclasm was more serious, as iconoclasm by its nature is more serious than fishing. Gall was a man set apart from the others of Columbanus's company by his instinct for languages. Gall did the preaching to the Alamanni at Tuggen, teaching them to worship the Trinity and keep the faith in its true form. But then, Walahfrid Strabo tells us, enthusiasm overcame discretion as Gall set fire to the Alamanni temples and threw the offerings on the sacrificial altars into the lake. The outraged Alamanni turned hostile, plotting death for Gall and expulsion for Columbanus and the others. Some friend to the new faith revealed the plot and Columbanus decided to leave Tuggen. Gall's biographer Walahfrid Strabo consistently attributes to Columbanus a fluency in cursing which finds no parallel in the pages of Columbanus's biographer, Jonas. According to Walahfrid Strabo, Columbanus laid upon the Alamanni of Tuggen the curse that madness would befall their children and they would fall victim to tyrants. Then Columbanus and the others left.

They made their way northeastward toward Lake Constance where there were Gallo-Roman villages, and reached the lake shore and the town of Arbon. Here they were greeted by a priest named Willimar with words almost forgotten by those inured to wilderness and barbarian: "Blessed is he that comes in the name of the Lord." Columbanus replied, "The Lord has gathered us out of the lands." Willimar entertained them for a week and reluctantly saw them leave for what in the minds of all except Columbanus was to be their permanent settlement at Bregenz.

Today Bregenz is an Austrian city lying at the extreme eastern end of Lake Constance, now frequently referred to by its German name, the Bodensee. In Roman days it was a settlement called Brigantium. Traces of Gallo-Roman Christianity still lingered at Bregenz, where the tiny church of St. Aurelia survived only to serve as a temple to the Germanic gods the Alamanni worshiped. The monks acquired and restored it, and made it the focal point of their ascetic lives and missionary activities. Along with the more usual perversities of human nature, Father Theodor Schwegler, the historian of Swiss Catholicism, records (p. 33) that on one occasion Columbanus was confronted by an unexpected show of bibulous ecumenism, with Gallo-Roman Christians and Alamanni pagans toasting each other in what purported to be some sort of religious ceremony. He restored orthodoxy by raising the vat and smashing it upon the ground.

The days of Columbanus at Bregenz were numbered, however, partly by the hostility of the triumphant Theuderic and partly by a call to a new mission field. As we have seen, there was already burning into his mind a new and farther gleam that shone from Italy itself: the call to the land now held by the Lombards, their conversion from Arianism to Catholic orthodoxy, a mission in the very land of the Romans and the heart of Christendom. The result was the sad separation of Columbanus and Gall, which must have been sad by its nature even if one discredits the bitterness which Walahfrid Strabo says attended it. Gall, ill though he was, placed his belongings in a boat and rowed the fifteen or more miles from Bregenz to Arbon, where Willimar received and housed him, appointing two priests, Magnoald and Theodore, to nurse him back to health. It was not Gall's destiny to remain at Bregenz, but his memory remains there today. High on a hill above the lake shore town stands the parish Church of St. Gall, a sandstone structure built in the fourteenth century to oversee in protective fashion the town below.

After Gall was restored to health, he decided that the voice of Providence had spoken to him in his illness and had ordained that his mission field should be the Alamanni of the area near the lake. He proceeded to follow the long established pattern of Irish monasticism. Willimar had a deacon named Hiltibod who knew intimately the rugged uplands south of Lake Constance. Gall asked Hiltibod to bring him to some isolated spot in the wilderness, supplied with water and with a level bit of land that might be tilled, where he could construct his uncouth cell and live in pious isolation. Hiltibod knew of such a place, and knew as well that wolves and bears frequented it. Undaunted, Gall set out with Hiltibod and came to the River Steinach, a mountain stream that tosses and tumbles down to the lake but has as well its quiet, trout-haunted pools. They found such a pool, and Gall found quick success in his favorite pastime. Hiltibod set about to kindle a fire while Gall withdrew to pray. Gall proceeded to stumble over a tree root and to fall, and here once more he saw the intervention of Providence. This place, by the trout pool where the land was level, would be the site of his cell. Walahfrid Strabo tells us that he fashioned a cross of hazel twigs and hung from it his precious pouch with its relics of the Virgin Mary, St. Maurice, and Bishop Desiderius. That night, as Hiltibod lay seemingly asleep, Gall withdrew to pray. As he prayed, a bear appeared and poked about their bivouac. Gall commanded the bear to pick up a log and throw it on the fire. The bear did so. Then Gall gave the bear a loaf of bread and commanded it to withdraw from the valley and never to harm it or its occupants, but to be free to roam wherever it chose in the neighboring woods and mountains. The bear lumbered off.

Hiltibod, however, had not been asleep. He had seen and heard all, and it confirmed his conviction that Gall was indeed a man of God. When Gall realized that Hiltibod had overheard what he had said, he commanded him not to reveal it this side of heaven. Hiltibod, however, saw fit to let Arbon know, and the story went the rounds of time and place until it reached the ears and so the pen of Walahfrid Strabo. Thereafter St. Gall and his bear were inseparable, and the story took on the inevitable embroidery. The bear lived in the cell with Gall. The bear's responsibility was to keep the fire going, and Gall's responsibility was to provide the bear with bread. One of the treasures of the abbey library of St. Gall is the Long Gospel. Its back cover is a tablet of ivory on which the ninth-century monk, Tutilo, carved the founding father of Sankt Gallen and his constant comrade, the former holding the loaf, the latter the log, and the hazel cross nearby with the relics. What Tutilo carved in the ninth century, the printing press reproduces in the twentieth. Gall and his bear are the inevitable trademarks of the city that bears the saint's name. The bear sometimes expands to tower above the saint, sometimes dwindles to teddy bear size. The hazel cross is sometimes present, usually not. The saint retains the size and expression appropriate to sanctity. Always he holds the loaf, always the bear holds the log. Few twists in the history of the emblem are more curious than the one that makes an Irishman of the seventh century the symbol of a busy industrial Swiss city of the twentieth, the center of the Swiss lace industry and one of the most attractive small cities of Europe.

The Sankt Gallen Grant

Another story is told of Gall which, when pruned of hagiographic embellishments, may well be grounded in truth. Gall had a solid reputation as an exorcist. It is part of his record that he expelled demons from the shores of both the Lake of Zurich and Lake Constance. Therefore, when the daughter of Duke Gunzo was possessed of a demon which stated that it would leave her body at the behest of none but Gall, the saint was sent for. He refused to come, and took refuge deeper in the mountains. He was found, however, and brought to the court of Gunzo, where Friedeburga, the victim of possession, was presented for his ministrations. She was deep in a coma, and seemed as if dead. When Gall pronounced the words of exorcism, the demon emerged shrieking, "Ingrate! It is to avenge thee that I have entered into the daughter of thy persecutor, and thou comest now to expel me again!" Gall then urged Gunzo to dedicate his daughter to the service of the Lord. This did not fit with prior plans, since Friedeburga was affianced to Sigebert, eldest son of Theuderic II who had just mounted the throne. Friedeburga was sent to him at Metz but escaped en route and fled to a church where she sought sanctuary. Sigebert, with a nobility not always achieved by Merovingians, brought her nuptial robe and bridal crown to the church and gave them to her with these words: "Such as thou art there, adorned for thy bridal, I yield thee to the bridegroom whom thou preferrest to me—to my Lord Jesus Christ." As for Gall, when Gunzo realized that he had rescued Friedeburga from the demonic clutches, he gave him whatever lands he desired between Lake Constance and the Rhaetian Alps. The grant included the site of modern Sankt Gallen.

More deftness perhaps than is humanly possible is needed to winnow the grains of history from this pious tale. Sense can be made of the expelled demon's words if only the *thee* charged with ingratitude could be Columbanus rather than Gall. Theuderic, the old nemesis of Columbanus, had conquered his brother Theudebert at this time and controlled the Alamanni. It is quite likely that Duke Gunzo, father of Friedeburga, was his unwilling tool and indeed Walahfrid Strabo states that Gunzo forced Columbanus to leave Bregenz. The willingness of Gunzo and Sigebert to see Friedeburga enter the religious life rather than the marital is not without precedent in seventh-century history. What is quite believable is the grant of land made to Gall. The strong likelihood is that the other aspect of the pattern of the Irish anchorite had emerged. The band of followers had come into being, as more and more Christian Gallo-Romans far removed from the isolated and timorous centers of the ancient faith found new strength and courage in the words of the resolute Irish monk, and perhaps more and more wondering pagans found an unsuspected truth and a new vision in what he preached. There is ample evidence that the Merovingians, with vast expanses of land at their disposal to bestow upon the servants of a God far more powerful than Thor and Woden, could have the generosity of the seventeenth-century British sovereigns who gave colonial grants from the Atlantic to the Pacific. In short, it is entirely possible that the Duke of the Alamanni did give a substantial grant of land to Gall and his followers and thus lay the foundation of what would become the abbey of St. Gall a century later. As for Sigebert and Friedeburga, and the abused, well-meaning demon, *"toute la reste est littérature."*

The Bishop of Constance

The next recorded event in the life of St. Gall occurred in 616. In the heart of the area occupied by the Alamanni was the city of Constance (Konstanz), on the tip of the peninsula which forms the strait between the Untersee to the west and the much larger Lake Constance to the east. Politically German since the 1805 Treaty of Pressburg, it is on the Swiss side of the lake and its history is part of the history of Switzerland. As its modern name suggests, Konstanz or Constantia was a Roman settlement and so a center of Gallo-Roman Christianity. Schwegler calls it the bishopric from which the episcopal structure among the converted Alamanni was erected, once the Frankish and Alamanni nobility accepted the faith and acquired an enthusiasm for furthering the Gospel. Even in Gall's day there was a bishop of Constance and when he died, Duke Gunzo selected Gall to be his successor. Gall, to whom a hermit's cell on the Steinach was far preferable to a bishop's palace in Constance, countered with the nomination of a man named John who, as a Rhaeto-Roman, could easily be accepted as a native. John was Gall's deacon and pupil, and his German teacher as well. Gall preached the consecration sermon at John's installation, the one piece of writing by him that has survived. It is a simple and clear exposition of the Bible story from the creation through the incarnation, crucifixion, resurrection, and descent of the Holy Spirit, delivered, as it had to be, in Latin in light of the occasion but evidently intended as a simple statement of fundamental belief for any Alamanni in attendance. It closes with an exhortation that the congregation keep the faith and persevere in good works.

St. Gall's Last Days

Once more the record is silent for nearly a decade. In 625 Eustasius, who had succeeded Columbanus as abbot at Luxeuil, died and Gall was elected his successor. Once more he declined a position of high distinction although a deputation of six monks, reputedly Irish, walked the hills and dales from Luxeuil to the Steinach to offer him the post. There remains in the scanty record but one other date, the date of his death. In 645 he went to Arbon to visit his old and dear friend Willimar. He sickened, lingered for two weeks, and on October 16 he died, an old man by seventh-century standards but hardly ninety as Walahfrid Strabo asserts. He was buried at Arbon where his name is perpetuated in St. Gallus Church. The monument to his life in the year he died was the tiny monastery on the Steinach, a cluster of huts where at first twelve monks had lived and worshiped with him. Destiny had in store for that cluster of huts a greatness of a sort very different from the greatness that make memorable Iona, Lindisfarne, Luxeuil, and Bobbio.

The Apostle of Switzerland

It is conventional to call St. Gall the Apostle of Switzerland, and this convention like many others is seldom put to the test of ascertainable fact. The simple truth is that we have no information whatever about the missionary activity of Gall, but there is a contingent fact of equal importance: the lack of evidence does not connote the lack of activity. What can be adduced as a substitute for evidence is a body of collateral facts. Gall acquired a substantial prestige during the thirty-five years he lived and worked among the Alamanni. He was given a lordly grant of land by Duke Gunzo to further the work. When the bishopric of Constance was open, Gall was Duke Gunzo's nominee for the post and Walahfrid Strabo reports that his election was unanimous. Some fifteen years after he left Luxeuil, which apparently he never visited in the interim, he was the choice of the monks of the abbey to be the successor of Eustasius as their abbot. After his death his name was perpetuated in the protomonastery which he brought into being, later in the great abbey which was its lineal successor, and finally in the city which today bears his name. All this is at least collateral evidence to the respect in which the man, and it would seem reasonable to add his works, was held by both the Alamanni and the Gallo-Romans of Switzerland.

There is strong evidence as well of a vigorous St. Gall cult in Italy. Brother Tommasini, whose *Irish Saints in Italy* records such matters with a wealth of corroborative detail, lists ten churches in Italy which bear the name of St. Gall. There is a village in Lombardy call San Gallo, a side altar in the village church is dedicated to St. Gall, and infants of San Gallo are often christened with the name Gall. High on a hill above Soligo in the province of Treviso is a "hermitage of St. Gall," built in the fifteenth century by a friar who had spent his early years in Switzerland and helped form a Swiss colony in the area which still bears the name Viezzers (Switzers). Even the American tourist pacing off the wonders of Florence may have encountered the saint as he walked the Via San Gallo from its start near the Medici Chapel to the Piazza della Liberta, where the Porta San Gallo stands. The irreverent may find interest in Boccaccio's "Lucifero da San Gallo" who chews the damned to bits, and the report that the Church of San Gallo, which stood until 1529 in what later became the ornamental garden area of the Piazza, was embellished with the picture of a devil with a number of mouths. Fra Tommasini's deflating interpretation is that the Lucifer of San Gallo is merely Leviathan whom St. Gregory was the first but not the last to consider a personification of Satan. Thus the evidence at least suggests that the title, Apostle of Switzerland, reflects the esteem in which St. Gall was held from the start.

When it comes to the problem of defining the area of his presumptive apostolate, there is little indeed on which to proceed. We have already seen that missionary work on the western borders of modern Switzerland, where the Burgundians and Franks penetrated, proceeded in the main from Luxeuil and should in logic be considered part of the story of missionary activity in France. One cannot discount entirely what may have proceeded from the bishoprics established from Rome in the centuries before the German migrations, specifically from Basel and Constance in what became Alamanni territory, and from Chur deep in the Grisons where the Rhaeto-Romans took refuge. There is no evidence that St. Gall's monastery was a seedbed of monasticism after the fashion of Luxeuil and Péronne. There is recorded however the establishment of two monasteries from the protomonastery on the Steinach, one at Kempten by a monk named Theodore and the other by one Magnus at Füssen, both in Bavaria. Probably the informed guess of the writer of the St. Gall entry in the *Dictionary of National Biography* is as accurate a guess as can be made: "Although no materials exist for an exact estimate of the results of his work, it would not be too much to refer to him the evangelization of the country between the Alps, the Aar, and the Lech."

The Abbey and the Mission

It is entirely possible that the missionary achievements associated with the name of St. Gall were in large measure those of monks from the abbey which bears his name. We have seen that what St. Columba was credited with was in large measure the achievement of the community of monks he established at Iona. The achievement of St. Aidan cannot be separated from the achievement of Lindisfarne, and even the greatest of them all, St. Columbanus, owed no small part of his fame to what the monks of Luxeuil did after him. As for St. Fursa, he was an inspiration to Péronne but nothing more. Thus what St. Gall started on the Steinach cannot be separated from what his companions and successors continued at the monastery of St. Gall, and those who came long after them in the city of Sankt Gallen. Today Iona is an attractive reconstruction, Luxeuil and Péronne are modest memorials to a past greatness, and Lindisfarne a romantic ruins, but Sankt Gallen has a magnificent cathedral and is a great center of scholarly research. The work of the others survives in a Christian Europe, but the work of St. Gall survives both in that form and in a visible, tangible form as well.

The history of the abbey of St. Gall would bring us far beyond our period and subject, but it cannot be passed over in silence. Briefly, there are records through which its eighth-century history can be traced. In 720 Otmar, an Alamannian priest in the service of the Count of Rhaetia, was appointed abbot. He formalized life in the abbey under the Rule of Benedict in place of the Rule of Columbanus, which had prevailed before. He built the Church of St. Gall, the first stone church built among the Alamanni, and added to it a hospital and a hospice for travelers. His later days, and consequently for a time the state of Sankt Gallen, was clouded by the hostility of two local counts who placed Otmar in confinement and subjected the city to the control of the bishop of Constance. Otmar, who today is honored in Sankt Gallen as co-founder with Gall of the cathedral, the abbey library, and indeed the city, died on an island in the Rhine in 759.

With great and protracted difficulty Sankt Gallen freed itself from Constance and in the ninth century resumed its independent development. The old church was torn down and a new basilica built, aided by a bishop who had been providentially cured of the gout by prayers to St. Gall. The basilica was built under Abbot Gozbert, who founded a library as well and engaged first Wettin and later Walahfrid Strabo to write the Life of St. Gall. Under later abbots the library grew, a school was started, or more accurately two schools, an outer school for boys not destined for religion, and a cloister school for novices, and Sankt Gallen was on the way to becoming the great center of learning which was to be its medieval destiny. Music became a specialty and at the abbey there were developed the musical cadences called sequences out of which ultimately developed the *Dies Irae* and the *Stabat Mater.*

Sankt Gallen and Ireland

A fascinating corollary to our subject is the long and close intellectual connection that persisted between Sankt Gallen and Ireland. One of the prime sources of the modern knowledge of Old Irish is the Irish glosses to the ninth-century text of Priscian preserved at the abbey of St. Gall. Another of less significance is the Old Irish addenda to the Life of St. Fintan, an Irishman whose Life was written at the abbey by a monk whose identity time totally conceals. Of a value artistic rather than linguistic are the Gospels in Irish script, splendidly illustrated with the delicate spirals, intricate interlacings, and the grotesque animal forms characteristic of Irish decorative art, with a possible touch of Anglo-Saxon influence in the last. The Priscian already mentioned was the work of five Irish scribes who wrote a large, cursive hand with words now and then in Ogham at the top of the pages and an occasional prayer to St. Patrick or St. Brigit in the margin. To distinguish between what was done at the abbey by Irish monks and what they brought there is probably beyond the powers of scholarship, but the very existence of such work by Irish hands is proof of a long and close connection between this abbey in distant Switzerland and the island to which it owes its existence.

The visitor today to the elaborately beautiful, splendidly proportioned Library Hall with its ceiling frescoes depicting the first four ecumenical councils, its rich and radiantly gleaming wooden walls and doors may study the display cases with the great treasures of St. Gall—the oldest Virgil in existence; the unique B-text of the *Nibelungenlied;* one of the two texts of the *Parzival* of Wolfram von Eschenbach; the oldest form of the *Pater Noster* in German; the catalogue of the library drawn up in 847 in two lists, one of books "written by the Irish" *(libri scottice scripti)* and the other of other books. If he further ponders the fact that in the cases or out of sight are some two thousand ancient manuscripts and a hundred thousand printed books, many priceless, he needs no excessive imagination to envisage the twentieth-century debt to the Irish *peregrinus* who was too ill for Italy; found a cell by the Steinach, some say shared it with a bear who exchanged a log for the fire for a loaf of bread; brought the Word to a people still barbaric but capable of culture in its finest form; and was the founding father of one of the world's great centers of scholarship and a continuing place of serene beauty, artistic richness, and intellectual inspiration. The abbey library of St. Gall is indeed what the inscription over the entrance states: Psyches Iatreion, "Medicine Chest of the Soul."

Pirmin of Reichenau

There is relatively little that can be recorded about the mission to Switzerland beyond the biography of St. Gall and the history of the abbey of which he was the protofounder. Next in importance to the abbey of St. Gall, but next by a very substantial margin, is the Reichenau monastery. Midway in the smaller western extension of Lake Constance known as the Untersee is the island of Reichenau. Like the city of Constance, it is politically part of Germany but in terms of the seventh century it was well into the territory of the Alamanni. In 724 Pirmin, a Benedictine monk and a reputed refugee from the Arab invasion of Spain, was sent by Charles Martel to found a monastery on the island of Reichenau. He built a small monastery there, the first in Germanic territory to hold completely from the start to the Rule of Benedict. Known at first merely as Au, its name was later embellished with an ennobling prefix and became Reichenau. It is probable that Pirmin added missionary activities to his administrative duties at the abbey, but this is merely a matter of surmise. There exists from his pen a short account of man's salvation; a commentary on the Apostles' Creed; and a list of duties of the Christian, known collectively as Pirmin's *Scarapsus.* The last is essentially a student's compilation from various canonical works, and the faint mark it has left in literary history arises from the fact that it contains the earliest copy of the Apostles' Creed as now known. For a reason inextricably sunk in the obscurity of time Charles Martel sent Pirmin to Reichenau as a theological dairy farmer and his pietistic writing bears an alternate title, *The Farmer's Sermon.* There are three villages on the island, Oberzell, Mittelzell, and Unterzell. Out of Pirmin's modest beginnings there emerged in the ninth century two Carolingian structures, a cathedral at Mittelzell and a basilica at Unterzell, both of which still stand. Like the abbey of St. Gall, Reichenau achieved distinction in art and scholarship in the early Middle Ages, a distinction to which Walahfrid Strabo, St. Gall's biographer, contributed substantially during his time as abbot.

There has been a great deal of speculation about the nationality of Pirmin, whom Fuhrmann calls "a saint without a country." Rabanus Maurus says that he left his native land to seek the nation of the Franks. This absolves him of Frankish blood, assuming the accuracy of Rabanus Maurus. The statement that he was a refugee fleeing the Arab invaders of Spain has given rise to the suggestion that he was a Visigoth. The argument that he was English rests on the fact that he was a Benedictine, but the Rule of Benedict was too widespread by the time of Pirmin, who died in 753 or 754, to be helpful where his nationality is concerned. The argument that he was Irish depends on the fact that his first field of endeavor in France was Meaux, where there was an Irish hospice; that Reichenau was a favorite stopping place for Irish pilgrims en route to Rome; that St. Patrick's Day was always celebrated there; and that a century after Pirmin's death Abbot Ermenrich of Reichenau wrote to Abbot Grimoald of St. Gall, "How can we ever forget Ireland, the island where the sun of faith arose for us and whence the brilliant rays of so great a light have reached us?" There is at least as much reason to claim him for Ireland as for any other country, but that is a good point at which to let the claim rest.

From Reichenau, Pirmin proceeded to an establishment the history of which is almost totally engulfed in the oblivion of time. It

would seem that late in the seventh century Irish monks had formed
a community near Murbach in Alsace. With the aid of a local nobleman, Count Eberhard, they built a monastery dedicated to the memory of Eberhard's grand uncle, St. Leodegar. Pirmin now appeared
at Murbach, but in a capacity that cannot be determined. There is
no evidence that he was abbot, and indeed it is the belief of Fuhrmann that Pirmin's work was to bring into being a Benedictine
congregation of monasteries. If so, it was from Murbach that he
functioned and he may well have been partially instrumental in
paving the way for Murbach to achieve its eighth-century destiny as
the largest and most influential monastery in Alsace.

There were many aspects of Murbach reminiscent of Irish practice: it was free of episcopal jurisdiction, it had its resident bishop, it
was called *Vivarius Peregrinorum,* the wanderer's refuge, and the
very term *peregrini* was a synonym for Irish monks. Such monastic
chains were regularly constructed in Ireland and existed as well, as
we have seen, under Irish direction in England and Scotland. Links
in the chain had reciprocal relationships that implied both privileges
and responsibilities. The difficulty is that no reliable list of monasteries combined into a *Congregatio Peregrinorum* exists, nor is there
a list of monasteries founded by St. Pirmin. Yet the fact remains that
the charter of Murbach and the charter of a later foundation, Arnulf-
sau, testify to the reality of the congregation, and with it the other
fact, that Murbach enjoyed a primacy in eighth-century Alsace similar to the primacy enjoyed earlier by Luxeuil, Péronne, and St. Gall.
As is so often and so sadly true in these matters, conjecture can only
patch inadequately the chinks in the wall of reliable history. Reichenau had certain earmarks of an Irish foundation, and the congregation that centered at Murbach was in the tradition of Irish monasticism. There is little beyond that to justify the inclusion of Pirmin
among the Irish *peregrini,* but neither is there anything beyond the
silence of reliable history to lessen his undoubted importance in the
conversion of the Alamanni of central Switzerland and the Franks of
Alsace.

St. Fridolin

Next to what Pirmin did, but again by a substantial distance, was
the achievement of St. Fridolin, an Irish monk of reputedly noble
parentage, who crossed to France according to his almost uniquely

unreliable Life and passed through Poitiers, Strasbourg, Constance, and Chur, establishing churches as he went. Then, led by a vision, he proceeded to the island of Säckingen, an uninhabited bit of land in the Rhine some twenty miles east of Basel, where he established a monastery and built a church. At this point the ground appears to be solid even if the inspiration was visionary. Fridolin did establish on the island about the middle of the seventh century a double monastery. Furthermore there is reason to believe that he was in some sense associated with the Church of St. Hilarius in Chur. What fragmentary evidence can be gleaned from the pietistic and highly imaginative pages of the monk named Balther who wrote the Life of Fridolin in the eleventh century has been put in order by Schwegler, the already mentioned historian of Swiss Catholicism, but it amounts to nothing more than the above. As for Säckingen, the name is perpetuated today in a small town on the German side of the river above Basel. In the Church of St. Fridolin, an eighteenth-century remodelling of a thirteenth-century structure, is the Shrine of St. Fridolin. It was not the destiny of Säckingen, however, to achieve greatness. Forty miles upstream is the city of Schaffhausen, with an eleventh-century Munster and a secularized monastery which today is one of the primary museums of Switzerland. In the natural course of ecclesiastical development Schaffhausen replaced and eclipsed the monastery of Säckingen, and led to its almost total obliteration.

Sigisbert

There remains one other monk and founder, probably the most shadowy of all. His name was Sigisbert and his achievement was to construct a cell at Disentis. At this point we enter as usual the thorny area of conjecture. If etymology is a guide, he was a Frank and he is so described by Schwegler and the Catholic Encyclopedia. But Patrick Fleming lists among the Irish monks who came from Bangor with Columbanus one Sigisburtus and it is recorded that he was among those expelled from Luxeuil with Columbanus, a group supposedly Irish to a man. It is possible, then, that Sigisbert was either a name which he took or a Germanic approximation of an Irish name, and that St. Sigisbert is grist for our mill. As we have seen, when Columbanus reached Bobbio he had but one companion. Sigisbert had been his companion farther than most, but the St. Gotthard Pass turned him back and he made his way by the peaks and glaciers of

Crisalpt to the high sources of the Rhine and there, at least in the Irish fashion, he found his remote, isolated, barely accessible hermitage. Today the locale is known to German-speaking Swiss as Disentis, to those who speak Romansh, as Mustér.

The full name of the village, if one traces the name back to its origins, is Mustér Disertina, *Monasterium desertum,* "monastery in the wilderness." The noun remained in Romansh, the adjective suffered a sea change in German to Disentis. Tourists who have ridden the Glacier Express from St. Moritz to Zermatt, through the Grisons and under the great shield of the Bernese Oberland, up slopes no train should undertake and down inclines that seem impossible in retrospect, may recall that just before the train achieved the Oberalpass and drifted down to Andermatt they passed the village of Disentis, or if one prefers, Mustér. The region is Switzerland at its most lordly magnificent, but one can only pause in quiet wonder at a man who would penetrate what then, as in such large measure now, was a grim, inhospitable, perilous, if entrancing wilderness and there contrive his cell, plant his crude cross before it, and seek his own salvation and that of the Rhaetians driven into the heart of beautiful desolation by the pressure of Germanic invaders to the north. Sigisbert was joined by a Rhaetian named Placidus and there the two men lived, worked, and died. In the mid-eighth century Bishop Ursicin of Chur erected a small monastery over their graves, staffing it from the Rhaetian monastery of Pfäfers. Three churches were built at Disentis, which has never ceased to be a religious landmark of the Upper Rhine. There is still a monastery and school at Disentis, and it is a center for the study of Romansh literature and life. Before departing from Sigisbert and Disentis one should add that Schwegler reduces to a footnote what he terms "the later tradition," that Sigisbert was a companion of Columbanus, and he never mentions the possibility that he might have been Irish. There is no evidence whatever that Sigisbert founded even a rudimentary monastery. He and Placidus were the inspiration of those who came after them, and Schwegler quite properly points out that they stand to Disentis in the same relationship as St. Gall to Sankt Gallen and St. Meinrad to Einsiedeln.

The Irish and the Swiss Mission

The fragmentary and inconclusive nature of our information about the mission to Switzerland makes impossible an entirely accurate appraisal of the Irish contribution. One must start by taking into consideration the physical pattern of Switzerland as it was in the seventh century, and the logical limitations that physical pattern imposed on the infiltration of Christianity. Switzerland was then an undefined part of the gigantic North European forest which stretched from the Atlantic farther eastward than man could tell. Its undulating, forested terrain was punctuated by seven major lakes, all of them relatively long and narrow with a tendency toward a crescent shape. From these lakes, and even through them, mighty rivers ran. South of the lakes the forest soared upward, the trees grew sparse and stunted, and there towered above a mighty shield of rock, great fields of snow, and rivers of eternal ice, rising and falling from one massive peak to another. The Alps then were a forbidden land, as remote from human habitation as the Brooks Range of northern Alaska is today. Here and there the likes of Columbanus could thread their way through lofty passes and rugged defiles to the plains of Italy beyond. The Switzerland in which man could live was north of the Alps, and mainly on the shores of the lakes and rivers.

The historical results follow logically from the physical pattern of the land. The oldest Roman settlement north of the Alps was Solodurum, modern Solothurn, northeast of the Bielersee on the River Aar. Farther downstream on the Aar there was an ancient Roman settlement at what now is Schönenwerd. By the first century of the Christian era there was a Roman town called Turicum, now the city of Zurich on the lake that bears its name. In 44 B.C. the Romans had reached a likely spot on the River Rhine for a settlement. It took the name of Augusta Raurica and today, with its center some miles downstream, it is the city of Basel. Modern Konstanz, with its strategic setting on the peninsula that almost divides Lake Constance, was Roman Constantia. Lucerne, again on the lake of the same name, is of immemorial antiquity. Geneva was tangent to the Roman province of Gaul in Caesar's day and Sion on the Rhone has a cathedral the oldest parts of which date to the ninth century. In a word, a century after the birth of Christ the chief cities of Switzerland were fairly close to what they are today.

One other community, similar in history to those mentioned above but very different in locale, should be added to the list. In 15 B.C. the Romans conquered the canton of the Grisons and adopted the name the Etruscans are said to have given it, Rhaetia. They established a military post to guard what then was the favored route from Italy to Lake Constance, the route past Lake Como, up the Inn River to a point near modern St. Moritz, then over the Julier Pass, which was deemed relatively safe from avalanches, down to the Rhine. On the Rhine they built Curia Rhaetorum, modern Chur, one of the oldest of all Swiss communities. In a crypt behind and beneath the high altar of the Church of St. Lucius at Chur is a tiny chapel that dates to the age of Charlemagne.

The bishoprics of Switzerland established before the Germanic invasion and the subsequent missionary period were where one might reasonably expect. In west Switzerland which the Burgundians were to people the bishoprics centered at Geneva and Sion, in the great central area that would be Alamannian the seats were Basel and Constance, and in Rhaetia one was at Chur. There were ancient Gallo-Roman churches in the Burgundian region at Lausanne, in the Alamanni area at Solothurn, Schönenwerd and Zurich, but none are recorded in Rhaetia. The last is logical, since the Gallo-Romans were driven down into that previously most thinly populated region by the invading Alamanni. Schwegler's compilation (p. 34) indicates that at the close of the eighth century, when the conversion of the Germans was virtually complete, there were six monasteries in west Switzerland. Granval and St. Ursanne were foundations from the Irish center at Luxeuil and Romainmoutier might be called an Irish restoration. There were five monasteries in the central Switzerland of the Alamanni. St. Gall and Säckingen were Irish, and Reichenau may have been Irish. There were also five in Rhaetia, of which Disentis may have been Irish. Thus, of the sixteen monasteries of Switzerland, as many as seven may have been Irish and five certainly were. Four of the nine foundations that were not Irish were deep in the Grisons, in the region most accessible from Italy and therefore to the surge of monastic activity set in motion by the Italian Benedictines. The field of greatest Irish activity was where one would expect, in west Switzerland which was within the orbit of Luxeuil and in central Switzerland north of the Alps.

There are limitations to this statistical approach. Luxeuil was a great seedbed of monasteries, St. Gall was not. Yet the homage paid from the start to the saint and to the monastery that bears his name is testimony of the most convincing nature to the role both played in the conversion of Switzerland. At a time when the institutional

Church had recoiled within the walls of Basel and Constance, and a few other communities well to the north, St. Gall and his companions boldly planted the cross in the heart of Alamanni territory and preached its message to barbarians whose willingness to hear it came slowly and with great reluctance. A cell by the Steinach, with a monk inside in prayer, while one would like to believe that a bear tended the fire, became a group of cells, a protomonastery, a monastery, and then a center of religious inspiration and secular learning. It is today what it became in the Middle Ages, one of the world's great repositories of books, a memorial to a greatness that was brought into being in the remote, barbaric past, that matured as civilization triumphed over barbarism, that withstood all the challenges of time and man's perversity, and that stands today a place of beauty and inspiration. The question that Ermenrich of Reichenau asked Grimoald of St. Gall cannot be answered in statistical terms: "How can we ever forget Ireland, the island where the sun of faith arose for us and whence the brilliant rays of so great a light have reached us?" Christianity, first kindled in Switzerland from Rome, was rekindled there, in large measure as it was in France, by Irish *peregrini,* simple hermits who sought the wilderness and were found there by peoples thirsting for the living water.

Bibliographical Note

There are three early Lives of St. Gall, the first fragmentary and very old, the second by a monk of Reichenau named Wettin, and the third by his pupil Walahfrid Strabo, abbot of Reichenau from 842 until his death in 849. They have been edited by Bruno Krusch, *MGH: Scriptores Rerum Merowingicarum* IV, pp. 280–337. The Life by Walahfrid Strabo has been translated, with a valuable Introduction, by Maud Joynt, *The Life of St. Gall* (London, 1927). St. Gall's sermon at the consecration of Bishop John of Constance is in Jacobus Basnage, ed., *Thesaurus Monumentorum Ecclesiasticorum sive Henrici Canisii Lectiones Antiquae* (Amsterdam, 1725), vol. I, pp. 785–92.

The missionary period in Switzerland, including an appraisal of all the figures treated in this chapter, is described in P. Theodor Schwegler, O.S.B., *Geschichte der Katholischen Kirche in der Schweiz* (Stans, 1943); see especially pp. 32–49. For St. Gall specifically, see Fritz Blanke, *Columban und Gallus: Urgeschichte des schweit-*

zerischen Christentums (Zurich, 1946); B. and H. Helbing, "Der heilige Gallus in der Geschichte," *Sweizerische Zeitschrift für Geschichte* XII (1962), pp. 1–62; and L. Hertling, "Saint Gall in Switzerland," in John J. Ryan, ed., *Irish Monks of the Golden Age* (Dublin, 1963), pp. 59–72. On the St. Gall cult in Italy, see Anselmo M. Tommasini, O.F.M., *Irish Saints in Italy*, trans. J.F. Scanlon (London, 1935), pp. 252–64. For the history of the abbey of St. Gall, see J. M. Clark, *The Abbey of St. Gall as a Center of Literature and Art* (Cambridge University Press, 1926); on the continuing Irish influence in the St. Gall *scriptorium*, Johannes Duft, *Irish Miniatures in the Library of the Abbey of St. Gall* (Berne, Olten, and Lausanne, 1954).

There are three Lives of St. Pirmin, of the ninth, eleventh, and thirteenth centuries respectively; they are in the Bollandist *Annales*, 3 Nov. II i; pp. 33–50. Pirmin's *Scarapsus* is in Migne, *Patres latini* LXXXIX, col. 1030 ff.; his version of the Apostles' Creed was reprinted by the Henry Bradshaw Society, *Facsimiles of the Creeds*, in *Proceedings*, vol. 36 (London, 1909). On the early history of the abbey of Reichenau, T. Mayer, "Die Anfänge der Reichenau," *Zeitschrift für der Geschichte des Oberrheins* 101 (1953), pp. 305–52. The eleventh-century Life of St. Fridolin by Balther is in *MGH: SRM* III, pp. 350–69.

Schwegler believes that the Abbey of Disentis was established from the Rhaetian Abbey of Pfäfers on the site chosen by a Frankish monk, Sigisbert, and his Rhaetian associate Placidus in 720 and built above their graves; see pp. 38–39. He dismisses the link between Sigisbert and Columbanus as a later tradition. The Catholic Encyclopedia (1967) accepts the link with Columbanus but calls Sigisbert "a Frankish disciple." The evidence is presumably contained in I. Muller, *Disenter Klostergeschichte (720–1512)* (Einsiedeln, 1942), a work I have not seen. Montalembert accepts the thesis that Sigisbert was Irish (*Moines d'Occident*, vol. 1, p. 584).

For the statement of Abbot Ermenrich of Reichenau about Ireland, "where the sun of faith arose for us," and in general the possibility that Pirmin was Irish, see J. J. Dunn, "Irish Monks on the Continent," *Catholic University Bulletin* X (1904), pp. 307–28.

10

St. Virgil
and the Mission to Germany

ON the island of Honau, several miles downstream from Strasbourg, a monastery was established a few years after 720, the
year in which the land for it was granted. Today not only has the
monastery vanished, but so has the island. The Rhine gradually leveled off and washed away the island, and the current of time has
similarly washed to oblivion the memory of St. Michael's monastery.
Yet for several generations it was the most active center of Irish
missionary work in the Rhineland, and it would seem to have continued at least a checkered and precarious existence into the thirteenth century.

We have seen the Irish missionary trend toward the East at work
in the northeast of France and Belgium. Such monasteries as St.
Roding's at Beaulieu and St. Omer's at Sithiu are examples of the
former, Nivelles and Malines of the latter, but the proliferation of
missionary activity from Péronne is the most striking example. By
the end of the seventh century, activity from Murbach in Alsace may
well have rivaled in intensity and scope the activity from Péronne,
and Alsace had become a primary field of activity for Irish *peregrini*.
St. Disibod, to whom we shall return, had founded with Irish compatriots a monastery at a site on which was bestowed his name, Disibodenberg. St. Fridolin, as we have already seen, had his insular
monastery in the Rhine not far from Basel. At least the contention
has been made that two seventh-century bishops of Strasbourg, Ar-
bogast and Florentius, were Irish, and that during the episcopacy of

Florentius a *monasterium Scottorum* named St. Thomas was established in Strasbourg. While as Kenney says the written record of their work has almost entirely perished, there is evidence enough to show that numerous Irish monks were working among the Germans of the Rhineland in the later years of the seventh century. The logical starting point from which to consider the mission to Germany is that tiny, vanished island in what is neither Germany nor France, the River Rhine near Strasbourg.

Honau

What is known of Honau is known through the labors of an eleventh-century canon of the monastery whose name was Leo. In 1079 he transcribed onto vellum certain charters of the monastery. These came into the hands of a canon of St. Peter's Church, Strasbourg, named John Le Labourer, who in turn gave them to Dom Mabillon for his Benedictine *Annales*. They were a few of an extraordinarily large number of documents dealing with Honau, once preserved at Strasbourg and now vanished into nothingness. Jodoc Coccius, the sixteenth-century biographer of King Dagobert II of Austrasia, whose benevolence toward Irish monks no doubt made its substantial contribution toward their work in the Rhineland, tells of seeing thousands of documents in the Strasbourg archives dealing with the Honau monastery. As for the benevolence of King Dagobert toward the Irish monks, it arose from the fact that when his father died Dagobert found it politically expedient to take refuge in Ireland where he lived in Irish monasteries for nearly twenty years.

The immediate benefactor of Honau was Duke Adelbert of Alsace, whose sister St. Odilia conducted a convent at Hohenburg and whose son Eberhard gave the land for the monastery at Murbach. The island was turned over piece by piece to the Irish monks until, by 750, the entire island was theirs. One of the oddities of Honau is that unlike every other monastery we have considered, the institution dwarfs the founder and not the other way around. The names of successive abbots are known: Benedict its founder, Tuban, Thomas, Stephen, and Beatus. Beatus died subsequent to 810, when his name appears in a charter, and the name of no abbot after him has been handed down, although in 884 Emperor Charles the Fat confirmed the right of the monks to elect their own superior. Mabillon's *An-*

nales records the fact that in the eleventh century secular canons headed the monastery, and at some date after 1079 the college of canons transferred from Honau to St. Peter's Church in Strasbourg. Erosion of the island forced the removal of the rest of the community to Rheinau in 1290.

It would appear that the abbacy of Benedict, the founder, was brief, since King Theodoric IV appointed Tuban as his successor in 724. Charlemagne proved to be a particularly benevolent protector of the monastery, confirming its exemption from judicial supervision and exempting it from all tolls and taxes. The legal instrument to this effect confirms the fact that the monastery was Irish, referring to Abbot Beatus "of the Irish monastery called Honau, which Bishop Benedict newly erected in honor of St. Michael and in which the body of its venerable founder rests in peace." Almost bewildering evidence of the size and importance of Honau is to be found in the testament of Abbot Beatus which was witnessed by seven Irish bishops, bishops rejoicing in such names as Echodh, Maucumgib, and Caincomrihe. These names Gallic Dom Mabillon found barbarous, and Bishop Reeves, a Celt and Adomnan's editor, testily found quite pronounceable to those who would bother to learn Irish pronunciation. There is collateral evidence enough to make one suspect that Honau was an Irish monastery even if such were not an established fact: its location on an island, its independence of diocesan authority, the double role of bishop and abbot assumed by the founder Benedict, and the later presence of resident bishops. The one unique feature is the presence of seven of the latter. No other Irish monastery, at home or abroad, approached that number.

The creation of these bishops, all without bishoprics, gives oblique evidence at least to the influence of Honau in the conversion of the Germans of the Rhineland and Alsace. The historian of the Church in Alsace attributes to Honau the establishment of communities at Lautenbach and Rheinau, and the cathedral at Ergau which Fuhrmann identifies with Aschaffenburg. In his testament, Abbot Beatus refers to seven churches under the jurisdiction of Honau of which the Church of St. Paul at Mainz, often referred to in early documents as *ecclesia Scottorum,* is the best known. The evidence is very early, quite fragmentary, and difficult to assess in terms of reliability, but the balance of evidence supports the view that the conversion of Alsace and the part of the Rhine in the neighborhood of Strasbourg proceeded in large measure from Honau. Strasbourg itself was, of course, Roman and the Church was first established there by Gallo-Romans, but the likelihood that it was a beleaguered Church, shrinking from the barbarian rather than bringing the Gospel to him, would be in the seventh-century pattern. The evidence of the charters that have survived is adequate to verify the size and importance of the monastery at Honau, and the very existence there of seven bishops is evidence that the work of conversion was followed by the work of confirmation and ordination. The creation of a native clergy was an invariable part of Irish monasticism, whether the field be Scotland or England, France, Belgium, Switzerland, or Germany.

Even the island of Honau, washed away by Rhine waters, seems substantial compared to the shadows of names that Kenney faithfully records. There is St. Wendelinus, a hermit of Trèves out of whose cell there developed the abbey of Tholey. His late Life, recorded in the Bollandist *Annales* under the date October 21, states that he came from Ireland. This may be, and beyond this one cannot go. There are the so-called apostles of Bavaria whose Lives are recorded in both prose and verse, Saints Marinus and Annianus. Their legend states that they were Irishmen who made the pilgrimage to Rome early in the seventh century, entered the mission field of Bavaria on their way back, centered their work at the village of Aurisium where Marinus was martyred by the barbarians and Annianus, symmetrically, died of natural causes on the same day. They had at least physical reality, since their bodies were buried at the monastery of Rott am Inn in Upper Bavaria. The ground becomes somewhat firmer when we reach St. Disibod and the Disibodenberg which he established. His Life was written by the medieval mystic Hildegard, abbess of Rupertsberg, and written, the author attests, from supernatural revelation. With the acknowledgment that what is written by supernatural revelation, unconfirmed by the supernatural source, tends to fall short of the more austere requirements of factual accuracy, it may be said that Disibod was an Irishman who came with several companions from Ireland to Alsace, concealed his clerical orders so that it was not known whether he was a priest or a bishop, founded the monastery of Disibodenberg, and died there about 674. Of him Kenney says (p. 513), "Disibod is one of those Irish saints who stand out in high relief in continental ecclesiastical tradition but of whom history can hardly accept the existence." The case for his reality must rest on Hildegard's Life and on the fact that Rabanus Maurus (776–856), archbishop of Mainz, assigns to him September 9 in his *Martyrologium*.

St. Kilian of Würzburg

We reach firm ground again when we come to St. Kilian of Würzburg. Kilian, whose name appears in such variants as Cilian, Caelianus, and Quillianus, was born in County Cavan, about 640. Local legend makes his birthplace a house on the road which leads from Mullagh to Virginia. At the spot where the house is reputed to have stood are traces of a cairn, and at one time there was a church dedicated to St. Kilian. The church was dismantled stone by stone and transferred to Virginia, where it was reassembled and still stands as the village church. There is no evidence as to Kilian's education and clerical life in Ireland. It may be significant that his birthplace is only a few miles northwest of Kells, an educational and religious center of the first importance. There are two Lives of Kilian, each containing much that is fabulous but also much that is reliable. The second is basically an expansion of the first, with the expansion material of dubious value.

The Lives agree that Kilian was a bishop when he left Ireland with eleven companions and traveled to the court of the pagan Duke of Thuringia, Gozbert, at Würzburg. The Lives also have it that before traveling to Würzburg, Kilian had gone to Rome and secured papal approval of his German mission. This has been questioned, but there is more than a little reason to believe that papal approval of Irish missionary work on the continent was on occasion sought to strengthen the hand of the missionary against covert and sometimes open opposition from the institutional Gallo-Roman Church, and indeed from rival missionaries of other racial stock, mainly Anglo-Saxon.

Würzburg, which is on the River Main in Lower Franconia, is by a substantial number of kilometers the most easterly point to which we have traced the Irish missionary movement. One recalls, however, the identification of the cathedral at Ergau, mentioned as a foundation from Honau, with the city of Aschaffenburg. Aschaffenburg is little more than twenty miles west of Würzburg, and it may well be that the Irish penetration of Lower Franconia had at least started when Kilian reached Würzburg. The city itself antedates history, with archaeological evidence of a great antiquity and of a period of Celtic occupation before the Christian era. The Germans arrived in the area during the first Christian century, but Würzburg was not a Roman settlement, nor was there in it a Gallo-Roman church. This was a land of paganism, undiluted and unmodified, of the sort we have not seen since we followed Patrick to Ireland. Whether or not formally ratified by the Pope, Kilian and his companions undertook the virgin missionary field of Franconia and Thuringia. Details of their work have not survived, but the effects were such that its efficiency, at least as an initiating force, is beyond question. What is an unquestionable fact is that within a half century of Kilian's death, which some date to 689 and others to 697, Würzburg was the center of a bishopric, and the conversion of Lower Franconia was an accomplished fact. When this is coupled with the honor paid from the start to Kilian as the Apostle to Franconia, there is no reason to question the fundamental fact that he and his followers won to the Church a substantial number of Germans to whom the name of Christ had previously been totally unknown. This was not a field where Christianity, established by the Romans but long in timorous retreat, had to be revitalized. It was a virgin field, in which the names of Woden and Thor had never had a rival in reverence.

Kilian's most notable act of conversion was also the cause of his death. He had converted Duke Gozbert, but Gozbert had been living with his brother's widow. Kilian broke up the alliance, and Geilana, the displaced widow, successfully plotted Kilian's death. Kilian and two co-workers named Colman and Totman were murdered at her order. They were buried devoutly enough, but on July 8, 752, Bishop Burchard of Würzburg, the first to hold the post, transferred their bones to his newly completed cathedral. Today they rest in a crypt beneath the Neumünster Church. One might add that the Neumünster Church is not the cathedral of Würzburg but, as its name indicates, was originally a monastery church with a cloister garden, now called the Lusamgärtlein. One who seeks out this quiet sanctuary will be rewarded by finding a monument to the greatest of the minnesingers, Walther von der Vogelweide, who spent his last days at the monastery and is believed to be buried in the garden. The monumental cathedral nearby bears the name of St. Kilian, and Bishop Burchard is commemorated in a church that stands by the vineyards at the foot of the towering Marienberg Fortress. In the fortress itself is proof of the success of the Irish missionary effort in Würzburg. The tiny round chapel in the fortress was built in 706, by one calculation only nine years after the death of St. Kilian, and consequently one of the very oldest churches in Germany.

Monastery Problems

As the seventh century ended and the eighth century began, a new problem arose for Irish missionaries in both Germany and France. In discussing it, we face the problem inherent in the specialized, and therefore partial, view of the great panorama of human history. That the revitalizing of Christianity in France and the implanting of it in Switzerland and in central and southern Germany was fundamentally an Irish achievement is beyond question. But it is equally beyond question that the Irish were not alone in the missionary field, and as the eighth century began, rivalries and the less than sanctified emotions rivalries beget, which first arose in Britain, were transferred to the continent. The Anglo-Saxons had been the students of the Irish at Lindisfarne, but they were also the conquerors of the Celts in England and the Scottish lowlands. As we have seen, Roman concepts of church organization and such aspects of Roman procedure as the dating of Easter and the form of the tonsure had been accepted quickly by the Anglo-Saxons, slowly and reluctantly by the Irish, and at the period of which we now speak not at all by the Welsh. Conflicts over these matters, and especially over the first, which was obviously the most important, began to arise as soon as Anglo-Saxon monks followed their Irish instructors into the mission field. As we saw in the chapter dealing with the mission to Belgium, the Anglo-Saxons undertook the mission to the Frisians, which in a geographic sense means to northern Belgium and most of the Netherlands, while the influence of Péronne was felt chiefly in southern and western Belgium. Naturally the two spheres of activity met and imperfectly fused, and then the imperfect fusion continued as Anglo-Saxon missionaries penetrated southward into parts of Germany that first received the faith from the Irish. The fusion was imperfect not because of differences in dogma nor, except quite incidentally, in ritual but because of a basic difference in concept of church organization. Such an issue as the dating of Easter had the advantage of being tangible, understandable, and therefore a good bone of contention, but the struggle really concerned far more basic issues.

The Irish pattern of church organization was monastic, as we have seen throughout. A typical sequence of events, already amply illustrated, presents a religious recluse finding his solitary cell, being found by seekers of the truth, becoming the center of a band of followers, then the founder of a very simple monastic community. Out of these simple beginnings in time there grew a monastery, and quite possibly one that endured, became celebrated, a center of religious light and secular learning, and in some cases still is such today. At the heart of the matter, however, was the religious recluse in his solitary cell, and there continued to be a centrifugal tendency in Irish monasticism, with monks separating themselves for a time or permanently from the monastic community and living in contemplative solitude. Cohesion, organization, and formalized discipline were by no means lacking in the Irish monasteries, but they were less basic to the Irish concept of monasticism than to the concept held by other peoples.

There were other aspects to Irish monasticism. The monastery was a very practical institution for a country in which Christianity had to be revitalized or established. It made a focal point of religious endeavor, from which missionaries could go out into the field, from which they could be aided, to which they could return. When the natives proved hostile, it could be a place of refuge. It was a place of training for novices, a place of retirement for the aged, a place of study and teaching since the monks carried the torch of civilization as well as of religion. As a church structure in miniature, it required for its full functioning the various clerical orders including the episcopacy. Hence arose a new church functionary, the bishop-abbot, or even more characteristically, the presence in the same monastery of two functionaries, the bishop who administered the sacraments appropriate to his clerical rank and the abbot who managed the monastery itself. The bishop was without a see, naturally, except to the extent that there might be an informal see comprising churches manned from the monastery, and his duties were defined in terms of clerical functions rather than administrative responsibilities. The latter remained vested in the abbot.

Much of the history of the Irish missionary movement of the late seventh and early eighth centuries in Germany can never be written.

Kenney refers to the work of Columbanus and Gall, of Fridolin and the influence Luxeuil exercised east of the Rhine. But although he states (p. 511): "In the central districts, Thuringia and Franconia, and more particularly in the southern, Alemannia or Suebia and Bavaria, the main work of evangelization was done by Celtic, or Celtic-trained, monks and hermits during the seventh and early eighth centuries," he perforce also adds: "The written records of their work, however, have almost entirely perished." We can with safety say that behind the names that have survived, such names as he mentions and such names as Kilian of Würzburg and Virgil of Salzburg, are the nameless monks who poured into France and Germany from Ireland and the Irish monastic centers of Scotland and England in the late seventh and early eighth centuries and today are buried in the oblivion of time. Ironically, their existence can be demonstrated mainly by the difficulty they so often presented to the institutional Church.

There can be no doubt that as time went on, the *peregrini* tended to be succeeded by the *vagantes*. The exiles in the name of Christ were followed by wanderers in the name of restlessness, adventure, whatever benefit chance might throw in their paths. The wanderers could be bishops quite as well as priests, in a day when the bishop was so easily and lightly consecrated, and the bishop without a see who had absolved himself from monastic allegiance and responsibility certainly posed the problems inherent in insubordination and could be darkly suspected of the problems inherent in heresy. The Merovingians, bemused with a God more powerful than Woden and Thor because his disciples had miraculous powers that transcended nature and the gods of nature, in general welcomed the *peregrini* as wonder-workers and therefore saints. The Carolingians, more sophisticated in their religious concepts but only by comparison, by and large gave warm support to the Irish missionaries. The result was that the saints were followed by the less than sanctified, the *peregrini* by the *vagantes*, the likes of Columbanus and Kilian by the likes of Adelbert and Clement whom a synod at Rome had to anathematize.

The problem of the *vagantes* was one for the institutional Church to solve, but the institutional Church was in no position to solve it or even to recognize that it existed as long as it huddled behind town walls, strove to placate German princes whom it thoroughly feared and never understood, and was too preoccupied with its temporal position to concern itself with its eternal mission. The day was to dawn, however, in which the institutional Church would be revitalized by an organizational genius from the British Isles, and the concepts of the diocese, the bishopric, formal church organization, and discipline would again have vitality and importance. The genius was St. Boniface.

St. Boniface

Bonifatius is a Latin approximation of the Anglo-Saxon name Wynfrith. A West Saxon priest born about 675, Boniface joined the English mission to Frisia in 716. Two years later he made his first visit to Rome and, like Irish monks before him, had his mission authorized. He visited Rome again in 722 and was consecrated a bishop. He continued his work as a missionary in Frisia and extended it in to Hesse and Thuringia. In 738 he was made a papal legate and in 748 he became archbishop of Mainz and primate of Germany. One recalls that the Church of St. Paul already existed at Mainz, under the jurisdiction of Honau. Although Boniface's commitment was to the diocesan form of church organization, the founding of several monasteries is attributed directly or indirectly to him. The most important was founded in 744 by his disciple, Sturmi, the monastery of Fulda in Hesse, some seventy miles north of Würzburg. In 754 Boniface resigned all his dignities and returned to the mission field in Frisia. The next year he and his companions were killed by pagans at Dokkum on the Bordau River. His body lies today in the cathedral of Fulda and in the cathedral treasury are reliquaries of Boniface and Sturmi, and Boniface's episcopal staff.

The formal start of the attempt to restore church order and discipline in France and to introduce them to the nascent Church in Germany came in 738, when Boniface visited Pope Gregory at Rome and was appointed a papal legate. Boniface's lifelong dedication to ecclesiastical law and order makes safe the assumption that he had solemnly warned the Pope about the centrifugal tendency native to Irish monasticism and the lamentable results, which could range from insubordination to heresy. The immediate result was a letter from the Pope to the bishops of Bavaria and Alamannia which instructed them not merely to reject pagan ritual and teaching but also the ritual and teaching of British and other false priests and heretics. Kenney believes, reasonably, that the singling out of British priests, as distinct from Irish, reflected the fact that Wales still refused to accept the Roman dating of Easter. After Boniface returned to Germany, he received a letter from the Pope instructing him to set up four bishoprics in Bavaria and to ordain three bishops. Bishop Vivilo of Passau, whom the Pope himself had consecrated, was in good standing with the papacy. Bishops John of Salzburg, Erembert of Freising, and Gaibald of Ratisbon (modern Regensburg), were appointed. With bishops in Regensburg and Passau the Church was formally established in the Danube valley. Freising is some fifteen miles north of Munich. To this very day the official title of the Munich prelate is Archbishop of Munich and Freising, as what began in the eighth century was perpetuated by a distinguished ecclesiastical achievement in the early Middle Ages. Freising is still ornamented by a Romanesque cathedral and a Benediktuskirche of the twelfth century, and on the hills beyond, the Weihenstephan Benedictine monastery where beer has been brewed since 1040. As for the bishopric of Salzburg, that will be our subsequent concern.

The German Councils of the Church

Boniface then set about curbing the rebellious bishops and priests. On April 21, 742, the first general council of the Church in Germany was convened at a site that has never been identified. It passed an ordinance forbidding unassigned bishops and priests to perform their clerical functions unless they first met the approval of a synod. Two years later a similar council was convened at Soissons in France. It passed a comparable ordinance requiring unassigned clerics to secure the approbation of the bishop of the diocese in which they wished to officiate before doing so. It elevated to the archbishopric of Reims a priest named Abel and it condemned as heretics a Gaul named Adelbert and his Irish associate Clement. The pair was formally anathematized by Pope Zachary in 745 at a synod held in Rome, although it is curious that two years later the Pope asked that the case of the two be once more considered in council. This curiosity must stay unsatisfied since nothing more is heard of either. The claim of Adelbert that he had a letter which Christ had written and dropped from heaven tends to bolster Kenney's theory that he was a mountebank. As for Archbishop Abel of Reims, he was a priest of the abbey of Lobbes appointed to the post on the nomination of

Boniface. Folcuin, abbot of Lobbes, which is in Hainault, Belgium, states in his *History of the Abbots of Lobbes* that Abel was an Irishman and that his appointment made him successor to Archbishop Melo who had been deposed by the Council of Soissons. Folcuin further states that Abel met such opposition in the post that he resigned, returned to Lobbes, and became abbot there.

These details have broader significance than might appear at first sight. There is not a vestige of evidence that Boniface took restrictive measures against any Irish monastery or its members that was functioning in its proper fashion, or against any Irish or British bishop or priest performing his clerical functions in accord with the requirements of his station in the Church. There is evidence that he favored the promotion of Irish clerics to higher positions to which they were properly eligible. Archbishop Abel of Reims is one example, and it is quite likely that Bishop Erembert of Freising was another. The point is significant as a corrective to the implications of what follows, to a case in which Boniface was wrong in the accusations which he leveled at an Irish prelate and in the outcome was worsted. The case involved one of the most interesting and colorful figures to appear in the Irish missionary movement, St. Virgil of Salzburg.

St. Virgil of Salzburg

St. Virgil was born in Ireland about 710. His name was Ferghil which Latinizes naturally into Virgilius, in a fashion complimentary to a scholar for its overtones suggestive of the Mantuan Virgil. In Salzburg, with which his name is always and properly associated, Virgilius became Virgil, and as St. Virgil he is known and perpetuated in church art, holding his cathedral in the fashion customary for ecclesiastical founding fathers. In a field in which scholarship is never well off for biographical details, we are worse off than usual where Virgil is concerned. There is a short treatise on the conversion of the Bavarians and Carinthians which appears to date to the ninth century. It presents the oldest account extant of the continental career of Virgil but contains nothing about his Irish background. There is also a twelfth-century Life which leans heavily on the *Libellus de conversione Bogoariorum et Carantorum,* as the ninth-century treatise is called, but it adds little if anything of independent worth. One might add an epitaph of Virgil which is extant and a short poem about him by Alcuin. The one thing supposedly known of his Irish background is the fact that he was abbot of the monastery of Achad Bó, the foundation of St. Cainnech near Dublin, and Father Paul Grosjean, S.J., a Bollandiste and an authority on early Irish history, questions the certainty of even this. Virgil must have had a career of some significance in Ireland, however, since his name and pedigree are found in both the *Book of Leinster* and the *Leabhar Breac*. They make Virgil the son of a man named Moeliduin and a descendant of Niall of the Nine Hostages.

He came to the continent about 742 and went to the court of Pepin the Short at Quierzy on the Oise, in northern France. There has been surmise about the relationship of Virgil and Pepin that covers close to the entire gamut, ranging from close friendship to the charge that any friendship was mythical. What is not challenged is the fact that Virgil spent some time at the court of Pepin, mayor of the palace to the last Merovingian king Childeric III and the man who overthrew the Merovingians and established the Carolingian dynasty. Two other facts at least hitherto unchallenged are that in 743 Pepin had been fighting with his customary success against Duke Odilo of Bavaria and that Pepin sent Virgil to Salzburg about that time. Salzburg was then central to the realm of the Bavarians and close to the restless territory of the Carinthians, who were beset by the Bavarians from the north and the Avars from the east. Both the capacity in which Pepin sent Virgil to Salzburg and his intent in sending him have been given widely varying interpretations. No interpretation can be reasonably attempted without a prior consideration of the religious history of Salzburg and of the Bavarians.

St. Rupert of Salzburg

The Romans reached Salzburg in 15 B.C. They called the Celtic settlement there Juvavum and the district Noricum. They left Salzburg in A.D. 485 as part of the fifth-century contraction of the Empire. Thus there were four centuries in which one might reasonably expect the light of Christianity to reach Salzburg, but it was never a flame that burned in Noricum with a clear and steady light. After the Romans withdrew and the Bavarians took over the province in 530, there followed a century and a half of Germanic paganism with at the most a flicker of Christianity left from Roman days. In the

eighth century the Bavarian Duke Theodo became a Christian and
he sent to Salzburg the man known in history as St. Rupert of Salzburg to convert the city and the region. He arrived about 700 and
founded in Salzburg the monastery of St. Peter, which is still one of
the great religious shrines of the city. There is some reason to believe
that he staffed it with Irish monks, but there is no reason to believe
that Rupert himself was Irish. His name suggests that he was a Frank.
He might have recruited monks for St. Peter's from Luxeuil, Péronne, Honau, or any of their sibling monasteries that were Irish in
personnel and monastic rule.

As time went on, the Irish rule at Salzburg, which was presumably
the Rule of Columbanus, was replaced in the customary fashion by
the Rule of Benedict. In the Irish manner Rupert was both abbot and
bishop. In addition to establishing a monastery at Salzburg and winning the city to the faith, he founded the convent of Nonnberg, the
Church of St. Maximilian at Bischofshofen in the Pongau, some thirty
miles south of Salzburg, where the Romansh-speaking natives still
clung to the faith. Moving north, he built a church, also dedicated to
St. Peter, at Seekirchen on the Wallersee. He is reputed as well to
have encouraged mining for salt in the city that bears the name of
the trade, and this is the justification for the salt box in his hands
which is his hallmark in church art. The founder of Christianity in
Germanic Salzburg is remembered properly and even devoutly in
that fairest of cities. He might be called the ancestor of the Prince
Bishops who centuries ago made it what it still is today, a city of
churches and palaces, spacious squares and arcaded passageways,
monasteries with peaceful closes, and always music in the air.

Virgil Is Sent to Salzburg

St. Rupert died on March 27, 718, and was followed in office by the
abbot-bishops whose names are recorded in the *Fraternity Book of
St. Peter's,* a list of persons living and dead for whom the community
was to pray. Then came the appointment of Boniface as papal legate
to Germany in 738, and the instruction from the Pope to appoint a
bishop of Salzburg and create there a bishopric. A man of whom
history reveals nothing more than his name, which was John, was

accordingly appointed the first bishop of Salzburg who was not also abbot of St. Peter's. Five years later Pepin put down the insurrection of Duke Odilo and since the abbacy of St. Peter's was vacant, sent Virgil to fill the post. With the exception of the last point, the purported intervention of Pepin in the religious affairs of Salzburg, this much may be regarded as certain. It is possible that Virgil was invited to head the Salzburg community by its members; it was probably an Irish community in membership, and it was certainly an Irish community in terms of monastic observances. It is also possible that Pepin told the defeated Odilo that Virgil was to be his candidate for the abbacy, and that Pepin wanted a faithful òbserver of life in Salzburg and an influential formulator of its pattern. It is certainly not difficult to surmise that relations between the fledgling bishop of Salzburg and the abbot of the well-established and potent abbey of St. Peter would be at least delicate, could be strained; and, with the bishop the creation of the papal legate and the abbot the creation of the mayor of the palace, could even resemble an armed truce. There is another certainty to be added. So long as Boniface lived Virgil did not become a bishop. Boniface was killed in either 754 or early in 755, and within a year or two of his death Virgil was consecrated a bishop, "at the request of the people" says the *Libellus*. Whether Bishop John was living or dead is not part of the record. Indeed nothing about John is part of the record except his name and the Church rank to which he was elevated.

Virgil was not seriously handicapped in his earlier Salzburg years by the lack of episcopal rank. He had been accompanied from France to Germany, and quite possibly from Ireland to France, by an Irishman who had been raised to the post of abbot-bishop of the monastery of Chiemsee, east of Munich. His name was Dobdagrecus, which in the past was translated "Dubh the Greek," which made mediocre Latin of an Irish name, and less than mediocre sense. It is now regarded as the Irish Dubh da Crioch, which has been translated perhaps with more imagination than regard for sober etymology as Dubh of the Two Countries, that is, Ireland and Germany. Dobdagrecus did the confirming and ordaining for Virgil. Another associate of Virgil's from his days at court, Sidonius, later became bishop of Passau. His nationality is successfully concealed by a name more convincingly Latin than Dobdagrecus.

The Baptism Issue

The first passage of arms between Virgil and Boniface occurred in either 744 or 746, and concerned the baptismal formula used by a priest working the bush well to the east of Salzburg. He was reported to Boniface to have been baptizing *in nomine patria et filia et spiritus sancti.* The substitution, seemingly illiterate, of *patria et filia* for the linguistically and dogmatically correct *patris et filii* was enough in the view of Boniface to render invalid the baptism. He demanded that Virgil and Sidonius have the sacrament administered again in the correct form, and they refused on the grounds that the baptism was valid. The issue was referred to Pope Zachary who upheld Virgil and Sidonius. It is entirely possible that Virgil, Sidonius, and the Pope were the true linguists, and not Boniface. If the priest had been baptizing in the Alpine area, as Father Grosjean surmises, he was doing so in an area where Latin was still a living tongue and not a book language as in the England of Boniface's birth. Strange perversions were entering the tongue as Latin was gradually dissolving into Italian, French, and the other Romance languages of which the Romansh of the Alpine hinterlands was one. The Pope himself, in talking Vulgar Latin as he must have to the city if not to the world, undoubtedly used word forms and grammatical constructions calculated to strike terror to generations of Renaissance Ciceronians yet unborn. Father Grosjean's surmise that the priest's bad Latin was actually our oldest example of Romansh, and that the Pope recognized it as being at least the Latin of the country and therefore valid for baptismal purposes, has much to recommend it. In any event, the round went to Virgil.

The Antipodes Issue

The next passage of arms between Virgil and Boniface was over a most extraordinary matter. Evidently it had come to the attention of Boniface that Virgil held to a geographic belief that could be entertained by no sane man—to wit, that the world was round and there might well be antipodean dwellers on its under surface. He reported the charge to Pope Zachary and there is extant a long reply from the Pope. It is dated May first, but the year is uncertain. Kenney's surmise is that the Pope wrote in 748. The letter is worth consideration in its entirety. First, it concerns the matter of an Irish priest named Samson. This man held that the imposition of the hands of a bishop sufficed for admission into the Church and consequently that baptism was not necessary. This was obviously heretical and the Pope instructed Boniface to excommunicate the culprit. Samson would seem to have been one of the troublesome Irish *vagantes* whose theological aberrations were constant thorns in Boniface's side.

Pope Zachary then turned to that troublesome personage, Virgil. He was aware that Virgil and Duke Odilo were now friendly and that Virgil was reported to be striving to cause dissension between Odilo and Boniface. He assured Boniface that there was no truth to the claim that Virgil had the Pope's authority to receive a vacant Bavarian bishopric. But neither of these was the basic issue. The Pope also assured Boniface that if Virgil was convicted of teaching a doctrine as perverse as charged, that "there are another world and other men under the earth, and another sun and moon," he should most certainly be excommunicated. He added that he had written to Duke Odilo ordering Virgil to be sent to Rome for trial. The letter concludes on a slightly plaintive note: might not Boniface be patient where Virgil and Sidonius are concerned?

There the matter rests. There is no report that Virgil went to Rome, stood trial, or was excommunicated for such heresy. Indeed, the truth is the quite happy contrary. Not merely did Virgil hold his abbacy, but after Boniface died he was consecrated a bishop, and in 1233 Pope Gregory IX canonized Virgil as a saint in the Catholic Church. One may assume, therefore, that the cosmological issue between St. Boniface and St. Virgil had been resolved in Virgil's favor in the peaceable kingdom where the lion lies down with the lamb, the Celt with the Anglo-Saxon, and no doubt there are Australians and New Zealanders in abundance.

Virgil the Geometer

A curious pair of twentieth-century developments in literary and archaeological study have increased considerably the stature of Virgil. The first concerns his right to the title accorded him by his contemporaries, Virgil the Geometer. There has floated down from the eighth century a work of previously unknown provenance known as the *Cosmography of Ethicus Ister*. It purports to be the

Latin version of a work written in Greek by St. Jerome. The Latin is of incredible badness, with grammatical discordances that would seem to have taxed human perversity to contrive. The alleged translator explains its shortcomings on the grounds that the text was mangled in the first instance by a semiliterate Merovingian copyist. One paragraph in this work, which is dedicated to the thesis that the world is round and that people may well live down under, would seem most strangely out of place. It is a paragraph of comprehensive abuse of all things academically Irish: Irish schools, Irish teachers, Irish books. In 1951 a German scholar, Dr. Heinrich Löwe, demonstrated that Ethicus Ister was St. Virgil of Salzburg and that the *Cosmography*, which became an accepted work of geographic reference for centuries, served the double purpose of expounding the theory of Virgil the Geometer and of ridiculing his benighted contemporaries, among whom it would not be entirely unreasonable to include St. Boniface. The assault on Irish scholarship was, of course, part of the concealment process. As for the pen name, Father Grosjean translates it prosaically enough as "The Philosopher of the Danube," the Romans having called the Danube the Ister. Dr. Löwe offers a much more intriguing interpretation, translating Ethicus Ister as "a man from Ethica Terra" and identifying Ethica Terra with the Irish Tir Heth, that is, the Hebridean island of Tiree, not far from Iona and the site of a Columban foundation.

Presumably the writer of the St. Virgil entry in the Catholic Encyclopedia had this identification in mind when he made the birthplace of Virgil the island of Heth in West Scotland. If Dr. Löwe's interpretation seems farfetched, one might point out that there is a weakness as well in Father Grosjean's more obvious explanation. The Danube does not flow through Salzburg. If Löwe was right, light may also be shed on the curious fact that the Confraternity Book of St. Peter's Abbey includes in the list of those for whom prayers should be offered not merely the abbots of St. Peter's in Salzburg but also the abbots of Iona, starting with St. Columba and extending down to Slébténe, the fifteenth abbot, an exact contemporary of Virgil's and presumably Virgil's monastic associate if he had an Irish background that included Iona and its monastic offshoots. Before the *Cosmography* and the additional lustre the identification of its authorship sheds on the name of Virgil, one should point out that the theory of a round earth was a classical commonplace and that Virgil might easily have met it, among many possible places, in Martianus Capella whose *De Nuptiis Philologiae et Mercuriae* was a textbook in the Irish schools of Virgil's day. Naturally Virgil did not believe in a second sun and moon. On the other hand, what Boniface and possibly the Pope considered his heresy was not his cosmography but what they considered its corollary, that there was another race on earth which was not the human race that Christ came to save. It was the theological implication, not the geographical, which would concern the eighth century.

The Cathedrals of Salzburg

What archaeology has revealed is of greater importance. It has always been known that Salzburg has had three cathedrals, the Carolingian cathedral which Virgil built, the Romanesque cathedral which was built in the eleventh and twelfth centuries, and the present baroque cathedral which was started by Archbishop Wolf Dietrich von Raitenau (1587–1612). It was further known that on September 24, 774, Virgil dedicated the first cathedral to St. Rupert, moving his remains from the monastery church of St. Peter's where they had rested since his death in 718. Although Salzburg now had a cathedral, St. Peter's continued until 987 to be the see of the bishop of Salzburg, as it had been from its building. One recalls that Virgil was consecrated bishop of Salzburg on June 15, 767. To give Salzburg a cathedral was one of his first undertakings, but Bishop Virgil continued to be Abbot Virgil of St. Peter's.

There is something about the Salzburg cathedral reminiscent of the axe which in its century of existence had five heads and seven handles. The cathedral was destroyed by fire in 850, 1000, 1127, and probably in 1181. It was always restored and usually enlarged, but one dimension was sacrosanct. The width of the nave had to be forty-five feet, the width that Virgil had ordained. The Romanesque cathedral came into being by a slow process of accretion to what Virgil had built and what was restored after each fire. The choir was lengthened and a west front added by Archbishop Hartwick (991–1023); west towers were built by Archbishop Konrad I (1106–1147); after the fire that devastated the cathedral at an undetermined date after 1167, probably 1181, Cardinal Konrad III (1177–1183) brought into being what may with better appropriateness be called the Romanesque cathedral than may any of its previous stages. He enlarged the cathedral to five aisles and built a transept, a choir, and an apse at the east end. This was the cathedral which Wolf Dietrich undertook to modernize only to have great portions of it collapse, a disaster which he turned to advantage by resolving on a totally new, baroque cathedral. Ultimately it was completed, with everything it connotes today including an important axial change in its relationship to the Residenz and the Residenzplatz which it faces. To make it face the Residenzplatz squarely and to join it by archways to such adjacent squares as the Domplatz and Kapitelplatz Wolf Dietrich's cathedral has an axis 10 degrees to the south of the axis of Virgil's cathedral and the Romanesque cathedral. In front of the cathedral today along with Saints Peter and Paul are statues of Saints Rupert and Virgil, the one with his salt box carried by figures in the base of the pedestal on which he stands, the other with his cathedral similarly displayed. The theological founding fathers of Salzburg have never been forgotten nor indeed neglected.

Fire thereafter spared the Salzburg cathedral, but not war. On October 16, 1944, a bomb crashed through the dome wreaking havoc in the church. It took ten years to restore the cathedral, which was formally reopened during what was proclaimed Cathedral Week, May 1–7, 1959. As a quite unexpected by-product of aspects of restoration involving excavations in the Residenzplatz in 1957–1959 and again in 1966–1967, which had among other objectives the creation of a modern crypt for the burial of archbishops, much was unearthed of the foundation of Virgil's cathedral and much was thereby learned.

There are references in Carolingian literature to the "astonishing magnitude" of Virgil's cathedral. Not until the excavations of 1957–1959 was it realized how justified was this description. It is now known that the nave and two aisles were more than two hundred feet long and one hundred feet across. The aisles had straight ends but the nave had a square atrium at the west end and a curved apse at the east end. The visitor to Salzburg can now descend into the crypt and view for himself what remains of the foundations of Virgil's cathedral and its medieval successor. On the floor of the circular chamber of the crypt is a mosaic which shows the floor plan of Virgil's cathedral and the Romanesque cathedral in relation to the floor plan of the modern cathedral. The central chamber of the modern crypt which contains the altar corresponds to the east end of the south aisle of Virgil's cathedral, and the outer chamber corresponds to the Liutpram chapel, in the north wall of which Virgil's tomb was discovered as a result of the twelfth-century fire. The Romanesque cathedral was superimposed on Virgil's cathedral, since it was essentially a development of it by a process of accretion. It had a longer nave than that of Virgil's cathedral, two additional aisles, and an expanded east end. The earlier cathedrals, as explained above, have foundations at slight angles to the present cathedral, and it is noteworthy that the baroque cathedral which Wolf Dietrich built, a cathedral of great importance as a pioneer building in a new style of architecture as well as a magnificent structure in its own right, is slightly shorter than the Romanesque expansion of Virgil's cathedral.

The cathedral that Virgil built must have been a most extraordinary building to have been erected in the eighth century by a people new to civilization and with nothing of the architectural tradition of the classical world to guide them, and one might add with nothing in Virgil's Irish background to serve him as a model. By general consent Wolf Dietrich is the most colorful figure in the ecclesiastical history of Salzburg, as an extension of the more general principle that the lives of sinners are more interesting than the lives of saints. In terms of what we know, Virgil cannot compete in color with the overworldly prelate who built that tower of bliss, the Mirabell Palace, as well as the present cathedral, but enough is known to make it clear that Virgil the Geometer, with his mad notions of a round world and antipodean inhabitants, and with his ability to construct a church with dimensions by no means dwarfed by the magnificent edifice that is one of Salzburg's prime glories today, and to do it in the Dark Ages with no tradition to instruct him nor model to guide him, is one of the most intriguing and even exciting figures Ireland ever sent to bring the Word to peoples who had forgotten it or had never known it. It is right that he and his distinguished predecessor, St. Rupert, should rest side by side under the high altar of Salzburg cathedral. Much of what Salzburg became rests on what they did.

The Mission to Carinthia

Administration and building were more important aspects of Virgil's career than missionary work. This was due only in part to the fact that his natural role was administrative. He came fairly late in the period of Irish missionary activity on the continent, and much of the work had already been done. There was one natural and necessary mission field, however, not far from Salzburg, and to it Virgil devoted an important part of his attention. The field was Carinthia, and the Carinthians of the eighth century were Slavs.

Carinthia today is one of the states of Austria and among the most clearly defined geographic entities in Europe. It is a vast arena, bounded by mountains that form a great, slightly ovoid band about an elevated valley floor of fields and lakes. Relatively few passes penetrate the walls of Carinthia, and no one of them offers a particularly easy passage. When Carinthia first enters history it is an Alpine Celtic state that yielded to the Romans in the first century B.C. The Romans christened the area of which it is part Noricum, after its Celtic capital Noreia. With the contraction of the Roman Empire Carinthia became the homeland of the Slovenes and received the name Carantaria, of which Carinthia is a derivative. By the eighth century the Slovenes of Carinthia found themselves crushed in a vise, with the Avars crowding them from the east and the Bavarians from the north. The Avars were Tartars who left their historic domain near the Caspian Sea in the sixth century, pushed westward into the Danube valley, and then southwestward through the valley of the River Mur until they were at the walls of Carinthia and forcing their way into the fertile lands beyond. Simultaneously, the Bavarians were pressing downward from the north. The Slovenes, recognizing the greater menace in the swarthy, Mongol invaders from the east, begged assistance from their far from benevolent German neighbors to the north. A treaty was effected, the Duke of Carinthia became a Christian, and in 780 or thereabouts the Duke requested that Virgil receive his son and nephew into the Church. The boys were being held as hostages by Duke Tassilo of Bavaria. This request initiated the mission to Carinthia.

Only the scantiest of details about the mission survive. Virgil appointed as its head one Bishop Modestus and gave him a staff of aides from the monastery of St. Peter and from two monasteries founded by Duke Tassilo at Virgil's request, the abbeys of Kremsmünster and Innichen. The Slovenes of Carinthia were efficiently added to the Church, with the energetic assistance of the current Duke Chetimar, the nephew held hostage whom Virgil had converted. Later Virgil made a missionary trip in person to Carinthia, continuing into Slavonia and traveling to the point at which the River Drave empties into the Danube.

Virgil is the one Irish prelate of the seventh and eighth centuries known to have carried the Word into a Slavic land. This trip, which he took to the confluence of the Danube and the Drave (German, *Drau*), makes a useful one, because an exact one, with which to illustrate the distances traveled by Irish missionaries of the seventh and eighth centuries as they brought the Gospel to the German, or in this instance the Slavic, pagan. The Drave is the great river of Carinthia. Rising in the Alps, it flows east through Carinthia, crosses the northern tip of Yugoslavia, forms the boundary between Hungary and Yugoslavia, and then dips south to meet the Danube at a point about 150 miles south of Budapest and 100 miles northwest of Belgrade. One may assume with some assurance that Virgil proceeded south from Salzburg, up and over the 6900 foot Radstädter Tauern Pass, where today there is a Cemetery of the Unknown for the victims of the mountains, into the southeast part of Carinthia to the River Drau, as the Drave is there known, at the village of Obervellach. The assurance rests on the fact that there was a Roman road for this route.

Still proceeding by assumption, as one must in such matters, we may state that he went the rest of the way by water, with such land portages as the water route made necessary. The journey could not have been less than 800 miles round trip, every inch of it through territory where the Roman patina had won thin indeed and the Slavic natives spoke a language that might as well have been antipodean for an Irishman or a Bavarian. This was the journey on which an Irish missionary brought Christianity to a land at least metaphorically the antipodes to Ireland. The thread is naturally most tenuous, but there is a thread that links the mission which Virgil sent to Carinthia and later joined in person with the present day in northern Yugoslavia. The Slovenes of Virgil's day are most closely related to the modern Croats, who are Catholics, use the Latin alphabet, speak either Sloveno-Croatian or Serbo-Croatian, and incline culturally to the West rather than to the Hellenic East to which most of Yugoslavia is indebted for light and letters. For that matter there are still Slovenes in Carinthia, mainly along the Yugoslav border.

Virgil was not a founder of monasteries, although two of those which were founded by Duke Tassilo are believed to have been founded at Virgil's urging. They are the abbeys already mentioned, Kremsmünster and Innichen. Innichen seems to have been a name writ on water, but Kremsmünster survived triumphantly. Founded in 777 ten or so miles south of Linz, Kremsmünster was a Benedictine monastery from the start. The present building is baroque, of much later construction, but in its treasury is the chalice of Duke Tassilo, the finest example of the Carolingian goldsmith's work preserved in Germanic Europe and the one artistic rival of its type to the Irish Cong Cross of much later manufacture. The school at Kremsmünster became one of the great schools of Austria, and there is something at least symbolically satisfying, considering its link with Virgil the Geometer, that it was a center of astronomic study and its splendid library is still housed in its astronomic tower.

The Irish Mission in Summary

In summary, Irish monasticism never permeated Germany in the way it permeated England and northern France, nor is there any Irish missionary who might reasonably rival St. Boniface in a claim to the title of Apostle to Germany. On the other hand, the achievement of Irish monasticism in Germany was substantial, and as always it had the distinction of priority in time. The one area that it might with accuracy be said to have permeated is the Rhineland from Lake Constance west and north to the Dutch border and somewhat beyond. Such penetration proceeded in the first instance from Luxeuil, later from Honau, and intermittently from the efforts of individual missionaries carrying the light to wherever the light had not yet penetrated. In appraising the Irish contribution to the conversion of Germany, it is fair to add to the work proceeding from the known monastic centers what cannot in a literal sense be added, the work of individual monks who lived, worked, and died as individual *peregrini* and whose names today are written only in the Book of Life.

Next in importance to the work in the Rhineland was the work done in southwest Bavaria, centering around Munich and in Salzburg, assigning the latter to Bavaria in terms of eighth-century racial patterns. One recalls the unquestionably Irish Bishop Dobdagrecus who was bishop of Chiemsee, between Munich and Salzburg, the quite possibly Irish Bishop Erembert whom Boniface elevated to the

Freising see, which to the present day is inseparable from the see of Munich, and far more important than either the triumphantly Irish Bishop Virgil of Salzburg. The conversion of the southern Slavs was the work in the main of the Greek Church, but even in a region so remote from Ireland as Carinthia and the adjacent Slovenian parts of what today is Yugoslavia, Irish *peregrini* under the direction of Virgil planted the faith, and with it the pattern of writing, both of which survive there to the present day. Nor is it certain that there may not have been Irish missionary activity among the Slavs in a direction north and east of Salzburg. Archaeological excavation in Moravia, now a province of Czechoslovakia, has unearthed the foundation of an Irish type of monastic establishment, and the surmise has been voiced that Christianity may have been first brought to Moravia from Salzburg when Virgil was bishop and abbot.

The banks of the Main were ennobled by two major Irish foundations, the Church of St. Paul at Mainz which was an establishment out of Honau and the predecessor of the Neumünster Church at Würzburg which St. Kilian founded. To them may quite possibly be added the cathedral at Aschaffenburg. The Danube, on the other hand, was an Anglo-Saxon river, ecclesiastically speaking. The creation of key bishoprics at Regensburg and, in a sense, at Passau, was the work of Boniface and, except for the monastery at Kremsmünster, south of the river which flows through Linz, there is no record of an Irish monastery in the Danube valley. Passau, where the Inn River meets the Danube and southeast Bavaria meets Austria, is a city as ancient as it is beautiful. The Romans were there before the birth of Christ, and Passau was made a Celto-Roman bishopric by St. Severinus as early as the fifth century. At least a Celto-Roman fragment continued in the city after it was successively taken over by the Thuringians and the Bavarians. Christianity continued to exist in Passau but certainly not to thrive, and even the Bishop Vivilo, who enjoyed the favor of St. Boniface, was in office before Boniface became papal legate, owing his elevation directly to the Pope. The religious history of Passau, where people take a quiet pride in the fact that their cathedral is the mother church of the great St. Stephen's Cathedral in Vienna, is intricate, obscure, and even confused. The point is stressed because it was Passau and not the larger Ratisbon (Regensburg) upstream, or the far larger Vienna downstream, that was the historic center of Christianity in the Danube valley. Passau was the focal point out of which missionary activity and culture itself proceeded toward the east, and actually the seat of the largest diocese in the Holy Roman Empire.

Thus the *peregrini* labored extensively in the Rhineland, brought the faith to the Munich-Salzburg area, had their important foundations on the Main, and certainly brought the cross into what now is Carinthia and northern Yugoslavia and possibly elsewhere in the great formless unknown that in the eighth century was the Slavic world. The Danube and the great area north of it and east was outside their sphere of influence. It is true that one meets from time to time a *Schottenkirche,* an "Irish church," or at least the memory of one in Danubian regions. Examples are the Schottenkirchen of Regensburg and Vienna. These are establishments brought into being by Irish Benedictines, but they date to the early Middle Ages, not to the seventh and eighth centuries. There were limits beyond which a movement, even so spiritually explosive as the Irish missionary movement of the two centuries on which our study concentrates, could hardly be expected to be felt. In a very approximate way the limits of the movement in Germany were the Danube, the east banks of the Main and the Rhine, and the border of the Netherlands. But beyond the Alps lies Italy, and in these missionary centuries there was in Italy itself a field that once more had to be worked. What brought Columbanus to Bobbio so early in the movement seems to have brought others. To them and their work we must now turn.

Bibliographical Note

The most extensive description of the monastery of St. Michael on Honau is Joseph P. Fuhrmann, *Irish Medieval Monasteries on the Continent* (Washington, D.C., 1927), chap. 2, pp. 31–40. The testament of Abbot Beatus, with its references to the churches under the jurisdiction of Honau including the Church of St. Paul at Mainz, and the awesome names of the seven Irish bishops, are in Mabillon, *Annales* (1704), July II, pp. 581–97. See also James F. Kenney, *The Early History of Ireland: Ecclesiastical* (New York, 1929 and later), pp. 513–14.

There are two Lives of St. Kilian, known as *Passio prima* and *Passio secunda.* Levison who edited the earlier *Passio* for *MGH* dates it to about 840 but not earlier than 833; Emerich and Hefner (see below) assign it to c. 752. It contains much that is fabulous but the missionary labors and martyrdom of the saint are certain historic facts. *Passio prima* is in *MGH: Scriptores Rerum Merowingicarum* V, pp. 711–28. Both *Passios* are in Franz Emmerich, *Der heilige Kilian, Regionarbischof und Märtyrer historisch-critisch dargestellt* (Würzburg, 1896). Two recent studies of St. Kilian are J. Dienemann, *Der Kult des heiligen Kilian in 8 und 9 Jahrhundert* (Würzburg, 1955), and A. Gwynn, "New Light on St. Kilian," *Irish Ecclesiastical Record* 88 (1957), pp. 1–16.

The Correspondence of St. Boniface is available in J. A. Giles, ed., *S. Bonifacii opera*, 2 vols. (London, 1844); in Ernest Dümmler, ed., *MGH: Epistolae* III (Berlin, 1892), pp. 231–431; and in Ephraim Emerton, trans., *The Letters of Saint Boniface* (Columbia University Press, 1940). His Life by Willibald is in W. Levison, ed., *MGH: Scriptores in usum scholarum*, 1905. There is an English translation by George W. Robinson, *The Life of Saint Boniface* (Harvard University Press, 1916). For the baptism controversy, see F. S. Serland, "The Controversy Concerning Baptism under St. Boniface." *American Catholic Quarterly Review* 42 (1917), pp. 270–75; for St. Boniface's cosmological differences of opinion with Virgil, see below.

The one early account of St. Virgil's life, limited to his period on the continent, is the ninth-century *Libellus de conversione Bagoariorum et Carantanorum* ("Treatise on the Conversion of the Bavarians and Carinthians"). It is in Wilhelm Wattenbach, ed., *MGH: Scriptores* XI (Hannover, 1854), pp. 4–14. There is an eleventh-century Life of no particular value in the same volume, pp. 86–95. The *Libellus* was edited by M. Kos (Laibach, 1936). For a general description of Virgil's life and work, see Paul Grosjean, S.J., "Virgil of Salzburg," in John J. Ryan, *Irish Monks in the Golden Age* (Dublin, 1963.) Virgil's cosmological theories are described in Hermann Krabbo, "Bischof Virgil von Salzburg und seine kosmologischen Ideen," *Mittheilungen des Institutes für österreichische Geschichtsforschung* XXIV (Innsbruck, 1903), pp. 1–28. The red herring aspects of the *Cosmology* of Ethicus Ister and his identification with Virgil were revealed by Heinrich Löwe, "Ein literarischen Widersacher des Bonifatius: Virgil von Salzburg und die Kosmographie des Aethicus Ister," *Abhandlungen der geistes- und sozialwissenschaftlichen Klasse der Mainzer Akademie der Wissenschaften* 11 (1951), pp. 908–88 (also published separately, Wiesbaden, 1952). The Salzburg excavations and what they revealed of Virgil's cathedral are described in Franz Fuhrmann, *Die Chorkrypta des Romanischen Domes in Salzburg* (Salzburg, 1962).

For a general history of the revival of Christianity in Germany, or its introduction to the parts that were pagan, see Albert Hauck, *Kirchengeschichte Deutschlands,* Erster Teil, Bis zum Tode des Bonifatius (Leipzig, 1887).

11

The Farthest Light

IN the history of Irish missionary activity, Italy is a special, and a specially difficult, case. From the earliest days pilgrims of the Irish Church made their slow, painful, circuitous way to Rome. Some never arrived, others never returned. Some of those who never returned entered the monastic or eremitic life somewhere between the Liffey and the Tiber, often in Italy itself. Their mark in history is the faintest of traces, and frequently the illusion of such a trace has been mistaken for the reality. Therefore, a caution verging on skepticism is justifiable when one treats of the *peregrini* who remained in Italy. Cautious skepticism, however, is not disbelief. If there are those whose claims to Irish blood rest on the unsupported statements of biographers who came much later, there must have been many whose names have been swallowed by oblivion.

The two certain Irish foundations established in Italy within our period were the monastery at Bobbio and the monastery of the Holy Trinity at Rome, *S. Trinitatis Scottorum*. In 1910 the crypt at Bobbio was renovated at the request of Cardinal Logue, archbishop of Armagh, and the expense defrayed by the people of Ireland. The remains of St. Columbanus, the founder, were placed again in the beautiful sarcophagus designed by the fifteenth-century artist, Giovanni dei Patriarchi. The second and third abbots of Bobbio, both Italians, were placed beside the tomb of their founder, and beneath the new marble altar were buried the bones of twenty Bobbio saints —with one exception, all Italians. Bobbio was always an Italian monastery, not an Irish one. It was unfailingly hospitable to Irish pilgrims, however, and a close intellectual relationship was long maintained between Bobbio and the monasteries of Ireland, as the Irish manuscripts of the Bobbio library and the manuscripts done in the Irish manner by Italian monks attest.

The one foreigner among the Italian saints beneath the Bobbio altar was St. Cummian, an Irishman. What we know of Cummian we learn from his tombstone: he was a bishop and advanced in years when he left Ireland for Italy; he settled at Bobbio and lived there for four Olympiads. His period of residence was either seventeen or twenty-one years according as an Olympiad meant four or five years to the biographer of the tombstone. He died at the age of ninety-five on August 19, during the reign of King Liutprand which extended from 712 until 744. Thus St. Cummian, whose tombstone biography is long and leisurely but about whom history otherwise is silent, lived just a century after Columbanus. Perhaps other Irishmen were monks at Bobbio, before Cummian or after, but about their existence nothing is possible but surmise.

Irish Churches in Italy

The monastic Church of the Holy Trinity, the other foundation that was certainly Irish, appears on enough lists of Roman churches drawn up in the Middle Ages to make certain its quondam existence. A problem has been presented to church historians by the confusion of this Irish church with the Church of St. Thomas of Canterbury which belonged to the English College. Tommasini carefully distinguishes between them and warns of other possible ecclesiastical entanglements with English foundations. Nothing can be said with certainty about its date of foundation except that its absence from the catalogue of churches prepared in 806 by Pope Leo III may provide a *terminus a quo* for it. The earliest extant roll of membership dates to the late eleventh century, long after its presumptive ninth-century foundation. At that time it was an establishment almost painfully modest, with an abbot, two provosts, six monks, and seven other members. It does not come as a shock to learn that at some date before 1249 it was absorbed by the monastery of St. Gregory. It is difficult to controvert the judgment of the Benedictine scholar Dom Wilmart whom Tommasini quotes (p. 99): ". . . the monastery *S. Trinitatis Scottorum* can never have been in a very flourishing condition; the Island of the Saints was too far off, despite the wandering proclivities of the race, to provide this remote foundation with such a stream of recruits as would guarantee a future for it conformable with its origins."

When we leave Bobbio and Holy Trinity of the Irish we enter the thickets of conjecture. Two other Roman churches of the earlier period bear the Irish name, *S. Benedicti Scottorum* and *S. Salvatoris Scottorum.* There are adequate references to the former to make certain its existence, but in addition to its being St. Benedict *Scottorum* it is also recorded as St. Benedict *Sconchi* or *Sconzi.* The not unreasonable conclusion of Italian scholars is that the church bore the name of the Roman baronial family of Scotti. It is quite possible that the substantially more enigmatic church, *S. Salvatoris Scottorum,* the very existence of which is not beyond challenge, may also have shed luster on the distinguished Roman family and not on *peregrini* from beyond the seas.

There were certainly Irish hospices and hospitals in Italy during our period, two at Ravenna and one each at Piacenza, Vercelli, and Pavia. The Ravenna institutions existed primarily as way stations for Irish pilgrims, one outside the city and one inside, with the inner one actually a monastery, *S. Pietro degli Scotti.* The hospice at Piacenza was founded in 850 by St. Donatus, bishop of Fiesole and a person with whom to conjure. It appears that the year 829 found the people of Fiesole without a bishop. Very conscious of the weight of choice, they had assembled in prayer when Donatus, an Irish *peregrinus,* appeared. No properly devout resident of Fiesole could interpret the timely appearance of a *peregrinus,* and Irish at that, as other than proof positive of divine response to prayer. Donatus was straightaway made bishop and ruled with universal approval from 829 until he died in 876. His influence and activity obviously extended far from the hilltop bishopric of Fiesole, with its old and honorable history before it came within the orbit of Florence. The hospice at Piacenza, actually a nunnery dedicated to St. Brigid, he placed under the rule of Bobbio which was very much nearer to it than was Fiesole. Long residence and abundant honors in Italy would not seem to have erased from the mind of Donatus happy memories of his native land. McNeill quotes (p. 185) some translated lines from a poem he wrote about Ireland: ". . . a land of wealth and health, of milk and honey, free from savage beasts and venomous serpents, where only the Scottic race deserves to dwell." The hospices in Vercelli and Pavia were also dedicated to St. Brigid, although the Irish connections with the latter have been questioned.

Irish Saints in Italy

There remain three Irish saints who lived and worked in Italy, in an aura of sanctity no doubt, but at this remote remove in an aura of uncertainty as well. They are St. Ursus of Aosta, St. Frediano of Lucca, and St. Cathaldus of Tarentum.

Aosta is the delightful small city in the glorious valley that bears the same name, where the roads over the Great and the Little St. Bernard Passes meet, where St. Anselm was born in the eleventh century, and where shadows fall from Mont Blanc to the west, the Matterhorn and Monte Rosa to the east. Of St. Ursus it is recorded that after a French sojourn this very early Irish *peregrinus* settled at Aosta where he became archdeacon under Bishop Jucundus. The time was the early sixth century and the theological mountains to be mastered were hardly less formidable than Mont Blanc and the Matterhorn. The Ostrogoths, who had largely passed through, were Arians, as were the Lombards who remained in the Val d'Aosta. The Church itself was far from secure, as the Catholic Bishop Jucundus was succeeded by the reputedly Arian Bishop Plocean. The reported date of death of St. Ursus is 529. The difficulty of accepting Ursus as an Irishman is that one must believe an Irish monk held a high position in ecclesiastical Italy, battled the Arians, built the Church of SS. Peter and Ursus, and did it all before the time of Brigid, Columba, and Columbanus. This is obviously another difficulty of Matterhorn proportions. There is no problem about accepting the reality of Ursus himself. His coffin is preserved in the chapel of the tenth-century Church of St. Ursus in Aosta and there is reliable evidence of a hospital of St. Ursus that dated to the seventh or eighth century.

St. Frediano of Lucca was bishop of that northern Tuscan town from about 560 until 588. Lucca is a picturesque place with a cathedral old enough for Romanesque elements to mingle with the Gothic, in from the coast about ten miles north of Pisa. There are four Lives of Frediano, all twelfth century or later. They are in fundamental agreement that Frediano was an Irishman, son of a king of the Ulaid who became a hermit on Monte Pisano near Lucca and then was elevated by the people to the bishopric. We are told that he established a monastery at Lucca and that he founded or restored twenty-eight churches. Once more a healthy skepticism may be in order where the presence of an Irish bishop in Italy as early as the second half of the sixth century is concerned. Yet Frediano, whose Irish name may well have undergone a sea change to an Italian form, is mentioned in the *Dialogues* of Pope Gregory the Great, who wrote in the late sixth century; and Kenney records a document dated 680 in the archives of Lucca which refers to the monastery of San Frediano. To this must be added the fact that Lucca was always an important center of Irish influence, with Luccan manuscripts showing decisive marks of Irish handwriting. Perhaps one can go so far as to say that no grounds exist for rejecting the Irish birth of Frediano. The dates assigned him are very early but the sources all confirm his Irish birth and it has always been a part of his tradition. It is fascinating to speculate on the possibility of Irish monks holding positions of responsibility in the Italian Church prior to the coming of Columbanus to Bobbio.

St. Cathaldus of Taranto presents a problem in some ways similar, in others different. There is no conceivable reason for doubting his reality. His bones still rest in the splendid Chapel of St. Cathal at the cathedral of Taranto, at the head of the Gulf of Taranto or, in terms familiar to those who think of Italy in anatomical terms, at the inside top of the Italian heel. His career as recorded by the hagiographers was as follows: he was born in Munster, near Lismore, educated at the local monastery, and he embarked upon a career of miracles which led the king of Munster to denounce and imprison him as a magician. The king promptly died, whereupon Cathaldus was released and became bishop of Rachau. About 666 he went on pilgrimage to the Holy Land and returned by way of Italy, performing miracles en route with renewed vigor. He landed deep in Italy, possibly on the shores of the Gulf of Taranto, and proceeded into the city, working miracles as he passed. Understandably he was made bishop and after fifteen years of successful administration and miracle working, he died. His dating to the sixth century depends upon the dating of a gold benedictional cross of that period which bears his name. There is, of course, no bishopric in Ireland with the Germanic name of Rachau. Those who seek substance in the legend of St. Cathaldus find Rachau an intermediate variant in the valid Irish place-name Rath-Cua which, at least by hypothesis, passed through such forms as Rathan and Raghan and then, as Old Raghan, became Sen Raghan and so ultimately Shanrahan. There is a Shanrahan in the south of Tipperary, near the boundaries of Waterford and Cork.

All this, in Kenney's judgment, with which Tommasini concurs, is "manifestly fictitious." What is not fictitious is the fact that from an early date the Italian people of remote Apulia, deep in the south of Italy, believed that the miracle-working bishop their forefathers knew was an Irishman. The most intriguing fact about Ursus, Frediano, and Cathaldus is the fact that it added to their prestige to be considered Irish. Irish ancestry was as much an embellishment of their careers as the strings of miracles attributed to them. Furthermore, whether this distinguished trio was Irish or not, there can be no question that there were Irish monks in Italy in the ages commonly denominated Dark, bringing the light to the farthest reaches of the peninsula after barbaric invaders had plunged so much of it into darkness. One of the glorious cities of Italy is Palermo on the northwest coast of Sicily. It was a colony from Carthage, a center of Greek culture, a Roman stronghold, and the capital of an Arab emirate before it was a Christian city. One of its most impressive monuments is the great, soaring Norman cathedral of Monreale, five miles south of the city where a massive hillside gives it appropriate enshrinement. The cathedral that exists today, with twelfth-century mosaics that depict, in one hundred and thirty pictures covering six thousand yards of surface, the panoply of Old and New Testament story, is a monument to medieval art and aspiration, but Monreale was ancient when those now nameless artists gave Monreale immortality. There were Irish monks in Monreale long before their day.

Irish Monks in Iceland

There were Irish monks in Iceland as well. Very early in the ninth century a group of Irish and Scottish recluses revived the very primitive and rigorous forms of eremitic asceticism which we met at the beginning of our story. They were called Céli Dé, "the servants of God," a name that later was modified to Culdees. Their chief centers in Ireland were the traditional centers of Irish monasticism: Armagh, Clonmacnois, and Glendalough. St. Andrew's in Scotland is associated with their name. It is recorded that King Brude presented the island of Lochleven to the Scottish Culdees, whom he regarded as the spiritual sons of St. Andrew the Apostle, whose relics were reputed to have come to rest at what today is the golfer's sanctuary. The Irish and Scottish Culdees were hermits but not in the complete sense as they had at least a loose connection with monastic centers. Their complete renunciation of worldly goods and total dependence upon Providence suggests the Portiuncula and Monte Subiaso centuries before St. Francis. Probably the Culdees are best understood as throwbacks to Celtic monasticism in its oldest and least organized form.

Included in the pattern revived from the past was the instinct to wander. About seventy years before Ingólfur Arnarson brought the first Norse refugees from Harald Fairhair to Ultima Thule, the end of the world today called Iceland, a colony of Irish Culdees landed there. The year is uncertain, but there were Culdees on Iceland in 795. In 825 the geographer Dicuil, who may have been an early ninth-century monk of Iona, wrote his *Liber de mensura orbis terrae,* "Book of Terrestrial Measurement," the first medieval treatise on geography. He tells of meeting Irish monks who had lived in Iceland from February to August 795. He records their observations about Iceland: the sea around Iceland is not frozen during the winter, but the pack ice is only a day's sail farther north; in spring when the days were longest they could see at midnight to pick the lice from their shirts. The latter note is homespun, but it rings with authenticity. The Culdees who went to Iceland were not missionaries. Iceland was then uninhabited and there cannot be a missionary without a mission field. They were anchorites who brought the light to Ultima Thule, not that it might enlighten the farthest from human habitation of all mankind but that it might light their own way, in the fashion they understood, to the Shores of Final Light. Nor is there reason to believe that the Culdees played a part in that Celtic infusion which is an accepted part of the earliest Norse settlements in Iceland or in the christening with Celtic names of places there. There were Irish with the Norse in those early settlements, but it is most unlikely that their role was more exalted than that of slave since the Norse settlements in Iceland followed Norse conquests and settlements in the British Isles. As for the Culdees, the oldest records state that when the Norse came, they left, and this is probably the simple truth. The curraghs that brought them, in all probability from the Shetlands and the Faroes, would bring them back again.

The Schottenklöster

As the eighth century progressed, the Irish *peregrini* changed in character and purpose. The missionary impulse dwindled and the scholarly impulse grew. The early *peregrini* brought the Holy Gospel according to Mark and Matthew, the later *peregrini* brought the illuminated Gospel according to Kells and Lindisfarne. During the late eighth and ninth centuries, the major Irish contribution to the revival of civilization in Europe was in the arts and not in morals and religion. This also is an admirable story but, as Chaucer would put it, is for "an othere boke." As the tenth century opened, however, there was a revival of the old Irish missionary spirit and activity, mainly in the Germanic world. Once more it found its first expression in northern France and in the border area, notably Lorraine. In the eleventh and twelfth centuries it expanded into Germany and resulted in the establishment of an impressive series of Irish monasteries, the *Schottenklöster*, as they were known.

The movement started in Ratisbon, modern Regensburg, on the Danube eighty-five miles north of Munich and sixty miles northwest of the junction of the Danube and the Inn, where today Bavaria meets Austria. An Irishman known in Donegal as Muirdach mac Robartsaig and in Regensburg as Marianus Scottus had made the pilgrimage to Rome, returned by way of the Inn and Danube valleys, and reached Regensburg in or about the year 1076. He was a man of versatility and energy. It is reported that he could write with bewildering speed and had to his credit more copies of the Old and New Testament than one would care to count. He was a builder as well, with the monastery of St. Peter at Regensburg his chief monument but with other foundations attributed to him elsewhere in Bavaria and in France. St. Peter's was a Benedictine abbey headed by a long series of Irish abbots. About 1089 another Irish monastery was built at Regensburg, the monastery of St. James, and this was the mother-house of the *Schottenklöster*. Fuhrmann, who has put in systematic order what is known of these Irish monasteries, indicates that they were built in the communities listed in the following order: Würzburg, Erfurt, Nuremberg, Constance, Vienna, Memmingen, Eichstatt, and Kelheim.

Out of St. James at Regensburg emerged the farthest light of all. Shortly after it was founded the monks of St. James, led by a man named Lauritius and favored with the consent of the sovereigns of Bohemia and Poland, passed as trade emissaries of Emperor Henry IV into Russia. They were assisted in their venture, which had a private economic objective of its own and also a spiritual one, by St. Gertrude, sister of Casimir II of Poland, wife of Prince Izaslav of Kiev, friend of Emperor Henry IV, and patroness of Irish *peregrini*. They reached Kiev, came to terms with the Prince of Kiev, founded a monastic community at Kiev, and returned with enough Russian furs for the proceeds to pay for the rebuilding of a Regensburg church. Understandably, the church thus restored thereafter bore the name of two saints, St. James and St. Gertrude. From about 1089 until 1242 there was an Irish monastery at Kiev in Russia, the last pinpoint of light to shine from the Ireland of the Age of the Saints.

The story of the *Schottenklöster* belongs to a period far beyond the one proper to this book, but it should at least be concluded so that our study may have the antique quiet ending. In 1215 Pope Innocent III united these Irish monasteries into a *paruchia* called the Congregation of the *Schottenklöster*. As was proper, the abbot of St. James at Regensburg was its head, but propriety ended with the fact of his primacy. Although he bore the imposing title, "Visitor and Corrector of all Monks and Brothers of the Irish Nation in Germany," his visits were resented and his correction ignored. By the fourteenth century the Irish Nation in Germany was a sorry remnant, decimated by the Black Death and constantly reduced as time took its toll and the possibility of recruitments dwindled and disappeared. In 1515 the Benedictines of Dunfermline obtained from Pope Leo X what was left of the *Schottenklöster*, but they did no better under the Scottish name than under the Irish. In 1862 the last fragment of Irish medieval monasticism on the continent, the community of St. James at Regensburg, was dissolved by Pope Pius IX. The antique quiet ending was a fact.

Today there remain two physical memorials to this late revival of the spirit of the Age of Irish Saints and the establishment of the Irish Nation in Germany. On the Jakobstrasse in Regensburg is the Jakobskirche, the Church of St. James, the oldest parts of which date to the twelfth century. Its antique Romanesque doorway with Christ flanked by Saints John and James is one of the most esteemed treasures of a city especially rich in ecclesiastical art, but to the imagination the thought that this *Schottenkirche* was the intermediary through which a light kindled in Ireland was brought to Russia has a richness that is unique. The other memorial is even more impressive. Today a great multiangular boulevard, starting and ending at the Danube Canal, surrounds the old city of Vienna. Called the Ringstrasse, each of its constituent angles bears a name of its own. The stretch from the Danube Canal down to the University is the *Schotten Ring*, at the corner of the University property is the start of the *Schottengasse*, and on the *Schottengasse* is the *Schottenkirche*. Thus the inner city of Vienna has its memorial to the Irish Nation in Germany, its Irish Boulevard, its Irish Way, and its Irish Church. The church was founded in the twelfth century for the Irish monks from Regensburg by that colorful Viennese notable remembered after nearly 800 years by his favorite expletive, Heinrich Jasomirgott, "Henry So-Help-Me-God." It is a relatively unadorned church, even sparse by the standards of Viennese baroque, but it still stands as a memorial to the farthest light that Ireland ever cast.

The Light Is Dimmed

By the start of the eighth century the sequence of events that was to dim that light had already begun. Vikings had landed on the island of Lambay and the first drums of doom were heard. There followed the Norse conquests and settlements at Dublin, Cork, Waterford, and elsewhere; and even the fusion of Irish and now Hibernicized Norse that won the Battle of Clontarf under Brian Boru did not cause a basic change in Ireland's tragic destiny. By the twelfth century the Normans had arrived and for three and a half centuries Norman families held half Ireland. Later there came the Ulster plantations and more centuries of hardship and repression, as Ireland continued for one thousand years a land always in part captive, always in a measure repressed, always in some degree downtrodden. What the tenth century began the twentieth century finally ended, if indeed it may be termed ended until the north knows peace.

The Age of Saints was followed by a brief age of scholars and artists, and then the age of warriors, martyrs, and victims began. Our concern has been with the light and not the darkness, and the light when it was brightest. The sixth, seventh, and eighth centuries were the great centuries of Irish history, the centuries when the light from Ireland flooded Europe in its darkest hour of barbarism. The light shone over all Scotland and much of England, illuminated northern France, penetrated Belgium, brightened Switzerland, flooded parts of Germany and Austria, and its farthest beams reached into what now are Yugoslavia, Czechoslovakia, and Russia. Only once in the history of Christianity has this occurred, that one tiny nation should continue missionary work for so long a period, through so many lands, with such single-minded dedication, and with such abiding results. The roll is a noble one: Iona, Lindisfarne, Glastonbury, Luxeuil, Péronne, St. Gallen, Bobbio, Würzburg, Regensburg, Munich, Salzburg, Vienna, and Kiev. The record is sufficiently magnificent to justify rhetoric and exculpate exaggeration: the Irish monks of the sixth to eighth centuries effected the second conversion of Europe.

Bibliographical Note

For the Irish churches, hospices, and hospitals in Italy, see Anselmo M. Tommasini, *Irish Saints in Italy* (London, 1935), pp. 93–99. For the monastery at Bobbio, see chap. VI above, "Saint Columbanus"; also James F. Kenney, *The Sources of the Early History of Ireland: Ecclesiastical* (New York, 1929 and later), pp. 515 ff. For Commian of Bobbio, Tommasini, pp. 315–19. There is information about St. Donatus, the bishop of Fiesole, and the Piacenza hospice in John T. McNeill, *The Celtic Churches* (University of Chicago Press, 1974), p. 185; Tommasini, pp. 383–94; and Kenney, pp. 601–2.

There is an early Life of St. Ursus of Aosta in the Bollandist *Acta*, Appendix to Feb. I, pp. 936–39. See Tommasini, pp. 266–74. Tommasini refers to a nineteenth-century study by Canon Dondeynaz, *Vie de Saint Ours archidiacre d'Aoste* (Mensio, 1868).

There are four early Lives of St. Frediano of Lucca. Lives i, iii, and iv are in Colgan, *Acta Sanctorum* (see Bibliographical Note to chap. 7), pp. 633–51, and excerpts from Life ii are in the Bollandist *Annales* XI (1892), pp. 262 ff. See Kenney, pp. 184–85 and Tommasini, pp. 362–71. The early Life of St. Cathaldus of Taranto is in Colgan, pp. 542–62, and the Bollandist *Acta*, May II, pp. 570–78. See Kenney, pp. 185–86, and Tommasini, pp. 401–9.

Nothing is known about the Culdees in Iceland beyond the fact that they were there for a time. There is a modern edition and translation of Dicuil, *Dicuili: Liber de mensura orbis terrae*, ed. James J. Tierney (Dublin, 1967). For the Culdees in general, see

McNeill, chap. 12. For the Celtic element in early Icelandic life and literature, see Sir William Craigie, "The Gaels in Iceland," *Proceedings of the Society of Antiquaries in Scotland* (Edinburgh, 1966–1967), pp. 247 ff. and "Gaelic Words and Names in Icelandic Sagas," *Zeitschrift für Keltische Philologie* I, pp. 439 ff.

There is a comprehensive treatment of the Germanic Schottenklöster in Joseph P. Fuhrmann, *Irish Medieval Monasteries on the Continent* (Washington, D.C., 1927), pp. 73–104. For the monastery at Kiev see also McNeill, chap. 11, "Irish Scholars in European Lands," and John Hennig, "Irish Monastic Activities in Eastern Europe," *Irish Ecclesiastical Record* 65 (1945), pp. 394–400. McNeill refers to a study of the Kiev monastery by a Russian Scholar Mikhail Shaitan published in a *festschrift, Srednevekoi Byt,* Leningrad, 1925, pp. 179–205.

An Irish monk of the eleventh century named Mael Brigte (1028–1082) became an anchorite at Mainz in 1069 and wrote under the name Marianus a chronicle in three parts. Part III, which extends from the Ascension to 1082, contains considerable information about the Irish Nation in Germany. It is in *MGH: Scriptores* V, pp. 481–564.

Index